T0333221

RUISLIP, EASTCOTE
and NORTHWOOD
during the First World War

RUISLIP, EASTCOTE and NORTHWOOD
during the First World War

TANYA BRITTON

The History Press

First published 2011

The History Press
The Mill, Brimscombe Port
Stroud, Gloucestershire, GL5 2QG
www.thehistorypress.co.uk

© Tanya Britton, 2011

The right of Tanya Britton to be identified as the Author
of this work has been asserted in accordance with the
Copyrights, Designs and Patents Act 1988.

All rights reserved. No part of this book may be reprinted
or reproduced or utilised in any form or by any electronic,
mechanical or other means, now known or hereafter invented,
including photocopying and recording, or in any information
storage or retrieval system, without the permission in writing
from the Publishers.
British Library Cataloguing in Publication Data.
A catalogue record for this book is available from the British Library.

ISBN 978 0 7524 6200 4

Typesetting and origination by The History Press
Printed in Great Britain

CONTENTS

ACKNOWLEDGEMENTS

I WOULD LIKE to acknowledge and thank in particular the staff of Uxbridge Local History Library, the Public Record Office, the London Metropolitan Archives, the Ruislip, Northwood and Eastcote Local History Society, Eric Button, Nicole Nunn, Pam Pollicott, Margaret Raniwala, Joss Martin and Stephen Britton for the help given to me in producing this book. I would also like to thank the staff at The History Press, particularly Cate Ludlow.

INTRODUCTION

THE WRITING of this book, a result of many years of research, has been difficult. The people who lived through this terrible period are now gone along with their memories. The Home Front's contribution to victory during the First World War is important and is just one moment in time which requires recording, as it is now part of history.

Details of the servicemen who died in the First World War are taken from Ruislip, Ruislip Common, Eastcote and Northwood war memorials, including Rolls of Honour located in churches in these areas. Included are details of those based at Northolt Aerodrome who died while in the service of their country and who are buried in St Martin's church, Ruislip churchyard, and others tenuously connected with the borough (although from other parts of the country) who were buried locally. Kindly take note that where a record exists on the 'Ancestry' website, the details (in the main) have not been used.

Other details provided are as known, and come from a variety of sources – the eighty or so volumes called 'Soldiers Died', the Commonwealth War Graves Commission registers, the Urban District of Uxbridge Roll of Honour (to September 1915), De Ruvigny's Roll of Honour, Regimental and Divisional histories, local papers and archive material from Uxbridge Local Studies Library. Local papers can be notoriously incorrect. They also relied on families of the deceased to give as much information as they could, but the information they gave varied from sparse to rich accounts of how their relation fell in battle or died of wounds. Some of the details from the sources not only differ in the amount of information provided, but also occasionally conflict. Furthermore, not all soldiers who died in this war are listed in the volumes of Soldiers Died, and the Commonwealth War Graves Commission, apart from not having had, in some instances, any details from relatives of the deceased, also sometimes has problems locating names where no service number is available, especially in the case of common names. The *Ruislip Parish Magazine* for the years 1914 to 1918 – which, it is believed, contained far more details about those who died – seems to be missing from the archives.

Servicemen posted as missing in action were not declared officially killed until up to one year had passed and a military tribunal heard the facts relating to the disappearance. If the loss of records meant that a date could not officially be declared, then an arbitrary date was decided upon. A notification of 'missing in action' meant an immediate loss of income and the uncertainty of any pension rights, which was devastating for a married woman.

For the purposes of the Commonwealth War Graves Commission the dates of the First World War are 4 August 1914 to 31 August 1921; however, a number of men still suffered from their injuries and died some years later as a result of them. These men are not commemorated by the Commonwealth War Graves Commission, and local war memorials tend not to include men or women who died later than 1918. This could possibly be the case with the Revd Henry Meredith Bate, BA (Oxon) who served in the First World War and was seriously wounded in France in October 1918. He died on 29 July 1921, aged thirty-three, and is buried at Ruislip. Similarly, Sidney Thomas Cherry, who had spent his youth at Northwood, had served during the war and the hardships entailed in that service aggravated the nature of his last illness from which he died at Wendover in December 1921.

Please note that 'Died at home' can mean they died anywhere in the British Isles. Places of burial as recorded in local papers can differ from where the deceased was eventually buried or commemorated, as many burials were later disturbed by heavy fire.

Further details of prisoners of war can be found by contacting the International Red Cross at Geneva.

Every care has been taken in compiling this document. I apologise for any errors or omissions.

Tanya Britton, 2011

SETTING THE SCENE

THE PERIOD between 1902, when the Boer War ended, and the beginning of the First World War in August 1914 was one of peace and comparative economic stability, but not advance, although the period was a time of war scares. July was the time for holidays – 1914 had the most brilliant summer for years – and August was the time of annual training. The Territorial Army, and many of its units, were already mustered in camp, while others were about to go into camp that weekend. The local 'E' Company, 8th Middlesex V.B. Regiment, was on the outbreak of war at Salisbury Plain for its annual training. It had been there since July.

Although the suburban expansion of London in the nineteenth century was great and high rents were forcing workers to move to cheaper areas and commute – in some instances the population had doubled in the space of seven years – the modern-day London borough of Hillingdon was still largely unaffected by this spread. At the turn of the twentieth century, Uxbridge was the only town of any size, although Ruislip, Hayes, West Drayton and Harlington had small centres of population. The district of Ruislip-Northwood covered over 6,350 acres, the largest parish in the county of Middlesex, and was almost entirely residential. Ruislip's population in 1871 was about 1,100; this number also included the population of Eastcote. By 1891 the population was 1,198 and by 1901 had grown to 1,441 – or 3,566, including Eastcote. At the end of June 1905 the population of Ruislip-Northwood was estimated to be 4,515; by 1906 there were fifty more inhabitants; in 1909, the figure was estimated to be 5,906, and at the time of the 1911 census, the population of Ruislip, Eastcote and Northwood had risen to 6,217. There had been a growing awareness of the problems created since 1851 by London's rapid expansion. The new Housing Act of 1909 vested powers in Local Authorities to, should they wish, prepare town-planning schemes. The 1911 census showed that one-tenth of the population of England was living in overcrowded conditions and it was estimated that between 5 per cent and 10 per cent of urban workmen were living in slums.

In Hillingdon the dreaded workhouse, which had opened in 1747, was enlarged in 1838 to become the workhouse for Cowley, Hayes, Hillingdon and Uxbridge, West Drayton, Ruislip, Ickenham and Harefield. At one period in 1911 there had been as many as 282 unfortunate inmates, although for the following years the numbers tended to be less. In 1930, it became part of Hillingdon Hospital. The Isolation Hospital at Uxbridge served the Ruislip area, as did the Smallpox Hospital at Yeading. The former contained a scarlet fever block and diphtheria wards. House disinfection was carried out after TB, measles, whooping cough, chicken pox and other cases (at a small charge per room) – no charges were made in cases of poor people unable to pay.

At the turn of the twentieth century, Ruislip was still rural and isolated. In common with other places there were no pavements, and the roads were muddy in wet weather and dusty during dry spells. In general, household shopping was delivered, although some people walked over 3 miles to shop at Uxbridge, and twice a year a peddler with all sorts of wares came rattling along. Ruislip Church of England School (mixed and infants) had been built in about 1864 on land given by King's College, Cambridge, and could accommodate 199 children. In 1904, Mr J.H. Wallis had been hired to undertake refuse collection in Ruislip-Northwood. By 1914, a collection of house refuse was made once a week throughout the whole district – 1,097 houses were on the list for collection. Refuse was carted to Woodstock Hill Brickfield, where it was screened and the ashes used in the brick kilns. Every year until 1932 a pleasure fair was held in the High Street on 31 May. In 1904 the Metropolitan line was extended from Harrow on the Hill to Uxbridge and the station at Ruislip was opened on 4 July. At first steam locomotives were used, but by January 1905 the line had been electrified.

There was also the Great Western & Great Central joint line close by. Special trips into the 'country' were provided by the railway company, which offered special excursions on Bank Holidays and cheap weekend returns from inner London stations. Day trippers flocked to the many cottage gardens thrown open to them. During the summer James Bunce, assisted by his daughter and granddaughter, served teas at Bury Farm, as did Mrs Riddle in the High Street, Mr Hoar at the George and Mrs Weedon at Field End Farm. The Poplars Tea Garden was opened in June 1906 and the local girls employed as waitresses were all given flower names.

Orchard Bungalow, situated at the corner of Ickenham Road and Sharps Lane, opened at Easter 1905 and also catered for the day trippers. The Metropolitan Police X Division had arrived at Ruislip in the 1840s and was hoping to build a new police station to replace the house they had made use of at 17 High Street since September 1869. In 1906 the Great Western & Great Central Joint Railway opened a station at Ruislip for Ickenham, now named West Ruislip. With the opening of the stations, agriculture began to give way to housing developments. The increased building of estates necessitated a new station – Ruislip Manor Halt – which opened on 5 August 1912. It was only accessible from a path across a field.

Even before 1914 local landowners in Ruislip were finding that the sale of land was more profitable than farming upon it. Perhaps the most important of those approved by the Local Government Board in the London area was the Ruislip-Northwood scheme – a plan put forward by King's College, Cambridge, for the development of its estate as a garden suburb. King's College granted the rights of acquiring its entire estate to Ruislip Manor Limited so that a town-planning scheme could be organised and a new town with further services and amenities – churches, hospitals, public halls and shops – built.

A special town-planning competition was held. Sixty-two designs were submitted and the first prize was awarded to Messrs A. and J. Soutar, a firm of architects from Wandsworth. It was one of the largest development schemes yet proposed and was to have been the

Ruislip Village. (Courtesy of Hillingdon Local Studies, Archives and Museum Service)

first of its kind in England. The plan covered 1,276 acres and extended from Northolt Junction station in the south to the Rickmansworth Road, close to Northwood station. The site went as far as Ruislip Manor, and Bury Street marked its most western boundary. A shopping centre, churches, schools, open spaces and a cottage hospital were planned. Housing densities were proposed – three to an acre in Copse Wood, increasing to ten to an acre south of Ruislip Manor station. Land adjoining Northolt Junction station was zoned for use as factories and workshops, with a marketplace, church and school close by. A major spine road was planned from about South Ruislip to Northwood. The River Pinn was to be turned into a series of ornamental lakes with a major shopping and service centre overlooking Ruislip Reservoir. Mr Carr, clerk to the council, Mr Abbott the surveyor and Frank Elgood (whose son was killed in action) negotiated with owners of land and organised meetings and inquiries. By August 1914 a certain amount of building had taken place, but a considerable amount of work still needed to be done. In Manor Close, Ruislip, by 1914, eleven cottages for the accommodation of the 'working classes' had been built; at Ruislip Common in that same year, the council had prepared a scheme for the erection of twenty-two working-class cottages.

One ecclesiastical parish had been formed on 16 June 1854 from the civil parishes of Ruislip, Rickmansworth and Watford when Holy Trinity church at Northwood was consecrated. On 12 August 1904, Ruislip, Northwood and Eastcote were created an urban district under the name of 'Ruislip-Northwood'. In January 1909, two separate parishes were formed. Northwood was a farming area and in 1871 about 250 people lived there, but with the coming of the Metropolitan railway to Northwood in 1887, the population rose by around 2,000 people in the twenty years between 1891 and 1901, and between 1901 and 1911 the population rose from 3,566 to 6,217. Plans for just twenty-four new houses had been passed by the council in 1914. As the population increased still further, so the housing

Maxwell Road, Northwood. (Courtesy of Hillingdon Local Studies, Archives and Museum Service)

problem grew. Mr Frank Maxwell Hallowell Carew had acquired the Eastbury estate of over 700 acres in 1886, and over the next five years he sold ten pieces of land as building plots: the proviso was that the houses should cost at least £750, except for cheaper cottages in the High Street. The roads were named after him and members of his family. Harry Neal, of The Slade, Carew Road, Northwood, bought plots and built large six-bedroomed houses in Carew and Eastbury Roads, and by 1914 had established a reputation for himself. The Ruislip Manor Cottage Society had constructed twenty-two 'working-class' cottages at Northwood. Each had been let.

With the numbers of inhabitants growing, Pinner Road Council School at Northwood was opened in 1910 as Northwood Council School. It was situated on the Pinner-Rickmansworth road and at first accommodated 330 children. It was enlarged in 1914. Half Mile Infants' School had been opened in 1899 in the Mission Hall of Emmanuel church. It was later renamed Emmanuel School. Holy Trinity Church of England School on Rickmansworth Road, Northwood, opened in 1862 and enlarged in 1892 and again in 1899.

A private girls' school was moved from London to Maxwell Road, Northwood, in 1892-3 and became known as Northwood College.

Northwood Preparatory School in Sandy Lodge Road was founded by Francis Terry in 1910 – and known locally as 'Terry's'. Another private school, St Helen's, was founded in 1899 as Northwood High School. In 1912 the school moved to Moor Farm, Sandy Lodge Road. In about 1887 a purpose-built hospital, from 1905 known as 'Mount Vernon Hospital for Tuberculosis and Diseases of the Lungs and Heart', was opened in Hampstead. The hospital opened its country branch at Northwood in 1904 in grounds of some 105 acres, for patients from all over the country. All the wards faced south. Great difficulty was experienced in financing the hospital, and until 1907 only sixty-six beds were open. After a festival dinner which was very successful in raising funds, it was decided to open a further forty beds. The hospital had extended the Nurse's Home and had made arrangements for a considerable extension to make good the disposal of the hospital at Hampstead. A large sum of money had been placed at the disposal of the hospital to provide accommodation for 100 women and children, where it was hoped that school-age children would continue their education with the help of qualified teachers. The foundations to the new children's wing, which were almost as large as the hospital itself, had been already laid.

South Ruislip's open fields were almost uninhabited except for a few farmhouses. A station had been opened there as Northolt Junction on the Great Western & Great Central Joint Railway in May 1908. In 1914, four houses of an average rental income had been built in South Ruislip, with another sixteen planned. Eastcote was still a large, yet sleepy hamlet of Ruislip. It was rural in character with fields, cottages and several large houses, although the opening of Eastcote station on 26 May 1906 had brought an influx of Londoners who wanted to live in rural surroundings as well as just pass through it leisurely. In May 1911 St Vincent's Cripples' Home was transferred from its home at Clapham to Ruislip Holt, a former private house. As well as a hospital, it was also a school. Originally there were forty beds. In 1913, X-ray equipment was installed, and by 1914 there was an operating theatre and accommodation for 114.

Building development was progressing rapidly; plans for eight houses were passed during 1914 (as compared with fifty-four in 1913). The Ruislip Manor Cottage Society had built four cottages in Frog Lane (now Fore Street) for the working classes, and these were immediately occupied. The Old Barn House, Eastcote, originally perhaps constructed in

Scene near the junction of Frog Lane (now Fore Street) and Eastcote High Road. (Courtesy of Hillingdon Local Studies, Archives and Museum Service)

Church Road. (Courtesy of Hillingdon Local Studies, Archives and Museum Service)

about 1500, now a Grade II listed building, was much in demand as a boarding house. In 1913 the Bishop of London's Fund to build a new mission church at Eastcote purchased an acre of land from Ralph Hawtrey-Deane. Mr Hardy, the Anglo-American Syndicate and the Home Freeholds Co. had offered plots of land for sale just prior to 1914 and the growth of the parish necessitated not only a new church and new houses, but also a new school.

The Development of the Roads and Funds Act of 1909 brought the Roads Board into existence, and many conferences were held before and during 1914 by all the local authorities to consider the arterial roads question very carefully. The Roads Board agreed with Middlesex County Council that the Brentford bypass would be constructed by a process of tendering. The contracting companies would provide their own labour. The MCC also arranged to proceed immediately with the Great West Road, which was in urgent need of building. It was to be commenced at the Bath Road end of the proposed road. The Western Avenue was also one of the proposed roads recommended as of urgent necessity. In 1914 Ruislip-Northwood UDC, applied to the Road Board for grants in respect of road widening and improvements, which the council decided to carry out under their town-planning scheme.

The range of entertainment available to ordinary Londoners was not particularly extensive. In fact, there was not a great deal of leisure for most working people (except on Saturday night and on Sundays). On weekdays they could read, play card games or have a sing-song around the piano. Local dignitaries, besides providing employment for some, also promoted entertainments and social events. Silent films were well established before the war, and cinema was already popular. In Middlesex at the outbreak of the First World

War there were eighty cinemas licensed, but as yet there were no dance halls. Northwood's cinema, the Northwood Picture House, was opened in Church Road in 1913. The Licensing Committee allowed no Sunday films at this time. Other entertainments such as charity and variety concerts were also held in the cinemas. In about 1912, the Kings End Club at Ruislip introduced the Merrymakers Pierrot Troupe who entertained at the Parish Rooms. Boys of the Eastcote Joy Club, which met at Field End House, also entertained. Northwood Men's Club held its first sporting event in August 1907. Annual sports for the children of Eastcote had been started by 1908 and from 1904 annual sports were held at Ruislip. With the development of the district, the *Ruislip-Northwood Courier* was established by John King, who in 1880 had launched the *Uxbridge Gazette* and *Middlesex and Buckinghamshire Observer.*

Many sports clubs had started before the turn of the twentieth century, amongst them Staines and West Middlesex Golf Club (which was inaugurated in 1890, followed by Northwood Club on 25 April 1891, in extensive grounds of almost 14 acres of old gravel pits on the Pinner-Rickmansworth Road, with links of eighteen holes). The Sandy Lodge Golf Club was also in existence. Ruislip Lawn Tennis Club used grounds in Bury Street, and Ruislip Tennis and Croquet Club was inaugurated at the end of October 1911. Kewferry Lawn Tennis Club was situated in Kewferry Road and Northwood Bowling Club in Maxwell Road. Eastcote Institute Cricket and Football Clubs were in existence prior to 1914.

Northwood Cricket Club was established in 1877 on the Pinner-Rickmansworth Road. There were also clubs at Eastcote and Ruislip. The Uxbridge Cycling Club was formed

The Golf Links, Northwood. (Courtesy of Hillingdon Local Studies, Archives and Museum Service)

in 1890 and The Ship in Joel Street was the county headquarters for the Elgin, Kensal Rise and Paddington Cycling Clubs. The Cavendish Amateur Athletic Association was in Northolt Lane, Eastcote. An athletics ground was also situated at Eastcote. Rifle shooting was also a popular activity: Ruislip Rifle Club's range was in Ickenham Road, and in about 1907 the Northwood Rifle Club was formed.

The choirs of St Margaret's, Uxbridge, and St Andrew's, Uxbridge, St John's, Uxbridge Moor, Cowley, Yiewsley, West Drayton, Harmondsworth, Harlington-Hayes, Ruislip and Harefield had met annually for a festival service at Hillingdon on St John the Baptist day – 24 June. They had last met in 1913.

Unemployment was a problem immediately prior to the First World War and there had been plenty of unemployment parades. Some local men had been lured to new lives in Canada, New Zealand or Australia. Agitation was mounting on behalf of women's rights and the suffragette movement had local supporters. Groups had been set up, including the ones at Northwood and Uxbridge – The Northwood Women's Suffrage Society and the Uxbridge Women's Suffrage Society. By 1914 the movement had become increasingly more militant, although a meeting which had taken place in June 1914 at Lyon House, Manor Way, Ruislip, was poorly attended.

The European situation was getting blacker, although the impasse of Home Rule for Ireland was predominant in people's minds. War clouds were looming…

WAR IS DECLARED...

THE DECLARATION of war between Austria and Serbia on 29 July 1914 seemed sudden. All hopes of peace were gradually abandoned, and on the morning of 4 August 1914 Britain declared war on Germany. The announcement was greeted with relief by many. The war would be over by Christmas, the 'Hun' taught a lesson and victory would be won. Patriotic fervour was the order of the day.

Crowds of panic-stricken people flocked to all the local shops to buy food and provisions and as many goods as they could carry, and found that prices were rising. Although the Government's maximum-price scheme quickly put a stop to it, the price of sugar, which had hitherto been imported from Germany and Austria, immediately went up and the Government had to issue suggested prices for it; hoarding was made a criminal offence. As delivery boys went off to war, so people went in person to shop and provision shops stayed open long after their usual closing times.

Sentries on the Strand at Somerset House at the outbreak of the war: inside, stores and ammunition were being packed for the mobilisation of the London Territorials – 313,000 men were expected to mobilise within the week.

Above The suffragette movement declared their support for the war effort within hours of the announcement – a call that thousands of women answered. This image shows the Women War Worker's Procession at Buckingham Palace in 1918, as the end of the war approached.

Left The first contingents of British troops debark at Boulogne.

Every farm had its hayricks commandeered by the War Department, leaving only the bare minimum. Hay was baled by the Pioneer Corps and taken away to Cavalry depots. The authorities had lists of all tradesmen and others who were likely to be able to furnish draught and other horses and the War Office commandeered several horses from local traders.

Within hours, the suffragettes put their aims on hold. Leaders of the women's suffrage movement supported the war effort, urging men to enlist and women to work in industry, preferring to set aside their cause for the period of the conflict. Thousands of women answered their call. It also worked to combat the appalling poverty suffered by ordinary people.

Boy Scouts, some of whom were in camp, were urgently summoned back. Army units mustered in camps were immediately put on a war footing. Others en route for their annual camp were stopped mid-journey, their trains turned around to return to London. The local volunteers of 'E' Company, 8th Middlesex V.B. Regiment, returned home on 4 August. Two or three days later men left for Hounslow: they were first stationed at Sittingbourne and subsequently transferred, to their great disappointment, to Gibraltar for five months, after which they were relieved by their second-line battalions and saw service in France. Within days of war being declared a transit camp for troops had been established at Harrow Weald. Men who, more often than not, had ventured no more than a few miles from their homes were soon to find themselves in France or Flanders – or even further afield. On 7 August 1914, the first details of the British Army – the 'Old Contemptibles' – came down the gangway from a troopship at Boulogne – not as foes, but as allies.

The local councils found at first that supplies were difficult to obtain as the local traders had had their horses taken from them, but quickly got to work setting up committees and sub-committees, including the Belgian Guest Sub-Committee, the Food and Clothing Committee, the War Emergency Committee and the Ambulance Sub-Committee, chaired by Revd W. Grey, vicar of Ruislip.

The conflict, which was to be one of the greatest in the history of the world, was to grow to involve the whole population.

Left The 'Old Contemptibles' at the front, joyful though they may soon be facing death.

Below A group of deeply-interested young men reading the proclamation of war outside Horse Guards, London, on 4 August 1914.

HOUSING

THE WAR put an end to residential building and the growth of outer London ceased until some time after the end of hostilities. The building of houses and civil amenities in Ruislip-Northwood and the approved scheme for the new town were suspended. The contractor left trucks and bricks on a light railway from Ruislip station sidings, which became a playground. Harry Neal, who had been building on the Oxhey Woods estate (which he had bought in 1913), had to run down his business and was taken on by McAlpines as a contract manager employed building aerodromes, prisoner-of-war camps and hospitals throughout England. He later donated an ambulance to the Northwood VAD Hospital. The scheme to erect a new police station was scrapped, and they did not change premises until 1961! The Mission church planned at Eastcote was eventually built in 1922, and the plots of land for sale came to nothing.

Large premises in the borough, including private houses, were taken over for various purposes. Part of Field End Lodge at Eastcote was taken over as a hospital.

The Old Barn House at Eastcote was taken over by the military authorities after 1915 for the use of, amongst others, the Queen Victoria Rifles (who were on night duty close to Eastcote station). It is thought that Northwood Hall (now Denville Hall) became a boys' school – Tivoli House – during hostilities, with Baron Isidore Berkovitz as headmaster. Kelvin House School, one of the earliest private schools in Ruislip, was founded in about 1914, and made use of a house in King Edward's Road. Housing shortages, already a problem before the outbreak of war, began to get worse when a large storage depot in South Ruislip, named after the nearby Northolt Junction station, but actually outside that parish, was requisitioned to store explosives for the Hayes Filling factory. This dump was constructed by Higgs and Hill in late 1916 on the east side of West End Road, and stretched almost as far as Ruislip Manor and Eastcote, covering Bessingby Park. It consisted of twenty huts spaced far apart. There were two dressing rooms, a guard room, mess, boiler house, forge and general stores. Many local girls, including Gladys Wheeler-Field who lived at Eastcote, worked here. Maybe her twin sister, Sybil Sandeman, who also resided at Eastcote, accompanied her on her walk across the fields to work. Those who came from further afield were provided with railway passes by the Ministry of Munitions. Others lodged locally. Water from the Yeading Brook was stored in a reservoir in case of fire here or at Northolt Aerodrome. By the end of September 1916, sidings on the Great Western Railway and Great Central

Old Forge and Smithy, Eastcote. (Courtesy of Hillingdon Local Studies, Archives and Museum Service)

A rigid-framed German 'dirigible'. In order to allay the public panic about bombing, the *Illustrated London News* printed this picture alongside the assurance that the enemy had only ten to a dozen of such machines capable of reaching our shores.

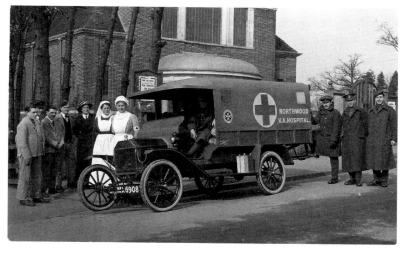

The ambulance donated by Harry Neal. (Courtesy of Hillingdon Local Studies, Archives and Museum Service)

Railway line at Northolt served the dump. When war ended, there were thirty-four men and two women employed breaking down ammunition.

Rooms in houses were also used to billet soldiers, although there was a regulation that soldiers would not be billeted in the house of the wife of a soldier serving abroad. For instance, in mid-August 1914 soldiers were billeted at and around Uxbridge as part of the general scheme for the outer defence of London. Almost 20,000 men were placed between Harrow, Uxbridge and Slough. The billeting of soldiers became a legal requirement, and many prosecutions took place. Landlords within a 10-mile radius of London were given an allowance to help with rent: this did not apply to any part of this borough, but it did apply to most parts of Ealing, and bad feeling was rife. Rents rose significantly in 1915, and were soon controlled by law and put back to pre-war costs so that extortionate rents could not be asked.

The influx of Belgian refugees and serving men, as well as the number of houses taken over as hospitals, all aggravated the serious housing shortage everywhere and after the first of the Zeppelin raids on this country, when air-raid refugees fled the capital, the demand for accommodation outside the capital became urgent. Following the 1917 autumn air raids there was further demand for apartments in this district, and fabulous prices were being offered. A large number of people, especially women with children, found that they could not find sleeping accommodation when they fled the London air raids, and were hence forced to walk the streets at night.

At Eastcote, to meet the demand occasioned by air-raid refugees, the Old Barn House's dance floor was partitioned into four rooms and a matchwood ceiling added. Northwood College was also used by frightened people who would huddle together on the first-floor landing of the Senior House at the first rumour of the approach of a Zeppelin. By 1915 there was a dearth of houses at Ruislip Common. In December 1917, residents in the Ruislip-Northwood district were asked to place their cellars at the disposal of the public should occasion arise during air raids.

The Warrender Institute, Ruislip church room, Pinner Parish Hall and Northwood Trinity Hall were all used for the 'visitors'. After the raids of October 1917, 2,000 refugees were reported at Northwood. The result of these 1917 air raids was, as reported by the Medical Officer of Health, overcrowding in the Ruislip-Northwood area during the August attacks, and in July 1918 the Eastcote Welfare Association reported an urgent need for additional housing. With the increase in population, the refuse collection in Ruislip-Northwood was taken over by Ruislip Parish Council and two more men were hired for the work, although by mid-1918 with the shortage of labour, house-refuge collection took place fortnightly rather than weekly.

After the late September air raids, on 25 September 1917, hundreds were unable to secure accommodation. Appalling conditions were experienced all down the lines of the GWR and the Metropolitan railway.

With the influx of so many people, the Government encouraged local authorities to provide more housing, although up to this time it was the popular belief that private builders would continue to provide all normal housing needs. This, however, had proved impossible, and with the lack of house building, serious problems were encountered after the war.

SCHOOLS

THE 1902 Education Act provided for the establishment of education other than elementary. Up until this time, the only secondary schools had been private. The war put a stop to the flow of educational progress and after the war the country's financial difficulties permitted few improvements.

In the spring of 1915, a circular was issued by the Middlesex Education Committee advising schools in the county to immediately prepare a plan of action in the case of air raids. It was advised that in the event of a raid the children should carry on working but be as far away as possible from the windows. They would not be released from the school until it had been ascertained that all danger had passed. The committee also advised a strongly worded letter be sent to all parents informing them that they would be unable to collect their children at such a time. In mid-November 1915, the Middlesex County Council ensured against enemy aircraft. In June 1917 the Middlesex Education Committee sent further letters to local schools advising them of the drilling of school children in preparation for air raids. Up to this time, each school had differed in its drilling arrangements. In some, when a whistle was blown, the children had to lie flat on their stomachs; in others children were told to get under a desk.

Most school children saved money that was collected for war savings and also contributed most willingly to fundraising and making 'comforts' for the troops – although not everything was appreciated by the Tommies. The scholars in Northwood Council Schools contributed the sum of £30 per month and at Emmanuel Infants' School money was collected each week for war savings.

Schooling suffered many interruptions. From almost the start of the war, Belgian refugee children attended local schools and the adults were given lessons in English. Air-raid refugees were also housed locally and it is known that their children were admitted to Emmanuel School, Northwood. Local authorities were under intense pressure to suspend the school attendance bylaws so that children could be released to undertake 'national work', and there was also a marked increase in early school-leaving to go to work. Summer holidays were mostly changed from August to July so that schoolchildren could help with the harvest.

By 1916, the price of paper had almost trebled. To save paper, school magazines reduced in size or were not printed at all and slates had to be used wherever possible.

For schools, the difficulty of the war years was mainly a matter of staffing, and towards the end of 1915 the headmasters of schools with an average attendance of no more than 350 were encouraged to take a class. In early 1916, it was reported that out of a total of well over 200 teachers in Middlesex County elementary schools, only ten had not joined the Colours or attested under the Derby scheme; in the secondary schools, out of 229 teachers, over 200 had enlisted or attested. By May 1918 more than 22,000 teachers had left the schools for the Colours, after a further call was made on the teaching profession by the Board of Education and the National Service Ministry. A few men under twenty-five – and a rather larger number under thirty-two – had been kept in the schools by local education authorities under the classification 'indispensable'. However, these men too were now to be called up, and a serious situation was expected in the schools. The Middlesex Education Committee requested that in the 'present crisis the staffing of the Schools should be on the basis of the actual Code requirements wherever possible and the committee would be glad if the Managers could see their way to release one of their teachers to assist in other schools if necessary.'

Headteachers often gave news of teachers' and pupils' service, and were very sad when they had to report the deaths on active service of former pupils or staff.

Corporal Harold Talboys, for example, the younger son of Mr R. Talboys of Hilliard Road, Northwood, had been educated at Northwood Elementary School and had enlisted in the 1st Rifle Brigade in 1911. In June 1915, he received the congratulations of his commanding officer for conspicuous bravery in the field, carrying despatches.

Amongst those from Pinner Road School who lost their lives were Percival Woodman and postman Charlie Tobbutt; Henry Blackford, a widower; William Bray; and Arthur and Harold Brill. Northwood College magazine from 1915 (until it ceased, to save paper, in 1916) gave details of those girls helping in War Hospital Supply Depots, working in VAD (Voluntary Aid Detachment) or other hospitals – and those, albeit few, who were in France. Miss Dorothy Clough left the Ruislip Schools, where she had been an assistant, on 25 June 1918 to take up service with the Ministry of Munitions, which positively encouraged the role of women. She had been a member of staff there since July 1913. Her brother, Thomas, was reported as missing in Mesopotamia on 2 February 1919.

LEISURE PURSUITS

CINEMAS WERE patronised by both soldiers home on leave or recovering and those billeted with local families, as well as those well-paid men and women who worked in the munitions and other factories. The escapism and morale-boosting films – along with comfort, warmth and safety at an affordable price – were all very well received, and it became one of the most popular forms of working-class recreation. When Bert Pope, manager of the Northwood Picture Theatre, enlisted in 1915, his wife continued running the cinema. Documentary films taken on the fighting front began in 1916 with *The Battle of the Somme*. In 1917, films changed over to a newsreel format. Concerts were also given at cinemas, like the Grand Concert, in aid of English and Belgian POWs, at Northwood cinema on 26 January 1916. By 1919 most cinemas were in a very strong position and at the beginning of their heyday.

Within the first weeks of war, over 1,000 local footballers who were registered with the Middlesex County Football Association had joined the Colours and this figure increased day by day. As young men joined up, many clubs were forced to close through lack of members. This resulted in land becoming earmarked, while other sports grounds had already been built upon. The MCFA cancelled all their coming season competitions and urged able-bodied men to join up without delay. As leagues and clubs disbanded, local sides found opposition from various Army units that were stationed nearby at Denham or Slough. All teams were encouraged to play matches to raise funds for war relief. The Great Western Suburban League suspended all football fixtures for the 1914-1915 season when ten clubs dropped out – Uxbridge and Southall were the only ones remaining. The Uxbridge and District League had already been disbanded. Professional football was stopped in July 1915 and replaced with regional leagues where players, who would only play on Saturdays, were unpaid. A London Works League and a Munitions League were formed for the employees of factories engaged in the war effort. Football matches were arranged between women working at local munitions factories and were held in aid of Red Cross funds. The Middlesex County Football Association had hoped that cup matches would be run in the latter half of the 1918-1919 season, but this was impossible with so few clubs being in a position to resume playing.

Cricket carried on in a desultory fashion for a time. Uxbridge Cricket Club was disbanded in 1915, having managed to play Slough, Northwood, West Drayton, the Royal Flying Corps and the King's Royal Rifle Corps stationed at Denham. The Ruislip

Tennis and Croquet Club was suspended in early 1916 for the duration of the war. By late August 1914, Uxbridge and West Middlesex Athletic Club had lost 25 per cent of its total membership. Golf too suffered. When, in the autumn of 1914, an Indian Field Ambulance Corps was set up, arrangements were made for them to go into camp for further training each weekend, from Friday night to Monday morning, at Eastcote, where a large sports ground was placed at the disposal of the corps by Mr Debenham, and convenient buildings in an adjoining ground lent by Mr Haywood.

On the other hand, during the early weeks of the war and thereafter, local rifle clubs reported that membership had greatly increased, while others were formed. The Ruislip Rifle Club opened its rifle range to anyone who wanted to learn to shoot. The Northwood Club, erected on the recreation ground in November 1914 in accordance with the requirements of the War Office, started charging 6d a month to new members and reduced the charge for ammunition. It was soon taken over by the council. In mid-1915 the club approached the council, which agreed that they should be permitted to use the range every morning and afternoon as well as the times fixed by an earlier agreement. Scouts, Girl Guides and members of the Church Lads' Brigade also had use of the club, using a wider range with no gas facilities. By January 1915, over forty members of the Northwood Club, past and present, had taken up military duties of one sort or another. By 1917, ordinary shooting had ceased, and activities were confined mainly to those members who were also members of the local VTC. The GWR/Metropolitan Railway also started a rifle range and butts at Wembley for their employees, together with drill and shooting squads.

Sports facilities for the women and the elderly remained largely unaffected. Indeed, a ladies' hockey team started at Ruislip early in 1915.

It took a number of years for sports clubs to recover from the war, in which some fine local players were killed in action. After the war ended, clubs made hard efforts and gradually reformed, albeit sometimes years later, and were successful in reviving the pre-war activities.

HEALTH

THE EARLY part of the twentieth century saw a great reduction in the more serious infectious diseases and the civilian population did not suffer unduly during the war years. Surprisingly enough, the civilian death rate in Britain actually fell, although 1915 and 1918 were years of high mortality.

Cases of typhoid fever remained relatively constant in the industrialised world, and with the advent of proper sanitary facilities and vaccines, had been virtually eliminated in many areas. In 1908 the total number of enteric fever cases in London was only 1,357, and all throughout hostilities there were sporadic cases of enteric fever throughout the borough. In July 1917, there was only one case in the district. In anticipation of war, the Army Medical Services had 200,000 doses of the typhoid vaccine stored for Army use. By the time of the end of the war, they had produced over 20 million doses.

A serum had been developed for the treatment of cerebro-meningitis, which was relatively rare in this country until 1915; an epidemic spread that year and there were several reports of local cases, mainly affecting only individuals. In the county of London, 712 cases were notified, and throughout England and Wales there were 2,343 cases. These were notifications amongst civilians only. In this year there were no reported cases of this illness, although a visitor to Northwood was diagnosed with cerebro-meningitis and placed in quarantine. A new and improved treatment arrived in 1918.

Scarlet fever had been a disease of great severity with a high death rate. Early in the twentieth century, however, it changed its virulence, causing, in the greater number of cases, a milder illness. A considerable outbreak of scarlatina in November 1914, mainly affecting those up to the age of fifteen, seriously strained the resources of the local isolation hospitals, and convalescents were moved to cottage hospitals. However, by the end of that year the numbers of notifications had significantly reduced, and in the spring of 1915 there were only scattered cases; by mid-June of 1915 it was in decline, although there was a small outbreak affecting a small number of people – a handful were reported at Northwood.

Diphtheria had been fairly widespread throughout the British Isles and had the greatest fatality rate, although mortality had greatly reduced after the introduction of an anti-serum which was first produced in some quantity in 1894. It came into general use in 1895. In 1914, twenty-one cases in Ruislip-Northwood were notified. Eighteen people were removed to the Isolation Hospital at Uxbridge and there were three deaths (one in Great Ormond Street Hospital from secondary complications traceable to diphtheria probably contracted in the district). In 1915 diphtheria was prevalent throughout the country and was the largest case of all infectious diseases for that year. By mid-July of that year, thirteen cases had been notified, with six more cases at the end of July, and several more cases over the next few months. By December 1915, there was another serious outbreak of diphtheria in the district, including forty-two cases in the north of the borough (mainly in Northwood School). Between 1 February 1917 and 26 March 1917, there were five cases of the disease, with two cases notified to the MOH in September. There were sporadic cases of diphtheria in 1918. A stock of diphtheria anti-toxin was kept for emergency use by the council and supplied free of charge to cases recommended by the medical man attending.

In 1872 there had been a severe epidemic of the dreaded smallpox. In the following year, a huge number of people were vaccinated, but despite the effectiveness of the vaccine, outbreaks of the disease still frequently occurred. A large outbreak began in Great Britain in 1901. In early November 1901, notifications rose to 227, and by January 1902 this had grown to reach 546 in a fortnight, the cases occurring all over London. By 1906, this outbreak had died down. From then on, the incidence of severe smallpox in any period was very small and it never became a serious Public Health problem again. During this war, about 7,000,000 people, mainly adult males, were vaccinated during their time in the Forces. This prevented the importation of the disease into the country and was welcomed by those who believed that the disease could be effectively controlled by the vaccination of contacts. However, several local cases were reported. In the spring of 1918, smallpox broke out again in the district. Patients suffering from smallpox and other infectious diseases were usually taken to Yeading Smallpox Hospital and Kingston Lane Hospital in Uxbridge. The Yeading Isolation hospital had an agreement with the Joint Hospital Board of other districts in Middlesex to reserve for their use a limited number of beds at the hospital in the event of an outbreak of smallpox.

Measles, a disease of high infectivity, continued unabated. In 1913 Middlesex had recorded a total of 377 deaths from measles – the highest recorded since 1900. In the spring of 1915 measles was prevalent, and it contributed to the upward surge in infant mortality. Infections rose again from 1916-1917. The disease did not become notifiable until late 1915 or even 1916. Between March and mid-June 1916, fifteen cases of measles had been notified to the local Medical Officer of Health. Between 1 February 1917 and 26 March 1917, there were thirty-one cases of the disease. In July 1917 there were eleven cases; August saw seven, and September, four. When in 1918 there was an epidemic, 202 cases were recorded at Ruislip and Northwood schools. In the first ten days of 1918, there were fifteen instances of measles, and between 25 February 1918 and April 1918 there had been fifty-six cases in the Ruislip-Northwood district.

Tuberculosis had declined during the latter part of the nineteenth century, but was still prevalent. It rose during the war, partly due to poor housing and overcrowding, exhausting work and worry over the dreaded 'knock on the door'. The disease easily spread with the influx of many people, but hospital beds were given to soldiers rather than tubercular civilians. Seven cases of pulmonary TB were reported in 1914, and three of non-pulmonary TB. Some of the patients were treated in open-air shelters and others, whose houses were in the favourable parts of the district, were treated at home.

In early 1918, Medical Officers noticed a large number of cases of gastric ulcers, and other districts had also noticed the growth. It was not thought that the diet, at that time, had anything to do with this increase, although many people in October 1917 were complaining about the ill effects of war bread. Overall bread consumption dropped by 22 per cent under rationing.

Mental health suffered with the strain that any war brings. The noise, sleepless nights and anxiety of the air raids and bombings – although these amounted in the end to almost nothing more than a nuisance in the area – and the war diet, the fear that came with every knock at the door (or for those better off, the long-distance telephone call), and the dread of the bad news that could arrive at any moment – if it hadn't already done so – left lots of people feeling drained.

It is thought that American soldiers unwittingly took the 'Spanish flu' with them into the war, although others suspect it began in 1916 in one of the many hospitals around Étaples. By June 1918 it had arrived in Great Britain, peaking in the second week of July and again in the first week of November. The final wave of this new strain of Spanish flu appeared towards the end of January 1919, peaking in the last week of February that same year. It was secondary pneumonia that killed rather than the flu itself. It was one of the worst plagues in history, and the illness affected everybody alike. People wore masks in streets, and in some towns the roads were sprinkled with disinfectants. Queues formed outside chemists' shops for medicines. In London, leaflets advising preventative measures were distributed to every house. Estimates differ, but there were probably over 22,000,000 deaths worldwide, 250,000 in Britain alone.

Local Pensions Committees were set up in 1916 to deal with the training and treatment of disabled men, to report on appeals against the findings of the Ministry of Pensions (who often claimed that incapacity was not a result of service), to deal with applications for alternative pensions by men and widows, make special allowances to wives and dependants in need and grants to meet sickness in a soldier's family. Servicemen posted as 'missing in action' were not declared officially dead until up to one year had passed and a military tribunal had heard the facts relating to the disappearance. If the loss of records meant that a date could not officially be declared, then an arbitrary date was decided upon. A notification of 'missing in action' meant an immediate loss of income and the uncertainty of any pension rights, which was devastating for the family of a married man.

Many general hospitals became inundated with injured soldiers and could hardly cope with civilian casualties. Mount Vernon Hospital was crowded with injured men and ill soldiers.

Concerns had been voiced for improvements to public health. One of the priorities was the fight against infant mortality. By 1918 there was a downward trend, but gradually medical arrangements were developed, and Ruislip and Northwood baby clinics had been established. By the end of 1918, the Government were committed to the idea of a new Ministry for Health to co-ordinate the service for health and national insurance and to take over the duties of the Local Government Board.

HOSPITALS

THE FLOW of casualties from the various theatres of war soon overwhelmed the existing medical facilities in the United Kingdom. The War Office had military hospitals erected in favourable districts, and towns set aside parts of their infirmaries for the wounded. In some cases they built hospitals and handed the buildings over, fully equipped, to the military authorities. Many wealthy people converted their residences into hospitals and bore sole charge, while others handed their houses over to the Red Cross Society, or to be used as hospitals or places of convalescence.

On the outbreak of war, Southampton became the number one military embarkation port, and the port of departure for the British Expeditionary Force, as all railway lines led directly or indirectly to it. The first convoy of 111 sick and wounded men arrived here on 24 August 1914 and were taken in the War Department Ambulance Train to the Royal Victoria Hospital, Netley. The new Marine station at Dover, which had not yet been completed, was ready on 2 January 1915 to receive up to two hospital ships and six ambulance trains at the same time. It had been a rush job to finish the Marine station. The stream of wounded from Flanders seemed never-ending, but finally it was decided to complete the station within a week. Work started on 23 December and by working day and night right through Christmas, the work was finished to schedule.

There were four ambulance trains in service in 1914. By July 1916, there were twenty-eight. Over seventy-five hospital ships were in service during the war. In the end, the total number of sick and wounded British and Commonwealth servicemen from all theatres of war conveyed in ambulance trains to British ports up to April 1919 was 2,680,000, divided fairly equally between Southampton and Dover (apart from a small number landed at other ports). The vast majority of those arriving at Southampton and Dover were the wounded from France. Those from various Eastern campaigns were landed at Avonmouth, Devonport or Liverpool.

There were almost 200 railway stations in Britain which received convoys of the sick and wounded. Denham and Southall, on the Great Western Railway, were the nearest stations to this area which received military ambulance trains which had been sent from either Dover, the principal port for the transport of the wounded, or from Southampton, or from both.

The distribution of patients after their arrival in this country was complicated. Their destination depended very largely on the nature of their disability. It was essential that

A motor-ambulance filled with wounded troops of the Middlesex Regiments rushes these wounded men to ambulance trains heading for hospitals around the country. By the end of August 1914, the hospitals of the capital were already beginning to fill up with desperately injured soldiers: 300 wounded men were at Woolwich and 316 at the London Hospital alone.

certain cases should go to hospitals specialising in particular types of treatment. For instance, the chief surgery for facial wounds was the Cambridge Hospital, Aldershot, until 1917, when a new hospital for facial injuries opened at Frognal, near Sidcup in Kent. To begin with, casualties returning to Britain would receive initial treatment in British hospitals, and would be transferred to convalescent hospitals to make way for new arrivals from the front. In many cases these were in large houses lent by their owners. Australian, New Zealand and Canadian casualties usually went to hospitals which their own medical personnel had established in Britain. Indian wounded troops were treated in the Royal Pavilion at Brighton, where separate provisions were made to meet the dietary and religious requirements of the different religions.

To facilitate distribution, advanced information was cabled about the various categories of patients (lying and sitting patients) on each hospital ship and the estimated time of arrival. These categories were subdivided into the number of officers, nurses and other ranks, with further subdivisions into surgical, medical, infectious, mental, and any other special cases. Patients were labelled with one of the five areas corresponding to their home area – London and Southern, West of England, Midlands, North England and Scotland and Ireland. This meant there was a possibility that patients would be sent to a hospital close to where they lived. Each area's 'home commands', showing the bed situation in their larger and specialist hospitals, sent daily notifications.

Private individuals generously offered their houses for the use of the wounded. The Admiralty and War Office had decided that most offers of houses for auxiliary hospitals should reach them only through the British Red Cross Society. A flood of offers (5,000) poured in. The Red Cross Society had an onerous task examining and sifting through all of them. Several large houses and other institutions in the area were offered, including the house of Mr and Mrs Hoare of Duckshill, Ruislip, which was turned down.

It was for voluntary hospitals that VAD nurses had been recruited and trained, and it was in these hospitals – about 1,600 of them countrywide – that most VADs spent their war service. These hospitals were set up to receive the sick and occasionally the wounded from the battlefields. At the end of June 1916, hospitals were ordered to clear out all convalescents and prepare for a huge rush of wounded. Most VADs were unpaid and worked full or part-time; they were under-trained nurses, recruited locally or through the Red Cross from Devonshire House in Piccadilly. The County Director of the Middlesex Territorial Force Association received all offers for the registration of temporary hospitals and detachments. In Middlesex, by April 1916, there were twenty men's and thirty-eight women's VADs, with a total strength of almost 3,000 (of which over 1,400 had been mobilised) – men for transport and women for nursing in the auxiliary hospitals in the county (of which, by that time, there were twenty-one, a total of almost 1,500 beds). The local VAD was often called upon to help with the removal of wounded soldiers, transferring them from ambulance trains to various hospitals in Middlesex. By the end of the war, the local VAD had assisted in the transport of thousands of men.

The tin church of St John's, in Hallowell Road, Northwood, opened in November 1914 with twenty beds, honouring a pledge made prior to the war. On 19 November 1914, the first patients arrived. For six months Presbyterian services were held in Northwood College's gymnasium. At the end of March 1915 the need arose for more beds to accommodate sick men sent from camp at Windsor. A house, Lea Croft, next door to the hospital, was then hired and ten extra beds were installed there. The hospital office was also situated at Lea Croft. Between 1 November 1914 and 30 June 1915, 172 soldiers had been admitted – seven of these were Belgians and the remainder British.

In addition to this, there were three civilians recovering from a nasty accident which had taken place on the new Presbyterian building in January 1915: men engaged in fixing the rafters on the roof fell when a scaffold pole broke. The institution had also treated eight military outpatients.

From its opening until 28 June 1915, the hospital had been under the official control of the ADMS, Royal Herbert Hospital, Woolwich, on which date it transferred to the control of the ADMS, Edmonton Military Hospital in north London.

In 1916, the permanent Presbyterian church in Hallowell Road was taken over by the hospital. In July 1916, due to the increasing numbers of casualties returning from the Somme, the accommodation was enlarged from 50 to 100 beds – a further 25 beds were also added in April 1917 when the Presbyterian church premises were entirely given up by the congregation. From May 1917 until the end of the First World War, services were held in Emmanuel church, Northwood.

In December 1915, the premises were supplemented by the addition of a new ward in temporary buildings, the McAlpine Ward, which had been presented by Mr T. Malcolm McAlpine. It had surgical, electrical and other equipment, a large day-room, kitchens, bathrooms and a storeroom, and it stood at the corner of Green Lane and Hallowell Road.

Green Lane, Northwood. (Courtesy of Hillingdon Local Studies, Archives and Museum Service)

Mrs Ellen Darlow, wife of the Revd Thomas Darlow, a congregational minister, was commandant of the hospital. By early 1917 the hospital had lost a lot of its staff: some had resigned, while others had gone to work in Military hospitals. The future of the hospital's resources and staffing levels looked bleak. The Government hinted that compulsory service might be required and appealed to women to volunteer in large numbers for service of national importance.

Over 2,000 wounded soldiers had been nursed here in Northwood by January 1919 and the total expenditure was £25,837. Apart from the matron and sisters, the nursing was carried out by members of the Northwood VAD (Middlesex X) which was founded under the Territorial Branch of the St John's Ambulance Association, which had also defrayed the expense of one trained nurse from London. It had begun its training in September 1913 and registered as Middlesex X at the War Office in June 1914. Further recruits were trained and enrolled in October 1914. A number of local women helped as cleaners, cooks and ward-maids. Members of the Northwood Men's VAD (Middlesex V) acted as orderlies and bath-men. Local contributions – subscriptions and donations from residents, road collections (a number of beds being named after the contributing roads) and church collections – supplemented War Office payments of 2s per patient per day originally, later rising to 3s 3d.

There were also donations of food, clothing and 'comforts'. The Northwood War Supply Depot provided most of the surgical dressings and bandages required. The Metropolitan and Great Central Railway companies allowed temporary buildings to be erected in their field, behind the hospital, to be used for recreation. The Colne Valley Water Co. supplied water free of charge, and the Pinner Gas Co. supplied gas at a reduced rate and donated gas-stoves free of charge. Ruislip-Northwood Urban District Council exempted the hospital from rates.

At a meeting which took place on Wednesday, 12 August 1914 at the church room, Ruislip, the Ruislip and Eastcote Hospital and Ambulance Corps was inaugurated. The vicar told the people present of the 'patriotic offer of Mr and Mrs B.J. Hall to permit the greater part of their residence, Field End Lodge, Eastcote, to be used as a hospital for wounded soldiers'. It had been intended, until the offer by the Halls, to use the church room itself as a hospital for the wounded. Field End Lodge opened as a hospital in about November 1914 with twelve beds in three wards, later increased to fifteen beds. By late 1915 it was equipped with twenty-eight beds. It was at first affiliated to the Northwood VAD Hospital. Loans and gifts were immediately forthcoming – blankets, sheets, cutlery, dishes, surgical dressings, splints and a fully-equipped bed, amongst other things. After the battle of the Somme, thirty-five more beds were added. When war ended, the thirty remaining patients were transferred to Northwood VAD Hospital.

The hospital did not receive any contributions sent to the Northwood hospital, but War Office payments were sent to Northwood and then paid over to Eastcote. It became an independent unit on 22 April 1915 and was staffed mostly by local girls. St John's Hospital, a hospital for infectious diseases at Uxbridge, did not, except in rare instances, admit patients from outside the area, apart from the church Lad's Brigade of the 1st King's Royal Rifles at Denham (who were charged at 6s a day in 1914). In 1916 this exception was extended to this VAD hospital. In June 1917 three seats at Eastcote were constructed for the use of the wounded soldiers. Messrs Tapping and Sons provided the wood free of charge. In December 1917, there were sixty wounded soldiers being cared for – some with their

Northwood and Pinner (Memorial) Hospital, as it was in the 1970s. (Courtesy of Hillingdon Local Studies, Archives and Museum Service)

wives living within easy reach of the hospital. In total, 1,028 patients were treated at this hospital, mostly those who had been seriously wounded and requiring operations.

By 1914 St Vincent's Cripples' Home had an operating theatre and X-ray apparatus. As this was the only institution in the area, at that time, to have these facilities, a considerable number of wounded soldiers from the Northwood and Eastcote hospitals were able to be X-rayed locally. This was done at a nominal charge.

Mount Vernon Hospital's planned new children's wing was delayed because of hostilities and was eventually abandoned in 1921. At the outbreak of war, the hospital, which had lent equipment for one ward at the Northwood VAD Hospital, placed beds at the disposal of the authorities and these were immediately filled with servicemen and refugees from Belgium suffering from tuberculosis. Later on in the war, surgical cases from the front were admitted, as were patients suffering from heart problems. The special X-ray and cardiographic equipment owned by the hospital was placed at the disposal of the military authorities and were continuously used for investigating the nature and extent of wounds and for heart cases.

Before war broke out there had been 18,000 hospital beds throughout the British Empire, and by the time hostilities had ceased, this had reached 637,000, more than half being in the United Kingdom.

To all of them went a constant flow of medical equipment and drugs, despite rationing. When the war ended, the McAlpine Ward, with surgical, electrical and other equipment, was taken over and transformed into a cottage hospital as a memorial to those who had died during the war. After considerable repairs and alterations, Northwood and Pinner Memorial Hospital opened on 10 March 1920 and the monument unveiled on Sunday, 13 February 1921.

TRANSPORT

UNDER SECTION 16 of the Regulation of the Forces Act 1871, the Government was given power to control all railroads. This control was to be exercised through an executive council composed of general managers of the railways and was set up in 1912. It consisted entirely of the general managers of the nine leading British railway companies. On 5 August 1914, the Government's Railway Executive Committee took over all the railways of Great Britain. All Government traffic was carried without charge and had precedence. During the fortnight of mobilisation, 632 special troop trains, including 186 to bring back Territorials from their summer training camps, were run over the Great Western.

Railways became an indispensable part of the war machine, not only abroad but also at home. Ambulance trains, trains carrying soldiers and sailors on leave (or back into action), workmen's trains and general war traffic – as well as the passage of civilians – placed great stress on the railway companies. In early 1915, the Metropolitan Railway, in conjunction with the Midland and South Northern systems in the north and with the South Eastern and Chatham to Brighton systems in the south, had (by reason of its lines under the 'Circle' near Farringdon station) charge of the conveyance over these lines of no fewer than 2,738 troop trains. During the dispatch of the British Expeditionary Force, as many as fifty-eight troop trains a day passed over the Metropolitan lines without any interference with the ordinary passenger traffic. Special workmen's trains were later started on the Metropolitan line. However, after the air raids long queues formed for the workmen's trains, mostly of people who had arrived locally to escape the raiders. This exodus of people so taxed all railways that in the spring of 1918 special restrictions on the issue of tickets were introduced: on the tubes men in uniform travelled free (as they did throughout the country on trams and buses). In the end there were so many troops this also had to be withdrawn.

Thousands of railway workers, many of whom were Reservists or Territorials, joined the Colours, and eventually a restraining hand had to be placed on them. Amongst those locals who enlisted was Mr W. Clow of St Cecilia, Hallowell Road, Northwood, the Great Central Railway Co.'s superintendent of the line: he joined the Military Railways Department with the rank of Major in early 1917. Joseph Norman Rostern was serving as a Lieutenant in the 2nd/7th Manchester Regiment, and was reported missing at Peronne. He was the youngest son of Joseph Rostern, CBE, Chief Goods Manager with the Great Central Railway, and Clara Rostern of 'Prestwych', Dene Road, Northwood.

Old bus on a new route: London motor bus transporting wounded soldiers between Antwerp and Ghent.

Sadly, 130 men who were employed on the Metropolitan Railway were killed in action, including Gilbert Bruce and Ronald Welby King, both of Northwood. Charlie Kingston of Uxbridge had worked on the Metropolitan Railway at Uxbridge and Ruislip, where he was a clerk. He was killed in action on 30 August 1918. His brother, George (also of Uxbridge), who worked at Farringdon Street station, had been killed in action on 14 April 1917. Lawrence Johnson, who lived at Uxbridge, had worked in the Engineering Department at Ruislip as a platelayer; he died of enteric fever at Nantes. Henry Skey (Royal Field Artillery) was the youngest son of Arthur Skey, stationmaster at Ruislip station. He accidentally drowned at Alexandria on 23 September 1915. Almost 500 men who had been employed on the London, Brighton & South Coast Railway also lost their lives, including James Finch, a porter at Paddington station, and Guy Glyn, both of Northwood. Other railway companies were equally affected, and local lads were amongst those who were employed by them. Leigh Partington, who worked for the Great Northern Railway, lost his life. Robert Stevens and William Williamson were killed, and Harry Boreham, who held a post in the Chief Accountant's office at Euston station, also died; all three were employed by the London North Western Railway and all lived at Northwood.

In July 1915 a new booking office was erected at Eastcote station, but with the shortages of staff, shut-downs of stations on all lines began in 1915 (with further closures in 1916).

The newly built munitions factories were turning out war material at high speed and relied on continuous transport, but there were not enough trains to carry the material they had made to the front. As a result, as a matter of urgency, on 1 January 1917 ordinary passenger fares were raised by 50 per cent, restricting public travel, and a large number of stations were closed. Ruislip Manor station was one of these: it was closed on 12 February 1917, and reopened on 1 April 1919.

A great deal of traffic on the Great Central line came from both Northolt Aerodrome and the National Filling Factory's dump at South Ruislip. By mid-1918 a special train from Ruislip conveyed the large number of men then working in the district to and from these sites.

As the railways had come under considerable strain, road transport grew rapidly, but the more the roads were used the more they fell into a state of disrepair. Councils carried out repairs to local roads, mainly tarring; sometimes POWs were used to carry out this work. The major road repairs were carried out in conjunction with the military authorities. By March 1915, the War Office was requiring improvements to Kingsend and West End Road, and a private road which ran from Northolt Junction (South Ruislip) station opposite Hundred Acres. In September 1915 the Road Board requested the improvement of a private road running from Northolt Junction to Northolt Road. West End Road, between Ruislip station and Northolt Aerodrome, was in urgent need of repair due to the extraordinary amount of traffic by mid-1917. In September 1917, a section of West End Road between the entrance to the Northolt Junction station and the boundary of Uxbridge Rural District was repaired and reconstituted.

The London Territorials depositing their colours at St Pancras Church in August 1914. 'Fear God and defend your country,' was Princess Louise's message for the troops. 40,000 men had mobilised by 5 p.m. on the day after war was declared, and all vacancies were instantly filled.

Men were still working on the West End Road when an urgent letter, addressed to Ruislip-Northwood UDC, was received from the Road Board: it discussed the need to construct and improve roads for military purposes to access a proposed training store depot at Ruislip. The council was asked to undertake the work, the whole expense being borne by the Road Board. Two additional men were hired and the military authority required that as a matter of urgency, overtime be worked, paid at the rate of 1s per hour, as from 22 February 1918. The Road Board had previously requested urgent repairs to Kingsend in June 1917. The roads in Ickenham were, by March 1918, falling into a sorry state, worn out by the frequent traffic – including tractors and heavy lorries – using them. Mr A. Bayley wrote to his council, Ruislip-Northwood UDC, complaining about the condition of the roads in Eastcote in May 1918. Ickenham Road, Ruislip, was, by November 1918, in a poor state of repair due to the excessive speed, weight and extraordinary amount of Government lorries travelling along it, conveying goods to the aeroplane stores at Ickenham. A petition to the council was sent by the ratepayers to both repair the road and reduce the speed of heavy vehicles. The section of road from Eastcote station southward to the Uxbridge Rural District Council's boundary had been damaged by a large number of Government traction engines, trailers and lorries. In these cases, Councils claimed a proportion towards paying the cost of repairs from the Road Board.

The proposed building of the Western Avenue was deferred. The Road Board had agreed grants for certain road-widening schemes and improvements in Ruislip in 1914 under their town-planning scheme, but this had to be abandoned until 1919. Again, in 1916, all councils considered arterial road development, especially for the profitable employment of surplus labour in any period of unemployment after the war. In late 1918, the Road Board again investigated the various schemes and their reports on the suggested Western Avenue and the North Circular Road were issued as a parliamentary Paper. It was recommended that the Western Avenue would be an almost entirely new road over 15 miles long.

Thousands of women were employed on public transport. They acted as ticket collectors, porters, ticket inspectors, booking office clerks, etc. As from the early summer of 1916, a number of women were also employed as conductresses on buses and trams. These women, who wore blue uniforms, had to undergo a special course of training prior to employment.

RATIONING AND THE CULTIVATION OF LAND ORDER 1916

Britain imported much of the food needed for her population of around 45 million. This position remained secure as long as the Navy could ensure safe transit from suppliers oversees. During 1915, however, almost a quarter of British ships had been requisitioned. With this shortage of ships, fewer goods were imported and by February 1915 various commodities had increased in price. Although controls on food had begun at an early stage in the war, by 1916 there was no real shortage of food in Britain (although both prices and wages had begun to rise). By 1916, however, food substitutes were used to a limited extent and by the end of that year, less food was being produced than before the war. Although the convoy system cut the sinking of our ships, our food supplies were insufficient to go round at reasonable prices. The poor potato harvest of 1916 reduced poorer British residents to hardship, and on 13 January 1917 the first food riot occurred. By this time the average working-class family needed at least an extra 15s to pay for food and a further 1s 10d per week for rising fuel costs.

At the end of 1916, Germany was beginning to recognise that she could not win the war on the Western Front and decided to seek victory by waging unrestricted submarine warfare in the Atlantic – that is, to starve Britain into submission. By the winter of 1916-17, German U-boats had sunk 632,000 tons of British shipping, in intensified submarine blockades. By April 1917, one ship out of four leaving Britain's ports never returned, and British shipping losses reached their peak, losing 526,000 tons – the highest loss in any month of the war. Britain's food situation became serious, taking Britain to the edge of defeat.

Furthermore, the British wheat acreage and production had declined significantly since 1861, and wheat prices fell steadily from the spring of 1915. When supplies fell seriously short, owing to a poor world harvest and following the closure of the Dardanelles, Russian wheat could no longer be obtained. In 1916, British wheat-fields had been reduced further by a quarter of a million acres: the general production of home-grown food fell by 12 per cent between 1915 and 1916. The price of wheat, barley and oats had not been so high, by early 1918, for at least 100 years. The Government had to respond by fixing the prices. For the first time queues appeared at shops, though this was not on a large scale (despite the influx of people, both to work and to seek shelter from the air raids).

To make matters worse, farmers and farmhands had been gradually called up, and not much food was being produced. As so many people had come to the area, not only to work but as refugees, billeted soldiers, and wounded men in hospital, there was not enough

The royal household adopted voluntary rationing in order to inspire other households to do the same. However, they also hosted several teas for wounded troops. Here the Duchess of Sutherland arrives to 'wait' at Buckingham Palace in 1914, serving the three contingents of wounded soldiers from London hospitals scheduled for tea that day. Some of the injuries were very severe, including men who had lost both of their arms, or both legs. Many of the titled families of the county (including the Duchess of Devonshire) also served food and drink, as did Prince Albert.

food to go round. Shopkeepers were by now selling their wares to everyone (as it had been made illegal to only sell to regular customers), and queues therefore grew more frequent – and prices rose.

A special Department of the Ministry of Food was set up to promote the inauguration of National Kitchens for 'all classes', a large proportion of the expense, in the first instance, be provided by the Exchequer.

The first National Kitchens were opened in (or close to) London at Westminster Bridge Road and Acton. Several residents petitioned the Local Food Control Committee of Ruislip-Northwood on 26 February 1918, but they decided not to try the scheme in the area (although discussions still took place right up until the Armistice).

As time went along, people became anxious and appeals were made for voluntary rationing. By mid-April 1917 the King, Queen and Royal Household had adopted a policy of voluntary rationing and, inspired by this, the people who followed the scheme wore a badge of purple ribbon. Lord Devonport, a rich grocer, head of Kearley and Tonge's (provision merchants) and since 1909 chairman of the Port of London Authority and native of Uxbridge, was appointed the first Food Controller at the Ministry of Food in December 1916 and quickly put into place the restriction of the price of food; he launched a voluntary rationing scheme in late May 1917.

The first national rationing scheme, applying to sugar (two-thirds of which had come from Germany and Austria-Hungary), came into force on 1 March 1917. The quantity was reduced again in July 1917, but throughout that year local authorities introduced rationing schemes of their own. Sugar substitutes were available and some housewives resorted to using these. There was a shortage of bacon locally by the beginning of October 1917 – as well as tea, bread, margarine, lard, condensed milk, rice, butter, paper and some other commodities. Prices rose further.

By 1918 the food situation was at its most serious. The local paper, the *Advertiser and Gazette*, was amongst the first of the journals to advocate compulsory rationing. Local Food Committees were set up, and in May 1918 a Food Control office opened at the Poplars in Ruislip. In the spring of that year the country had only two weeks' supply of food left. Even hospitals and schools suffered. Mount Vernon, in common with other hospitals, had considerable difficulty obtaining supplies, and there was a serious shortage of milk at St Vincent's Cripples' Home. Food, as well as drugs, was in short supply, putting up prices, and food rationing applied to patients and staff alike. The compulsory rationing of certain foods – meat and bacon, butter and margarine (from the end of 1917, local bakers were already using cocoa-butter as an indifferent substitute to margarine) – came into operation in the last week of February 1918 and affected London and Middlesex, Hertfordshire, Essex, Kent and Surrey. Early in April the rest of the country was also rationed. Food was distributed almost equally between the rich and the poor, perhaps more than ever before. Customers were allotted to particular retailers who would be supplied by a specific wholesaler. Each household was issued with two ration cards, one for butcher's meat and bacon and the other for butter or margarine. Mrs Miller of Eastcote Lodge Farm became a registered dealer in margarine. As part of the Food for Britain campaign, food parcels were sent out from all over Australia for distribution amongst widows.

Dinner for the wounded at Buckingham Palace. The King and Queen circulated amongst the men, shaking hands as they went.

Mouth Vernon Hospital. (Courtesy of Hillingdon Local Studies, Archives and Museum Service)

As this rationing took effect, queues all but disappeared. However, there were various summonses for people selling products at too high a price. In May 1918, cheese was rationed at Ruislip-Northwood. The council took control of the supply and took 75 per cent of all cheese consignments for distribution amongst certain classes of workmen. It was commonly thought that wartime shortages of food would lead to illnesses and possibly also to early deaths in certain civilian communities.

Rationing was not only confined to food. Coal, which by early 1915 had risen in price by 20 per cent, was another necessary commodity of which there was a shortage in Greater London during the winter of 1916-17, and queues of people, in which children predominated, besieged the coal dealers. Coal rationing was introduced in London in the summer of 1917 and was extended to the rest of the country a year later. The order applied to all consumers of coal, coke or other fuel for heating and cooking (or purposes other than industrial use): every customer was required to purchase or obtain fuel only from a registered coal merchant or licensed coal dealer and then only from one merchant or dealer. One way of saving coal was put forward – to fill drainpipes with one part cement to nine parts coal dust, ramming this mixture down and adding water. It was supposed to burn for hours.

Church services were confined to daylight hours, followed by theatres, cinemas, music halls and restaurants. In the summer of 1916 the Daylight Saving, or Summer Time Order, came into effect. This enabled industries to make fuel savings. Restrictions on petrol were imposed early in the war and became tighter as hostilities progressed.

By 1916 the cost of paper had almost trebled. On 14 February 1916, the Middlesex Education Committee wrote to all the managers of council and non-provided school:

In view of the great increase in the price of paper and of the great difficulty which will be experienced in obtaining paper, I am directed by my Committee to ask you to be good enough to instruct your Head Teachers to be as economical as possible when ordering exercise books, drawing books, examination paper etc., and as far as possible to commence using slates in stock at once…

Instructions were also issued that both sides of the paper were also to be used. School magazines either ceased altogether or became much smaller. By mid-1917 parish magazines were printed on inferior paper and were reduced in length, while costing more. In January 1918, because of the enormous increase in the price of raw materials, the local paper increased its cost by ½d to 2d. National newspapers, which were under Government censorship and monitored to ensure they maintained morale, were in 1918 reduced to four pages. Sunday papers had stopped being published by this time. The *Uxbridge Gazette* had also reduced in size to save paper, and already, by early 1916, could only be obtained by regular order. In late 1917 or early 1918, the *Gazette* was one of the first local papers in the country to organise a house-to-house collection of waste paper. In the spring of 1918, local milkmen were asking for their payments as they no longer had the paper to write the bills.

The *Evening News* in mid-August 1914 had carried advice on which vegetables to plant for food supply to those who had gardens or plots of land. This advice came from the Royal Horticultural Society and was also printed in the local paper. The importance of producing food for others was stressed. Before 1916, allotments were virtually unknown, although in about 1885 the Harefield, Ickenham and Ruislip Horticultural Society was formed, and horticultural shows were arranged. In 1907 the Small Holdings and Allotments Act was introduced, and by 1911 the Ruislip-Northwood Small Holdings and Allotment Society had been formed, holding its first horticultural show in 1912. Already, by late 1914, eight men from Northwood had been willing to take up, at 9d per pole, the allotments adjoining the cemetery field, near Hilliard Road.

By Christmas 1916 the allotment campaign was well under way, spurred on by the gravity of the food situation. The Government issued a Cultivation of Lands Order facilitating the acquisition of land for smallholdings and market gardens in January 1917. With this order, parish councils and urban district councils scheduled land for cultivation after touring the locality. It was thought that some land would be suitable for farmers, for allotments or as grazing land – although sometimes it meant new fencing, which was not available. In January 1917, the district council of Ruislip-Northwood invited tenders to plough 3 acres of grassland situated at Northwood.

The Ruislip-Northwood War Agricultural District Committee was established in 1917. Thirty-eight farmers attended a meeting held by the chairman of the Ruislip-Northwood Council. These committees responded willingly to the guidance of the Central Food Production department at the Board of Agriculture who conferred upon them powers for the acquisition of land, within or without their own urban area for food growing, provided that the land could conveniently be cultivated by persons residing within the urban area. Private gardens were also turned over to vegetable growing. Allotment patrols were organised and growers took turns to guard their own and neighbour's plots.

When the railway line had been built between Harrow and Uxbridge, sufficient land had been taken for four tracks. This provided 6 acres within the fences, acres which, together with Metropolitan fields at Eastcote and Ickenham, were turned over to cultivation.

Ploughing was commenced on the railway embankment of the Metropolitan Railway between Eastcote and Rayners Lane in early 1917 to provide food, including potatoes, for workers, and logs were cut down for war hospitals. The Metropolitan Railway War Services Corps were also engaged in agricultural work along the line to Uxbridge.

Ruislip-Northwood Council took an active interest in food production and had, in 1916, resolved to maintain and increase the growth and production of food in the district. A Food Production Committee was appointed to look into the dispersal of surplus food that had been grown in the district. In April 1916 the council offered land adjoining the recreation ground at Northwood rent free for a term of three years (from 25 March 1916) to existing allotment holders in the district. This land would be equal in extent to the holder's existing allotment, as far as land was available. When only two allotment holders took an interest in the extra land, the council issued notices offering the land on the terms that the rent payable for the whole of the 5 acres would not exceed the total rent paid by the existing allotment holders. By June the whole of the council's allotments had been taken up, staked out and cultivated. In October 1917, land in Frithwood Avenue, Northwood, was being used for food cultivation. Further land was also made available which the council offered to any resident who could undertake the cultivation of an allotment. Three acres of land adjoining the cemetery, which had hitherto been cultivated by the council, was given up completely for allotments. The council itself was cultivating over 5 acres by July 1917, followed shortly afterwards by a 4-acre field adjoining 'Harescombe', near Frithwood Avenue and other land in Frithwood Avenue (including about 5 acres, 16 poles of land temporarily given to the council by the executors of the late Mr Jonathan Longbotham, and the available land at the sewage works – in all, a total of 10 acres). By late 1918, 9½ acres adjoining the cemetery at Northwood and other land, including part of Poors Field in Joel Street, plus a plot of land at Ruislip belonging to Mr George Young and let to Dr Jepson, amounting in all to 13½ acres, was available. Eleven acres of land adjacent to the River Pinn had, by mid March 1918, been taken over and ploughed up by the Middlesex War Agricultural Committee without notice to the council, who presented a claim for damages and rent.

The bottling of fruit and vegetables was demonstrated at the Warrender Institute at Ruislip on 5 July 1917. Northwood's church hall was the venue for the demonstration the following day, and on 31 August a demonstration was given on fruit and vegetable drying by Mrs Bodell, an official instructress from the Food Production Department of the Board of Agriculture and Fisheries. In April 1918 Mrs Bodell gave a number of practical demonstrations on food preservation in Northwood, Ruislip and Eastcote. In the same month a lecture, illustrated with lantern slides, was given in Northwood by an officer of the Food Production Department. More lectures and demonstrations on fruit and vegetable growing and on the proper preparation of soil and fertilisers were delivered at St Emmanuel church hall on 1 November 1918 by Mr John Odell, a member of the Scientific Committee of the Royal Horticultural Society. On 18 July 1918, Ruislip-Northwood Food Control Committee organised a vegetable market at Northwood which sold vegetables,

Cultivating surplus land besides the Metropolitan railway at Eastcote. (Photograph copyright of D.F. Edwards)

fruit, poultry, etc. In 1918 the Middlesex golf clubs, of which there were twenty-five, occupying about 2,000 acres, appointed a committee to inspect the land with a view to food production. Even Kew Gardens had 7 acres of lawn and flower plots prepared in February 1918 for growing potatoes and onions and 200 acres were under cultivation by Easter 1918. Shortly afterwards 7 acres of the royal paddocks at Hampton Wick were taken.

The Southern Federation of Allotment Holders, affiliated to the National Union of Allotment Holders, covered the area of London and southern counties. It was reported in February 1918 that membership in the last month had increased by almost 5,000 to 15,000 members; by the end of hostilities it exceeded 40,000. The demand for houses was so great that, in 1920, some allotment holders from all around the borough were notified that their plots were required for building purposes and that their right to rent the land was to be revoked.

As the war went on, more and more women were required to fill the gaps caused by men going off to war. By mid-1915, a party of five of the Women's Defence Relief Corps started work in the hayfields of Mr W.R. Goschen of Sigers, Eastcote. For about two weeks they lived in a shed on the farm where they had their own hammocks and cooking facilities. More than likely other farms in the locality also hired women at this time.

In February 1916 there was a call for 400,000 women to carry out agricultural work previously carried out by the men, who were now being called up for duty. In the summer of 1916 the Minister of Agriculture foresaw a serious shortage of horticultural labour, although all available soldiers were working on farms during the pressure of harvesting.

Land girls in Ruislip High Street. (Courtesy of Hillingdon Local Studies, Archives and Museum Service)

In January 1917, when a new minister took office, the Women's Land Army was born, funded by the Government. The Land Army was divided into three sections – agricultural, timber cutting and forage (for Army horses). Women signed on for either six months or a year. If an application was successful, the Government offered an initial wage of 20*s* a week and a free uniform. After passing an efficiency test, the wage was raised by 2*s* a week. Various training schemes were set up in different parts of the country and women were expected to go to whichever part of the country the Selection Board thought most fit. Many women also worked on plough teams. On 21 August 1917, the Corn Production Act 1917 was passed. It provided for the fixing of minimum rates of wages applicable to everyone employed in agriculture, including work on farms, market gardens, orchards, nursery grounds, woodlands and osier land. By the end of the war there were about 250,000 'land girls'. In 1919 the local paper reported that over 5,000 women in the Land Army wished to remain in agriculture.

When war ended the demand for allotments had taken hold and, in common with the Second World War, rationing continued long after the conclusion of hostilities. Indeed, it was not fully abolished until three years after the war ended.

FUND RAISING AND COMFORTS

FROM THE moment war was declared, relief funds were started, far too many to mention here. A relief fund was opened for Middlesex, which was divided into districts, with local sub-committees. These sub-committees were given the power to act at once. Public meetings were held, and at a well-attended meeting at St John's Presbyterian church, Northwood, on 12 August 1914, an emergency committee was appointed and relief measures quickly set up.

These committees dealt with the local effects of the war, including ensuring food supplies and co-ordinating other aspects of the war effort – including the care of the wounded at home. Local funds were opened. Ladies' Committees were set up, which in the Uxbridge area divided work into five smaller committees to collect money and organise other work. There was a visiting committee, a committee for needlework and a committee for food depots. Public houses in the district were supplied with collecting boxes for local relief funds. Eventually local relief funds amalgamated into the National Relief Fund, which had been inaugurated by the Prince of Wales and aimed to centralise the work. However, by and large, the anticipated levels of distress were not realised and much of the sums raised went to other causes, mainly the Red Cross.

Local offices of the Soldiers' and Sailors' Families Associations (SSFA), which for many years had alleviated the difficulties arising where the breadwinner had gone off to war, were started with voluntary staff. Their biggest work was visits and the advancing of money to distressed families in cases of delayed separation allowances, supplementing these allowances where necessary. The association at first itself supplied the money required, but later it was financed from the Prince of Wales' Fund. It only dealt with NCOs and men. By the end of 1914 Lady Hillingdon was president for Middlesex, as she had been during the Boer War, with Dr Christopher Addison of Northwood as vice-president and the Revd Prebend C.M. Harvey, vicar of Hillingdon, treasurer. The Uxbridge division covered all of the modern London borough of Hillingdon and also included Northolt and Cranford. Local sub-committees were set up. It appears that only records covering the period between the commencement of hostilities and towards the end of 1915 are available. During this time, thirteen cases of hardship had been dealt with in the Ruislip-Northwood area. A Thrift Club was already run by the SSFA in Northwood, and women were encouraged to knit for the soldiers. War Pensions Committees were also set up.

Troops initially wore soft caps knitted by women across the country. However, in March of 1916 a soldier stood up in the House of Commons and called out, 'I'm asked to ask you to protect the heads of British soldiers against shrapnel fire.' This image shows a London factory, staffed by women – as many factories were as the war ground on – who gave up their holiday to work, producing the first steel helmets for the front. These helmets reduced head wounds from 25 per cent to half a per cent of injuries tended.

Work quickly got under way to raise money for good causes, knit and sew garments for the poor or for the troops, sew bandages for the wounded, prepare parcels for prisoners of war, etc. Working parties were set up all over the place, flag days sprang up for various causes and funds were started to raise money for some or other purpose. Girls knitted socks, mittens, mufflers and helmets for the troops. The Middlesex Cinema War Fund was also set up in September 1914 for the relief of widows and children of Middlesex soldiers and sailors killed in action.

In the months of September and October 1914, when only a relatively small percentage of men were registered as unemployed, the percentage of women standing idle was three times as great. Queen Mary stepped in and inaugurated the Queen's Work for Women Funds, for women who wanted to work rather than receive charity. A grant was made out of the National Relief Fund. The money had come from a response to that appeal and was paid into the National Relief Fund for the sole purpose of the various projects and relief purposes for women. Over 300 branches were established throughout the country. Comforts for the troops – clothing, blankets, respirators, etc – were all made, and money was collected.

The Queen had formed Queen Mary's Needlework Guild (QMNG) in 1914 and voluntary needlewomen mobilised themselves everywhere. War Hospital Supply Depots were formed at Battersea, Blackheath, Hampstead, Market Harborough, Plymouth, Streatham and Wimbledon. A Branch Guild of the Northwood Ladies, under the auspices of the War Hospital Supply Depot, was set up and a depot was opened in a flat above the offices of Messrs Densham and Lambert on 9 November 1915. The voluntary workers each week subscribed to the running expenses of their depot, and the whole of the sums coming in from the public were solely devoted to the purchase of material. Many sewing parties of voluntary workers, also engaged in making shirts and other garments for troops, sprang up all over England and did valuable work.

The workers of the Primrose League, a Conservative Party organisation which had begun in 1883, and was divided into district 'habitations', helped in many ways, laying aside all political activities. Lady Milman was appointed chairman of the Needlework Committee of the Primrose League and working parties were held at the Central Office and at the local habitations, of which it is known that there was one at Uxbridge. There may also have been habitations at Ruislip and Northwood and elsewhere at this time. Vast numbers of garments were sent out to the Queen's Needlework Guild, the Order of St John and the British Red Cross Society.

War Savings Associations were set up under the National War Savings Committee. Children purchasing War Savings Stamps or subscribing through a War Savings Association, or adults purchasing on behalf of a child, were issued with pictured stamps on demand – one for each 6d spent. The Government spent the money on all kinds of things, from paying for the war and the reconstruction of housing schemes to health reforms and education after the war; money also went towards finding work for demobilised men. The Government continuously borrowed money at short notice by means of Treasury Bills, and in order to repay them money was required – money which could only be obtained by all the citizens of the state continuing to purchase War Savings Certificates and War Bonds.

Ladies' Red Cross meeting at Claridge's in 1914. These ladies are making woollen shirts for the troops. Queen Mary's Sewing Guild was set up in 1914, and a distribution office for the items made by ladies like this was quickly set up in St James' Palace.

A special War Committee launched the YMCA Huts Fund in November 1914, to provide dining halls and recreation rooms (for munitions factories and servicemen) and sleeping accommodation, amongst other things. It was a nationwide appeal for £25,000, but later increased by another £25,000. In the first two years of war the subscriptions amounted to £830,000. Harrow School in 1915 gave a complete building. A YMCA hut for servicemen was also opened at Northolt Aerodrome on 18 April 1917, prior to which the church room at Ruislip had been used.

The *Gazette* started a fund for supplying Middlesex 'Tommies' at the front with cigarettes almost as soon as the war broke out. Various other funds were also set up, including those for soldiers and sailors, prisoners of war and Belgian refugees. The Ruislip Vegetable Products Committee received gifts and subscriptions, fruit and vegetables for sailors of the Fleet.

Of the schools, Northwood College sent money to the Red Cross Fund for prisoners of war in Germany and the girls also knitted for the soldiers and sailors; scholars at Northwood Council Schools contributed 30s per month.

DEFENCE

IMMEDIATELY AFTER war had been declared, precautionary protective measures were taken by arrangement with the military authorities and taken in hand by the railway companies. The police, Boy Scouts, Cadet Corps and others were also called upon to guard the railways, although no unarmed watchman could serve on lines of primary importance. Our network of railways constituted indispensable lines of communications for troops, supplies, guns, ammunition, conveyance of the wounded, the supply of foodstuffs etc. There was also a possible threat from enemy aliens who might amass information as to the vulnerable points – bridges, viaducts, tunnels, etc. Therefore, precautionary measures to protect them from attack and interruptions had to be made. At first, policemen guarded all the railway bridges in the district day and night. Gradually Regulars or Territorials began guarding local stations, bridges and tunnels.

Local Volunteer Forces, affiliated to the National Voluntary Reserve, were begun, and Local Volunteer Training Corps (VTCs), allied to the Central Association of Voluntary Training Corps, were formed to help protect the country from possible invasion. They were composed of men not eligible for the Regular or Territorial Army for various reasons and were expected to encourage recruiting and undertake a certain amount of military training. The men were expected to remain in the Corps for the duration of the war. Voluntary contributions and subscriptions met expenses, and Northwood Volunteer Training Corps, 7th Platoon, B Coy, 5th Middlesex Regiment was formed in 1915. Drills were held at Holy Trinity School on Mondays and Thursdays at 8.15 p.m. and on Saturdays and Sundays at Nichol's Farm at 10.00 a.m. The 6th (Northwood-Pinner) Platoon, 3rd Battalion Middlesex Volunteer Regiment, held drills on Wednesday evenings and parades at the weekend.

The second platoon, the 7th, was raised later. There was also, by September 1915, a 'D' (Uxbridge and Yiewsley) Company of the Harrow Battalion, Middlesex Volunteer Regiment. At first the only uniform was a red cloth armband with 'GR' in black, worn over civilian clothes. By the summer of 1915, the uniform consisted of a grey-green tunic, cord breeches and puttees. The War Council issued an official khaki armband. General training carried on as before. A permanent camp of instruction for the Middlesex Volunteer Regiment was formed at Nazeing in Essex, and opened on Monday, 27 September 1915. The Volunteer Act of 1916 made a considerable difference. Official khaki was issued to those who passed a test of comparative fitness. They were armed with Lee-Enfield rifles and

Canon Bridge, Ruislip. (Courtesy of Hillingdon Local Studies, Archives and Museum Service)

issued with a Lewis machine gun for instruction purposes. There was a final examination on the Lewis gun at the Wellington Barracks. At first, air-raid warnings brought out a strong muster of members. Defence guards were undertaken at various establishments, including the dump at South Ruislip. Cadet Companies were also formed: a Ruislip platoon was formed in about May 1915.

In April 1916, National Guards and the Royal Defence Corps were created, mainly from old soldiers invalided from the fighting fronts. The Royal Defence Corps was later known as the National Reservists.

Much of the bombing of Britain was indiscriminate, although military targets were in most cases sought. Usually the bombing was sporadic, with only the occasional sustained attacks. Nevertheless, there were a considerable number of casualties and heavy material damage. Although fewer bombs were dropped by aeroplanes than by airships, more casualties and damage were caused by them. This was probably because attacks by aeroplanes were directed towards cities and towns, whereas airships dropped many bombs indiscriminately from great heights – and often in open country in order to lighten the airships.

By August 1914, only thirty anti-aircraft (AA) guns were deployed in the United Kingdom, and twenty-five of these were 1-pounder 'pom-poms' – remnants from the Boer War. In London there was an old 'pom-pom' and a naval 6-pounder, very clumsily mounted. At the end of October 1914 the Royal Artillery were placed in charge of defending everywhere but the capital, and the Admiralty was confirmed in the responsibility for the defence of London – with aeroplanes, guns and searchlights, temporarily assisted by four Royal Flying Corps aircraft from Joyce Green at Dartford and Hounslow, two at each – and of other large undefended towns, and for dealing with enemy aircraft crossing the coast. Military airships also guarded London.

After an airship raid on London, the city's first, on the night of 31 May/1 June 1915 killed seven people, other 3-inch guns increased London defences to eight. Until 1917 there were only sixteen guns, comprised of AA Defence Force fixed gun and searchlight positions, the Royal Naval Anti-Aircraft Mobile Brigade with, eventually, fourteen guns mounted on lorries and another mobile force equipped only with light AA guns, defending London, mostly manned by Royal National Volunteer Reservists (RNVR) part-timers.

The deficiency in these defences was emphasised by the raids of September 1915. On 1 October 1915, orders were issued by the Admiralty for guns, searchlights and aeroplanes to be brought to London as a precautionary measure against aerial attacks. Northolt Aerodrome, Hainault and Sutton's Farm all received two of the very best machines then available – BE (Bleriot Experimental) 2Cs. Searchlights were installed near all aerodromes and mobile guns were also made available. By the end of 1915, aeroplane searchlights were situated at Harmondsworth, Uxbridge and Eastcote. Special constables were at first deployed to man the searchlights when difficulty was experienced in finding crews. By February 1916 the total number of guns in the London district amounted to sixty-five.

In September 1916, the country was divided into two AA Defence Zones. The 'Ever Ready Zone', where all defences were in permanently readiness for action, covered this area. In April 1917, this zone was divided and renamed as Zones 'X' and 'Y', and in May 1917, the Army took control of all defences and a 'London Air Defence Area' was created. Rings of defences surrounded the capital, with guns in the central area with an inner ring of AA guns at about a 5-mile radius. A cordon of 13-pounder mobile anti-aircraft guns and searchlights around the north-western fringes of London surrounded this, which was also patrolled by fighter aircraft. Beyond this arc was a circle of gun defences surrounding the Home Counties, with outlying gun areas in Kent and Essex.

Yiewsley, Ruislip and Uxbridge (in that order), formed up into the Middlesex Regiment.
(Courtesy of Hillingdon Local Studies, Archives and Museum Service)

London National Guard Volunteer Corps, or National Guard, marching past Buckingham Palace.

Outside this circle was another searchlight ring. London had balloon aprons, each consisting of three Caquot captive balloons 500 yards apart and connected by horizontal wire from which was suspended, at 25ft intervals, steel wires 1,000ft in length. Eventually the height was raised to around 10,000ft. This forced the raiders to keep above that height and so enabled the defending machines to hunt them more easily. Gun Defence Sub-Commands were formed, and from 1917 to 1918 London's Western Sub-Command, which covered this area, consisted of nineteen gun stations (with twelve fixed 75mm French guns on mounts), four 'mobile' 75mm French auto-canons, and three 3in calibre British anti-aircraft guns. The defences also included thirty-six searchlight stations, which extended from about 2 miles beyond Watford to 3 miles south of Bromley, and from Windsor to Grove Park. The Sub-Command HQ was established in the Metropolitan Waterworks at Putney Heath. Each gun-station was under the charge of an officer and manned by a Sergeant, a Corporal and between sixteen and eighteen men. There were double crews at each station in order that the crews could work on alternate nights. Central stations (such as Hyde Park, Paddington Recreation Ground, Parliament Hill and Deptford) remained in the charge of the RNVR. Beyond them was a ring of inner guns, such as Richmond, Hounslow, Hanwell, Acton, Horsenden Hill and Kenton, with an outer ring extending through Eastcote, Windsor, Staines, Hampton, Morden, Croydon and Bromley to Grove Park.

The searchlight stations were manned by a non-commissioned officer with from six to eight men, according to the various types of engines by which the electric current was supplied to the searchlight. Around London a circle of searchlights was gradually drawn so that by close to the end of the war there were over 200, many of immense power. Most gun-stations were served by two searchlights, which were known as 'fighting lights'. The Eastcote light served the Horsenden Hill gun. Each gun and searchlight station was provided with a table fixed in the open in the immediate vicinity of the gun or light. On this was a map of the immediate district. It was covered with glass and illuminated from underneath. All information reaching a station was at once carried to the table and the position of an advancing target established on the squared map. As soon as the target was definitely located from any station, the station immediately reported the fact, and also the squares through which the target was passing at that moment, together with other information such as speed, altitude and direction. These OP's became of considerable value as sources of information during raids. The police, up to a 60-mile radius, were instructed to warn the city on the approach of enemy aircraft.

An elaborate telephone system was adopted so that the searchlight stations could communicate with gun-stations to which they were attached and the gun-stations could then communicate with HQ. Each gun-station was also connected to at least two observation posts, which were situated in opposite directions and some way away from the guns in order to observe the bursts of the shells and to advise the gun as to the position of the bursts in relation to the target. There were no posts locally.

To deal with airships which evaded fixed guns, mobile defence was quickly improvised by the Anti-Aircraft Corps. Machine guns with high-angle mountings were installed on motor chassis, together with searchlights.

In the summer of 1917, ninety fire brigades in an area of 750 square miles were organised to give aid in London in any emergency. All Reservists were called up from the front, and engineer detachments attached to the firemen were doubled. When the first air-raid warning reached the fire brigade, its supports closed in from the outlying area towards the most dangerous points.

The National Guard digging trenches near the GPO. Training in home defence – drill, musketry, ambulance work – was part of their duties.

The searchlight station at Hyde Park Corner.

Women fire-fighters from the Women's Volunteer Reserve drilling at a London workhouse.

Many councils made their own warning arrangements as far as possible. Police with 'take cover' placards and whistles, Boy Scouts on bikes shouting warnings, factory hooters and later church bells were all used in the beginning to warn of an air raid. In June 1915, Ruislip-Northwood Council obtained placards – 'WARNING! FIRES DUE TO AIR RAIDS'. On 14 August 1917 the council received a letter from the Metropolitan police stating that 'the firing of signals to locations within a 10-mile radius in the case of air raids,' was to be suspended, and 'that warning by this means would not be given in this District'. However, by March 1918 the council decided that the air-raid warnings were altogether insufficient and ineffective and decided to purchase an electric siren to give warning of approaching raids.

The defence of London never did reach its intended potential, unlike Paris – which, after a raid on 29 January 1916 killed twenty-six people, thereafter developed its defences so well that the French capital was left unassailed by Zeppelins.

The Royal Flying Corps, originally formed into Military and Naval Wings, had been constituted in 1912 by Royal Warrant. In mid-1914 the Naval Wing was detached and became the Royal Naval Air Service. In June 1914, shortly before war was declared, the Royal Flying Corps – aeroplanes and personnel – was brought together at Netheravon so they could benefit from lectures, discussions and practical flying on tactical exercises, reconnaissance and inter-service co-operation. On 4 August 1914 almost the entire strength of the four RFC squadrons flew to France for duty with the Expeditionary Force, and by the end of August there were only a handful of trained pilots and a modest supply of flyable aircraft left. Car inner tubes were distributed amongst the pilots to be used as lifebelts in the event of forced landings. Mounting losses in France meant that within a few months new aerodromes, the sites selected by the War Office, were planned for Northolt as well as for Norwich, Castle Bromwich, Beaulieu and Catterick. On 19 December 1914 two aircraft and crews were ordered to stand by at Farnborough, Brooklands and Hounslow.

Northolt Aerodrome was built on the site of open arable fields at first wholly in Ruislip but later extensions took it into Ickenham. The site had previously been surveyed three times since 1910 with the intention to construct an aerodrome, but nothing had taken place, although a sort of aero shed had been constructed. The land requisitioned for the Northolt venture comprised Glebe Farm, part of Down Barns Farm and Hundred Acres Farm. The north-west valley, so near to London, yet with few inhabitants, was formerly the scene of several skirmishes both in the War of the Roses and the Civil War. Work started in January 1915 on clearing the site and putting up the necessary buildings. An army of carpenters and navvies erected huts for the troops and hangars, and a road was built into the aerodrome from West End Road to near its northern boundary. Three straight 'pitches' were laid out from north to south, starting with the hangars and they extended towards and across the brook near the line of where the Western Avenue is today. Iron plates were used to bridge the stream. Although the ground had been made almost into mud heaps by all the traffic during construction, flights still took place. The 283 acre site consisted of six flight sheds, each 200ft x 60ft and a twin hangar of the same size, workshops and long wooden barrack huts. In August 1915 road repairs and improvements were carried out at the request of the Local Government Board. The aerodrome was opened on 3 March 1915,

A policeman taking the vital message through the London streets.

on which date No. 4 Reserve Aeroplane Squadron, an elementary training squadron, arrived from Farnborough.

A little later the aerodrome was extended taking over Hill Farm and it was designated as one of the seven Home Defence Night Landing Grounds which formed a crescent around the southern edge of London. At some time sidings on the Great Central line were constructed. Primitive lighting was installed for night operations. One B.E.2C plane was kept on permanent standby. On 6 May 1915 the War Office instructed Farnborough, Brooklands, Hounslow, Northolt, Joyce Green, Shoreham and Dover to maintain at least one aircraft at readiness for the defence of London, and at each military station a pilot was detailed daily for night duty in the event of a raid. If an enemy craft was reported approaching London, the War Office would inform each of the grounds at what hour a machine was to take off. This time would be calculated so as to allow the pilot to attain a height of 8,000ft before the German machine approached. At this height the pilot would patrol in the vicinity of his own landing ground, unless he sighted a hostile airship or plane, when he would take any necessary action. If no craft was seen, the pilot was to land one and a half hours after the flight had started. In the case of bad weather, the War Office was told and machines grounded. Situated to the north-east of landing fields, a chain of observers were placed ready to send up a rocket if they saw anything suspicious passing overhead. These rockets varied in colour depending on the direction of the craft.

Northolt was also used for training pilots in night flying for home defence duties and 11 Reserve Air (Home Defence Training) Squadron was set up for this purpose on 26 October 1915. It was commanded by Major Leslie Penn-Gaskell, one of the first RFC pilots to go to France in 1914, and equipped with Martinsydes, Curtiss JN and B.E.2cs. Two B.E.2cs and crew were permanently available for home defence.

By September 1915, the church room at Ruislip was used by the RFC from Northolt. Here there was an abundance of periodicals, material for letter writing as well as light refreshments and a snooker table. It should be remembered that in these times such facilities were a luxury.

By the end of the year there were eighteen reserve squadrons and eight operational squadrons engaged in flying training at Northolt, all turning out a satisfactory number of pilots.

During the winter of 1915/16 serious waterlogging problems, due to lack of drainage, made flying difficult; in the spring of 1916, a square of 8 acres was laid with clinker, with clinker tracks leading from the hangars.

Aircraft arrangements were extended in 1916 and the War Office undertook to provide two B.E.2cs with night-trained pilots from reserve aeroplane squadrons. The patrol system was unchanged, with pilots operating within visual range of their bases. On 13 January 1916, all RAS became known as RS (Reserve Squadrons). Detachments of B.E.2cs were sent to various aerodromes around London, including Northolt, replacing those previously supplied by other squadrons. On 31 March 1916 the various RFC stations around London and all London defence detachments were grouped into the newly formed 18th Wing under Lieutenant-Colonel F.V. Holt.

On Friday, 21 April 1916 an experiment took place with mirror position finders and a 3in mobile QFAA gun (which had be transported by road from Kenwood Barracks, Hampstead). A preliminary practice took place in the late morning at 3,700ft and, in the afternoon experiment, at 5,000ft. West End Road was blocked for traffic for an hour both in the morning and in the afternoon, as the gun could not be placed at one of the mirror stations (it weighed 9 tons, and therefore had to remain in the road). A local schoolboy who had volunteered his services during his holidays helped, and as it was a bank holiday, a large crowd collected to view the spectacle.

By the summer of 1916 the training of pilots in night flying and the recognition of the most suitable machines and weapons for attacking Zeppelins had greatly improved the prospects of the country's anti-aircraft defence.

In August 1916 the specialist nature of night operations was recognised by the transfer to Home Defence Wing of No. 11 Reserve Squadron, Northolt, by now the principal night-flying training unit. Training consisted of firing Le Prieur rockets at a 'Zeppelin'

The searchlight at Charing Cross station pictured in action, sweeping the skies for the dreaded Zeppelins. This picture had an exposure time of five minutes.

The Victoria Cross, or VC. This could be won by both rank and file.

target on the ground and air firing from a Lewis gun at small hydrogen balloons in the squadrons.

In late 1916/early 1917, Billy Bishop, a famous Canadian air ace who was to win a Military Cross on 7 April 1917 for shooting down a German balloon (and later that year, a VC), was transferred to No. 11 Squadron at Northolt for an advance course which included night flying. Feeling that he had nothing more to learn, the twenty-two-year-old soon fell foul of the commanding officer, Major B.F. Moore. Bishop's instructor was Squadron Commander Tryggve Gran, a Norwegian and the only subject of a foreign neutral country accepted to serve in the Royal Flying Corps during the First World War. He had served with Scott's ill-fated expedition to the Antarctic. Bishop's memory of night flying was that it was a nightmare, but he consoled himself with the knowledge that there was no night flying at the front. J.A. Aldridge, who trained in May 1917, recollected that some of the instructors at Northolt carried a wooden mallet to lay out any pupil who panicked under instruction!

Because of the terrible losses of pilots and observers during the Battle of the Somme in July 1916, all the squadron pilots and observers had been posted to various squadrons in France. New aircrew arrived at Northolt and the squadron was brought up to full strength and re-equipped with long-awaited Sopwith 1½ Strutters. One of the flight commanders who joined at this time was Captain H.H. Balfour, later Lord Balfour of Inchrye. Five weeks later, on 24 January 1917, after also serving as home defence, the squadrons had been trained and were on their way to St Omer in France. Captain Balfour was detailed to take the squadron personnel by boat to France via Southampton. Unfortunately, however, the first aircraft airborne, flown by twenty-three year old Second Lieutenant Henry Addis, stalled and spun out of control, killing him and a terrier dog, belonging to Captain Balfour, which was in the rear cockpit. His mechanic, 1st Air Mechanic Frederick Foott, died from his injuries six days later at Southall Auxiliary Military Hospital. British casualties from the aerodrome were, until 1917, usually buried at Ruislip, close to where they died in hospital or in their home town. In 1917 an area of land in Brookwood Cemetery in Surrey was set aside for Commonwealth servicemen who died either of war wounds or from training accidents. By this time, women had joined the RFC at Northolt.

In 1915 the wartime Government had found Richard Fairey his own factory in Clayton Road, Hayes, which was shared with the Army Motor Lorries Limited and the Government supplied a workforce of Belgian refugees. Northolt Aerodrome was used for flight testing Fairey aircraft, fuselages being towed from Hayes and assembled on the aerodrome at Northolt. In 1916 Harry Hawker tested the first Fairey-built aircraft, a Sopwith 1½ Strutter. Fairey's only F.2 prototype's first flight was at Northolt on 17 May 1917, after which the Admiralty became disinterested in the project. The largest aircraft in the world at that time, the Kennedy Giant, made its first 'flight' at Northolt. Work began on the aircraft in 1916; it had been designed by J.C.H. Kennedy, who had returned to England in 1915 after working with Igor Sikorsky in Russia. Components were built at the Gramophone Company and at Fairey's Hayes site on the understanding that the Government would not fund the project unless it flew. Lieut. Frank T. Courtney, of 35 TS Squadron, agreed to make the first flight, which took place in November 1917. It made a short hop before sinking into the earth. No further attempts were made to fly it and it was moved to the west end of the aerodrome (where it remained for many years). After some legal wrangling, it was decided that the plane had indeed flown, and the Government eventually paid Kennedy. Northolt remained, until 1929, the main testing centre for Fairey aircraft.

In late 1917 No. 4 MU (Maintenance Unit) – a stores depot – was built at Ickenham near West Ruislip station; the stores were on land belonging to Home Farm, only a mile away from Northolt Aerodrome. It was sometimes known as the 'Four Stores'. The site was bounded by the road to Ruislip, Austin Lane and the two railway lines and included Fairlight House, which had been built by Ernest Sims in 1914. Mr Saich of Home Farm was contracted to provide horses and carts during the construction. Transport was carried out by traction engine, horse and cart. The horses were stabled south of the Great Western Railway line. The sheds were only one brick thick (with reinforcing columns) as it was expected that they would only be temporary. A series of rail tracks branched off from the Great Western Railway and served thirteen large sheds. Rolling stock, which was unloaded by means of an overhead crane situated in No. 4 shed, was brought in by two small diesel locomotives. The unit employed a number of local men, while Americans who were stationed there after their entry into the war were invited to tea in local houses where there were young people.

Many Americans, after the entry of the United States into the war in April 1917, received training at Northolt, as did Czarist Russian cadets from about the spring of 1917. These Russians were under the command of Major Arbacanovitch, a Cossack. At least three of these cadets – C. Novikov, G.V. Smirnov, and another named Kopyloff – were killed during training, as was Private Donald R. Frazier of the US Army: he was killed in early 1918 when a propeller struck him on the head while he was assisting with the start-up of an aeroplane.

Crashes, both in combat and accidental, were frequent, but not always fatal, although in 1917 there were thirteen fatal crashes at Northolt with sixteen deaths; the majority of these were caused by stalls followed by nosedives. In late September 1916, an aeroplane containing two military airmen fell into 10ft of water at Ruislip Reservoir (the Lido) just after 6 p.m. The two airmen scrambled to safety but the plane remained all night in the charge of two other airmen. The following day a party from the RFC pulled the plane to pieces and took it away to Northolt for attention. This spectacle attracted crowds. Another aeroplane crashed near Ruislip Manor station in May 1918 while flying over the district. Mr F. Lavender of Ruislip, who was working nearby, hurried to the scene and helped the airman out of the wrecked plane. The pilot was very badly injured and taken to Southall VAD Hospital. Another pilot escaped injury when, after entertaining locals with his antics, his aircraft crashed in the grounds of 'Helvetia' in Kings End Road, now Kingsend, in mid-March 1918. In those early days, what a sight seven aeroplanes flying in formation must have been for the local inhabitants! In late September 1918, unfortunately, a collision between two aircraft in such a formation over Ruislip left one pilot dead. Major Penn-Gaskell and Lieut. John Bailey's fatal crashes – and two others at other Home Defence aerodromes – caused great concern in parliament. It was alleged that unsuitable aircraft and inadequately lit aerodromes were to blame. The Government set up a committee to investigate the organisation of the flying services and its recommendations led to the formation in 1918 of the Royal Air Force.

After the Armistice, squadrons were disbanded. Several hundred Americans in the RAF left Northolt Aerodrome in mid-November 1918 for Liverpool, and by May 1919 Northolt was no longer a fighter training aerodrome.

As an auxiliary to home defence, the County of Middlesex Motor Volunteer Corps was formed in 1916. This movement quickly spread to other counties in response to an appeal from the Army Council, which expressed the wish that the owner of every commandeered car should enrol his vehicle in a recognised motor volunteer corps for use in the event of threatened invasion, or for the occasional work of transporting troops and material. The military tribunals could grant temporary exemptions on condition that the applicant joined the Motor Volunteer Corps.

RAIDS

A NEW AND frightening experience was about to take place. Never before had this country experienced air raids, but during the First World War, for the first time, the United Kingdom was to come under aerial attack by Zeppelins and bombers and, near the coast, by naval bombardment. Raids by plane were more destructive than the raids by Zeppelins, the main targets of which were defined as magazines, munitions factories, ports and garrisons. On 27 December the Admiralty introduced a larger air-defence scheme for London, whereby a screen of aircraft would be positioned between Grimsby and London to intercept airships flying from northern Germany, and between Dungeness and London for those flying from Belgian bases. Northolt was one of the earliest aerodromes to be built in the United Kingdom.

Between the beginning of the war in 1914 and the end of 1916, there had been forty-three airship and twenty-eight aeroplane attacks all over England, and almost every part of London apart from the west and south-west had been hit. Between 24 December 1914 and 17 June 1918 there had been a total of fifty-one airship raids and fifty-seven aeroplane raids all over the country. A total number of 8,578 bombs had been dropped – and by the end of the war, the total number of British air-raid casualties amounted to 1,414 dead, 3,416 injured and material damage amounting to almost £3 million. London suffered more than half of the casualties – 670 killed and 1,962 injured. However, the nearest raids occurred near Harrow and in Brentford, just over the boundary of Ealing. Only the raids affecting local services or people are mentioned below.

Although British air raids began on German towns in September 1914, it was not until 9 January 1915 that the Kaiser approved raids on British coastal areas, docks and military establishments in the lower Thames area. Later, the Kaiser permitted the air services to attack London without restriction (apart from royal palaces and historic buildings). The German Navy, unlike the German Army, was ready to start raids on the city. From April, there had already been raids elsewhere, but the first raid on London took place on the night of 31 May/1 June 1915 and was carried out by the German Army Zeppelin LZ38, which, unnoticed, dropped incendiary and explosive bombs and one hand grenade on the East End of London, killing six people and injuring thirty-five. Unfounded rumours circulated that two Zeppelins had come down near Uxbridge.

At 1.20 p.m. on 4 June 1915, two of the newest naval Zeppelins left Nordholtz to attack London and the Humber area. Two sorties flew from Northolt and two from Joyce Green in defence. The RNAS were also mobilised. Although the targets had been London and the Humber area, Shoeburyness and Gravesend were bombed by mistake.

London itself had mainly avoided attacks until the second week in September, when raids took place on two consecutive nights. The first air raid that seriously affected London took place on the night of 8/9 September 1915. Searchlight and guns in and around London were in action, and one of four German Naval airships, the L.13, commanded by Heinrich Mathy (without a doubt the greatest commander of the war and admired by friend and foe alike), reached London where some bombs were dropped. Searchlights had picked up the L.13, and all twenty-six guns of the London defences opened fire on her, apparently without scoring a hit. The district hooter at Watford alerted residents in the north of the borough to the raid. A few minutes later the explosion of bombs and the crackling of guns in the distance could be heard locally as bombs were dropped on Golders Green, followed by more along a line from Euston to Liverpool Street. Many local people journeying in and around London saw the enemy craft and the bombs dropping. The fire brigade, VDF and local special constables were called out for both of these raids. Commander Mathy's day was yet to come.

First-aid classes sprang up everywhere and at Ruislip in early 1915 home nursing courses were also being organised. Ruislip-Northwood UDC decided in June 1915 that an ambulance stretcher and another standpipe be brought and stored at the Ruislip sub-fire station. Official respirators for firemen and sand were also purchased. In August, council property was insured against damage by aircraft.

A Zeppelin raid took place in the night of 13/14 October 1915. Five naval airships, the L.11, L.13, L.14, L.15 and L.16, set out for the attack from Nordholtz shortly after noon. There seems to have been a very distinct tactical plan for this raid, which was carried out in proper squadron formation. The L.13, captained by Mathy (the leader of the formation), swept round by St Albans, but altered its course over Rickmansworth immediately after Mathy had seen L.15 under fire, and headed south over the course of the River Colne. Despite the weather, the slow, eerie, large cigar-shaped airship was audible as well as visible as it passed over on its way to Chertsey on its way home, but not before dropping incendiary missiles at Woolwich. All of London's guns were in action. RFC stations had been alerted at 17.00 hours, and at 19.55 observers reported that Zeppelins were over the Thetford area, heading south. The War Office ordered Hainault, Joyce Green, Sutton's Farm and Northolt to send up one B.E.2c each, weather permitting. The visibility at Northolt was so bad at 20.15 hours, when the general alarm had sounded, that even the flare party lost themselves on the aerodrome. Lieut. Long had tried to get the engine of his B.E.2c to start when the flare detachment reported that they could not find the flares in the field (which remained unfit for flying throughout). At 22.15 hours the flares, with difficulty, were lit in case any other machines were in the air and a bonfire was lit in the south-west corner of the aerodrome. Lieut. Long remained on stand-by until 02.15 hours when the order to dismiss came from the War Office. This raid was one of the deadliest of the war. Seventy-one people were killed – thirty-eight were killed in London alone, and a number of soldiers in camp at Hertford also lost their lives – 128 people were injured, and damage was estimated at over £80,000.

On the night of 31 January/1 February 1916, nine German Navy Zeppelins were spotted heading for Liverpool. Although they failed to reach their target, it was the first major Zeppelin raid, causing about seventy deaths in the Midlands. Twenty-two defence sorties were made from ten airfields of the RFC, ringing the capital – including one from No. 11 R.A. Squadron, Northolt. The first call came at around 17.30hrs and the next message came through at 19.30hrs, stating that if weather conditions permitted the first patrol should be sent up at 19.45 as Zeppelins were due over London at 20.10. At Hounslow, a pilot went up at 20.45 after the fog had lifted and was in the air for only 15 minutes, as he could not see the flares or the large fire marking the aerodrome. At Northolt, the visibility too was minimal. When an order came from headquarters to send an airman up, Major (and Squadron-Leader) Leslie Da Costa Penn-Gaskell telephoned back to say that it would be suicidal to send anyone up in the fog. Although it was the turn of Captain Sampson to go up, he was told by the highly experienced Da Costa Penn-Gaskell not to. Major Penn-Gaskell, a pre-war pilot who had on occasions flown as an observer, took off in his B.E.2C 2091 plane at 19.35 to investigate conditions before allowing less experienced officers to fly. As he took off, thirty-four-year-old Penn-Gaskell crashed headlong into a tree on the outskirts of the aerodrome. Two Corporals in a nearby shed pulled him out before the bombs exploded. He suffered from a cut to the back of his head and burns to his face, hands and legs, but appeared to have no broken bones. It was at first thought that he was not seriously injured. However, he was very badly injured indeed, and died five days later at the Royal Flying Corps Hospital in Dorset Square, London. He is buried at Ruislip.

For almost a week in April 1916, Zeppelins took off every day to strafe England. German Naval Zeppelins were heading for London on the night of 31 March/1 April 1916. At the same time German Army Zeppelins were attacking East Anglia. Twenty-four

On the same night that Lieutenant John Winkworth Bailey died, one of the attacking Zeppelins was brought down in the Thames. The crew of the L.15, two officers and fifteen men (one drowned during the crash), were captured before the vessel vanished beneath the waves.

defence sorties were made from both the RNAS and RFCs. There was a slight haze when thirty-three-year-old Lieutenant John Winkworth Bailey of No. 19 RA Squadron took off at 21.05 hours, the only sortie from Northolt. At first he seemed to climb normally, but suddenly his B.E.2c crashed, killing him instantly. He was an Old Harrovian and had graduated from Exeter College, Oxford, with an MA. He is buried at Ruislip.

The longest airship raid took place in East Anglia on the night of 2/3 September 1916, when sixteen Army and Navy Zeppelins airships attacked between the Humber and Ipswich. With the German Army and Navy combining for the first – and last – time to attack, this was the biggest airship raid of the war (it was also, for the Germans, an utter failure). It was to be the only time during the war that Army airships bombed the same target simultaneously. One airship, the SL II, commanded by Hauptmann Wilhelm Schramm, reached London, the place of his birth. Lt. William Leefe Robinson from 39 Squadron – who had received some training at Northolt, although he was stationed at Sutton's Farm at the time – won his V.C. on 2 September 1916 for shooting down the Zeppelin, SL.II, at Cuffley, near Potter's Bar, in Hertfordshire. The flash of the exploding SL.II could be seen over a radius of some 40 to 50 miles, and despite the time being 02.25 a.m. it was seen by hundreds of thousands of cheering people. It was very clearly seen by the local men on duty and as some of the local trains were so late many inhabitants were able to see the spectacle themselves. Others were woken from their slumber by the sound of anti-aircraft fire and fled into the streets half-dressed, as they had done before in moonlight raids and also were to do in later attacks. The news that an air attack was impending had spread all over London. The hospitals were ready for any emergency, fire stations were prepared to respond to any call, every special constable had been called up, at every police station surgeons and nurses had come on duty, as had ambulance men with stretchers at the ready. Every vantage spot was crowded with spectators as dozens of beams from the searchlights showed from every part of London and the outer sections. London had never seen such brilliant illumination and there were loud cheers from high streets throughout the metropolis. The next day was a Sunday and the news spread quickly. Soon all the lanes were choked with sightseers. The successes around London led to the formation of more Home Defence Squadrons.

A further raid took place at the end of September 1916. The districts attacked during the night and in the early hours of the morning were the south coast, east coast, north-east coast and North Midlands. Seven airships took part in this raid, which killed thirty-six people. Two Zeppelins, L.32 and L.33, both of recent construction, were brought down in Essex. The first airship was destroyed by an aeroplane, having evaded gunfire. The second airship was hit by gunfire from the London Defences.

During air raids the special constabulary was always on duty occasionally for five-six hours at a stretch. Over 100 calls were sometimes received in the night-time.

Just before midnight on 1/2 October 1916, Commander Matthy's Zeppelin, the new L.31, was brought down near Potter's Bar after meandering over Hertfordshire, coming as far south as Cheshunt, where he released most of his bombs before heading westwards. He had managed to avoid the ground defences but 2nd Lieutenant W.J. Tempest, patrolling between Joyce Green and Hainault, had noticed the cigar-shaped object lit up by the converged searchlights of north London and gave chase, bringing it down near Potter's Bar. Mathy and all his crew were killed.

A daylight raid on 5 June 1917, which left thirteen killed and thirty-four injured, had Sheerness as its target. Again the RFC and RNAS pilots were sent up – sixty-two sorties were made. No. 35 (T) Squadron took off from Northolt in new Bristol Fighters, in pursuit of twenty-two Gothas. This is the first recorded flight from Northolt. Captain C.W.E. Cole-Hamilton, A7122 Lieutenant Chad and A7136 Lieutenant Walmsley flew. Walmsley was forced to land near Barnet with engine trouble. Although the RFC and RNAS had no success, anti-aircraft guns situated on either side of the Thames Estuary did. Gotha 660, piloted by Vizefeldwebel Erich Kluck, commanded by Leutnant H. Franke and with Unteroffizier Georg Schumacher, crashed into the water. Only Schumacher survived. After this raid, St Mary's School, Northwood, issued instructions concerning the action to be taken during air raids or air-raid warnings.

On 13 June 1917, of the eighteen Gotha bombers which had taken off from St Denis Westrem and Gontrode during the morning, one aircraft had become detached and headed for Margate while over Foulness; three more peeled off and made for the Thames Estuary area. The remaining fourteen large aircraft flew in diamond formation and approached London from the north-west. One pilot of the RNAS had been able to bring his guns to bear on an enemy machine but had to break off when his Lewis gun jammed. The RFC were more successful and several pilots made contact with the enemy. New Bristol Fighters from No. 35 Training Squadron, Northolt, took off. A7135 (Captain C.W.E. Cole-Hamilton and Captain Cecil H.C. Keevil) took off at 11.19 hours; A7136 (2nd Lieutenant J. Chapman and 2nd Lieutenant F.G.C. Weare) left at 11.18 hours, returning at 12.45 hours. Captain Cole-Hamilton met three enemy machines flying eastwards over Ilford. He flew into position for his gunner, Captain Keevil, Royal Flying Corps and 18th Battalion West Yorkshire Regiment, to attack but return fire from the raiders killed the brave Captain. He is buried in Hampstead Cemetery. On this occasion no German aircraft were shot down, but 162 civilians in London, including 18 schoolchildren from the Upper North Street School who were sheltering in a cellar where the bomb fell, were killed; 432 were injured, including several people slightly injured at Headstone near Harrow, wounded by falling glass and masonry. In all, almost as many as the casualties of all the Zeppelin raids of 1915 put together, and damage amounting to almost £130,000. A public outcry saw the immediate improvement in anti-aircraft defences, and from September of that year, the Gotha aeroplanes were forced to attack at night.

The targets in the daylight raid of 4 July 1917 were Harwich and Felixstowe. In the early hours of the morning, twenty-five Gothas were despatched. There were 103 defence sorties. Eighteen Gothas were attacked by dozens of RNAS and RFC aircraft, including one sortie from No. 35 (T) Squadron, Northolt. A7136, Captain A.C. Wright and Captain Bagnall, left at 08.02 hours and returned forty-four minutes later. It was at the naval air station at Felixstowe, the main objective of the raid, that seventeen men were killed, mostly naval ratings.

Twenty-four Gothas were despatched for a heavy daylight raid on London on 7 July 1917, which killed 57 and injured 193 people. There were 108 sorties all together, amongst them two Bristol Fighters from No. 35 (T) Squadron. Bristol Fighter A7135 (Captain G.D. Hill and Captain R. Stuart-Wortley) left at 09.40 hours, returning at 11.15 hours with an unspecified Bristol Fighter, 09.30 hours-11.15 hours. Twenty-two Gothas were attacked.

It was on their homeward journey that one Gotha, already in trouble, was fired on by No. 50 Home Defence Squadron, which had flights at Dover, Bekesbourne and Throwley. The aircraft was brought down into the sea. Aircraft of the RNAS also brought down two other bombers as they flew back over the North Sea. Almost 100 British fighters and all guns attacked them, shooting down five.

Many underground stations had become a refuge for panicking people – as many as 300,000 on some occasions, whether raids were imminent or not. After the air raids of mid-1917, hundreds of air-raid refugees from London arrived in the district.

Ramsgate and Dover were the targets for the 22 August 1917 daylight raid by fifteen Gothas. Ten were attacked by 138 sorties from both RNAS and RFC. One Bristol Fighter flew from Northolt in defence; it was flown by A7173 (Lieutenant F.G.C. Weare, of No. 35 (T) Squadron). Guns based at Harrow and Hanwell, amongst others, were engaged.

Another raid occurred at about on 24 September 1917 when Navy Zeppelins targeted the Midlands and the North-East. Star Shells bursting in the air and lighting up the enemy's position could plainly be seen. The noise was awesome. On the next night, the south-eastern districts of London, Kent and London itself were targets of attacks from Gothas. Take-cover notices were evident in all the local villages. After this raid, huge rents were asked for locally.

These large Gotha aeroplanes also set out to bomb London, night after night, from 28 September to 2 October. They became known as the 'harvest moon raids'. Londoners had never heard such a bombardment: the raid took place on 28 September, and in the brilliant moonlight the barrage from north-west London was clearly visible.

By now, the increased density of the guns and lights around London had forced the Germans to fly even larger formations of airships – at night. From late September 1917 a small number of the huge Riesen aircraft – the largest used in either war – began to accompany the Gotha aircraft. The raid on the night of 19/20 October 1917 took place with a raging gale at very high altitudes above calm. The target was northern England, but the raiders were blown off course by the strong winds and some crossed London. Because of the mist the guns kept silent. The acoustic conditions muffled the noise of their engines and guns and became known as 'the Silent Raid'. Out of the eleven Zeppelins that set out, only six returned home – four airships were lost over France and one crashed on London. It was the biggest Zeppelin disaster for the Germans of the whole war so far. Both L.55 and L.45 passed the western outskirts of London. Most of L.45's bombs fell to the north-west of London. Some big bombs were dropped near Harrow from L.45 as it sailed over London, dropping more bombs on Piccadilly and Camberwell before heading for France, leaving thirty-three people dead and fifty injured. The force of the exploding bombs dropped near Harrow was felt locally. From then on, the Zeppelins mostly confined themselves to attacking British submarines in the North Sea. There had been 208 Zeppelin flights, leaving 522 people dead.

Following an interval of some six weeks or so, the area once again heard gunfire. On the night of 29/30 January 1918 a number of attacks were carried out by hostile aeroplanes between 10 p.m. and 12.30 a.m. About fifteen enemy planes, coming in small detachments, crossed the coast, and four Giant aircraft headed for London. It was about 8 p.m. when the warning was fired, followed an hour later by sound of the first guns. Most people made promptly for shelter but many continued in the streets until the guns were heard. The barrage guns were more distinctly heard in the Ruislip district during this raid than ever before, but barrage fire was only violent in those districts where enemy planes were attempting to break through. Two machines reached London where one was viciously attacked near Tottenham: it then headed for home, but not before dropping some bombs near Wanstead. Another aeroplane was attacked on its inward path: it turned at Hertford and headed for Brentford, where it dropped some bombs on Whitestile Road – killing the wife of Sgt Major Curley, who was serving with the Colours, their five children, a niece and an invalid lady who resided with the family and two men at the water works – before making for the Chiswick area (where yet more bombs were dropped). A salvo of guns in the neighbourhood proved the end of the raid. Another raid took place the following night. Local special constables were called out, and at Ruislip the specials turned out in strength; they remained at their post for between four and five hours each night. Public indignation had by now reached boiling point.

London was the primary target for the night raid that took place on 16/17 February 1918, and the local area was more than usually within the sound of the guns. Five German Giant aircraft had been dispatched and the Mercedes-engined Giants attacked Dover.

During night raids, factories ceased production until the all-clear was sounded and all trains, apart from those underground, were stopped.

To begin with there were no air-raid shelters, and air-raid warnings were unheard of. This continued to be the case in Hillingdon throughout the war – local people were advised to use their cellars, and to offer cellar space to neighbours should the occasion arise. The Lights (London) Order placed restrictions on the lighting of London (and 10 miles around) after dark from the beginning of the war but this did not cover the Ruislip area, so local councils made their own arrangements. By early 1915 a policy of subdued lighting was adopted at Hayes. Northwood was in darkness, although other places outside the modern London borough were fully illuminated. In late June 1915, councils received letters from the Metropolitan Police pointing out the advisability of extinguishing all street lights in the event of an air raid. Gradually houses, factories, railways and trams were all brought under regulations tending to increase darkness. By the winter of 1916 every house and shop had its windows carefully shaded with dark curtains and the street lamps had been reduced in number and obscured so as to give no more than a glimmer of light; the headlights of vehicles were reduced in power. Many summonses for showing light during raids were brought against local people and local businesses. In January 1916 Grace K. Davis was summoned for failing to screen light from her shop in December 1915. She was an assistant in charge of Cullen's Wine and Spirit Stores in Northwood. She was fined 10s. In May 1916, under a new order, Ronald Oakshott, Frederick Caddy and Wilfred Spear, all of Park Way, Ruislip, were all fined 2s 6d., while Hannah Weekly, James Woodman, Colin Still, Alice Raymont, Lizzie Clark, Emma Hampson, James Ordidge and Graham Wright, all of Ruislip, were all fined varying amounts. At the beginning of January 1917, Edward Savalle, Jules Homme and Walter Simonson, all of Northwood, were each fined 10s. In January 1918, under the order, the hour for the obscuration of lights was fixed at 6 p.m. instead of 5.30 p.m. The local police had noticed that many homes in the area had not properly obscured their windows, and in January 1918 they drew this to the attention of

Review of Honour for the London Ambulance Section in Hyde Park, 1918.

the residents through the local paper. William Candlin was one of those from Ruislip who appeared in court at Uxbridge, where he was fined £1. Church services were confined to daylight hours, as were theatres, restaurants and cinemas. The kerbs of many London streets were whitewashed so they could be visible to vehicles and pedestrians. People were also prosecuted for failing to have red lights on their cars. A spate of road accidents followed, caused by badly lit roads. After summer time was brought in, gradually things became more organised.

Once the raiders were spotted there was usually about an hour's warning that an attack was imminent. In that time all the preparations had to be made. The searchlights and guns in London were manned nightly and always held ready, but when a raid was expected ambulances had to be mobilised, the fire brigade – which was still manned largely by volunteers – had to have all its strength available (including the engineer troops attached to it for rescue and demolition work), all the airmen to stand to, the specials to be summoned and the hospitals warned. When air-raid warning bombs were heard, local police patrolled the streets with whistles and take-cover notices. Maroons were fired, factory hooters blared out and church bells were rung. Leaflets were delivered by uniformed firemen, who were all voluntary, to all houses in mid-1915. Take-cover placards were placed outside Uxbridge police station (these, by mid-1917, were red illuminated notices, reading on the reverse side 'all clear'). All of these were unavoidably associated with some alarm. Bugles also sounded the 'all clear'.

Although local inhabitants saw nothing of the actual bombing, they could see anti-aircraft fire and Star Shells bursting over the capital and the neighbourhood, and hear a good deal: the firing practice from Northolt Aerodrome – and, from December 1917, the Armament and Gunnery School at Uxbridge – combined with the sound of aeroplanes on flying practice going on overhead, military airships guarding London zooming low, extra traffic occasioned by the war, maroons, hooters and gunfire. All of this made Isobel, wife of Dr Christopher Addison of Northwood, complain about the constant noise. Explosions could also be heard from miles and miles away. Even the sound of guns from the distant battlefields of France and Flanders could, on occasions, be heard when atmospheric conditions were right. When at 3.10 a.m. on 7 June 1917, immediately before the British infantry assault, nineteen mines charged with over a million pounds of ammonal, which lay beneath the enemy position, erupted simultaneously from Ploegsteert to Hill 60, all along the Messines ridge, the noise of the explosion of a series of the largest and deepest mines ever used in warfare could be heard in London. Again, in July 1917 the guns from Belgium could also be faintly heard.

POLICE

THE EXISTING police forces of the country, which had largely recruited men discharged from the fighting services, had suddenly been deprived of the services of all their Reservists, both Army and Navy. Not only was the strength of the regular constabulary reduced and efforts were made to spread their work amongst those of their colleagues left behind, but the duties devolved to the police during wartime became more numerous and varied. In the Metropolitan area, all police leave was cancelled for the first year.

As it was at the time of the Boer War, it was those above military age, those in some essential occupation and men physically unfit for war services who were encouraged to join up as special constables, an amateur service created by the war. This new service sprang into action at the outbreak of war and all strata of society turned up in their numbers to enlist. By 24 August 1914, 20,000 men – and by the end of 1914, 31,000 men – had enrolled and were given the same powers, duties and privileges as a regular policeman. They had to take the King's Oath and were issued with a constable's warrant and a whistle. At first they wore a blue and white armlet, accessorised some months later with a blue uniform cap. A uniform came later still, but only after a certain number of drills and duty 'turns' had been completed.

A special constabulary force for the whole of the London Metropolitan Police district, an area which embraced all the environs of London and all London itself apart from the City, was amongst the very first to be established after the Home Office, through the Commissioner of the Police, appealed through the press. There were twenty-one divisions in the Metropolitan Police district, of which the Ruislip area formed part of the Northern District. Enrolment began in Uxbridge Petty Sessional Court and Northwood police station in the second week of August 1914. Thirty-three members from the parishes of Hillingdon West, Ruislip, Yiewsley, West Drayton, Uxbridge, Hayes and Hillingdon East, were enrolled. They began their monotonous duties later on that month and undertook night duties at vulnerable positions such as the Uxbridge Gas Works, observation posts, etc.

Each Metropolitan Police Division had its own motor-transport section and a fleet of London buses was given to the Metropolitan Police force to facilitate the transport of police officers between divisions when the need arose. A third of the number was always on duty and available for service. Thus, at a moment's notice, at a call for police into any of the London divisions, a hundred or more buses, if need be, could set off without delay to bring in police from other divisions. On Saturday, 7 July 1917, when a fleet of nearly thirty German aeroplanes

Whilst their sisters in service were on strike, transport had to continue at the front: here, the London General Omnibus Co. rush troops to a weak point in the line on the Western Front.

flying in duck formation raided London, Special police in their hundreds were collected from the division and despatched to East London, where the damage was the greatest.

They carried on until October 1917 when they were represented at almost every State function in London. British Landcruisers, later known as tanks, had been used in very small numbers on the Somme on 15 September 1916 (only sixty out of 150 had been shipped successfully to France, as many had broken down en route. Of the eighteen which went into battle, only nine survived). They were first seen in London at the Lord Mayor's show on 10 November 1917. On 27 November 1917, Inspector R.H.G. Stagg of The Greenway, Uxbridge, along with twenty special constables of the X Division (ten from Uxbridge and ten from Ruislip) took the first turn of guarding the 'Tank' at Trafalgar Square and saw the opening ceremony of the Tank Bank War Savings service. The tank was to remain in Trafalgar Square for two weeks.

The Uxbridge, Northwood, Pinner, Ruislip and Harrow special constabulary were also occasionally called on to attend in London in order to relieve the London specials during and after air raids, and in October 1917 were provided with steel helmets to protect them from the hail of steel fragments scattered by anti-aircraft guns.

During this time, at the Battle of Cambrai in November 1917, tanks were used en masse. So brilliant was this tank victory that the church bells were pealed in triumph the length and breadth of Britain.

In July 1918, Inspector Stagg took a small party of specials to London to help line the route for the royal Silver Wedding celebrations. In early October 1917, members of the special constabulary from Uxbridge, Northwood, Pinner, Ruislip and Harrow attended London to relieve the London specials after the raids which had lasted from 28 September to 2 October.

As time went on, the duties of the specials changed considerably: they became efficient and available in first-aid work, and the Ruislip-Northwood volunteer fire brigade trained the local police in fire-fighting. During the air raids the police would have hardly coped but for the specials, who were always on duty, helping patrol the streets for any signs of light, manning the observation posts, and arranging the take-cover notices. In the spring of 1916 they were given a room at the council offices at Northwood to use when waiting to be called up on the occasion of air raids. In 1916 it was the special constabulary, in one of their vehicles, who transported the traitor Roger Casement across London to Brixton Prison.

Growing industrial unrest in July 1918 caused widespread strikes. In August 1918 there was a strike of 11,000 London tram and bus workers for more pay for women workers. Suddenly and unexpectedly, on the night of 30 August, about 14,000 Metropolitan policemen stopped work for an increase in pay, including their war bonus, and for their union to be officially recognised. Not a single policeman was on beat duty and only a handful out controlling traffic. The specials had been called out, but according to common report the response was rather half-hearted. Although this strike went on for nearly three days there was no increase in the crime levels. Their demands for more pay were met.

In May 1918, more than 7,000 special constables paraded at Regent's Park to receive the Silver Star awarded to all specials who had enrolled prior to January 1915 and had served continually since. The duties of the special constables ceased on 23 November 1918.

In early October 1921, special constables were honoured in Hyde Park when the Duke of York presented long-service medals to members of the Metropolitan Special Constabulary. Every man who served in the war force and put in at least 150 duties was entitled to the medal. Service in the then present reserve also counted, but it had to be three times the length of that required in the war force. The officers and men present, 5,000 strong, represented twenty-four police divisions. All the chief officers of the 'X' Division were present. After an inspection of the whole reserve, the Duke of York handed out medals to staff, divisional and senior station officers. At the same time, commandants handed medals at tables nearby to the inspectors and sub-inspectors, who in turn distributed them to the men on parade. Chief Inspector W.O. Lovibond received his medal from the Duke of York and the medals to sub-inspectors Woodbridge, Winstone and Stagg were pinned on by Commander Inston. The medals to the men were presented by the chief inspectors of each section. The Ruislip section, under Chief Inspector Davy, and the Hayes section paraded with the Uxbridge section, with Chief Inspector W.O. Lovibond in charge. Four of the fifteen members of the Northwood special constabulary were present. They were Chief Inspector H. Beer, Sergeant A. Dallas, Sergeant J. Hickmott and Special Constable C. Fry.

BOY SCOUTS AND GIRL GUIDES

THE SCOUT and Guide movements had great appeal during the First World War. Scouts were active throughout the war, and within the first few hours after war was declared, the Scouts had taken up the duty of guarding important railway bridges, water-works and telegraph and cable lines throughout the country – day and night. The Army and the Territorial troops later relieved them. They patrolled cliffs with coastguards and provided a messenger service for the police, stood guard over strategic bridges and telephone lines and had bugles to alert the public sheltering from Zeppelins and aircraft that all was now clear. Guides carried out tasks such as helping out in canteens and in hospitals (where they acted as stretcher-bearers and first-aiders). They also entertained the wounded and soldiers lodging locally. Scouts were also to collect specific items such as jam jars, tin cans, string and cotton waste. In August 1918, the National Salvage Corps wrote to

Rickmansworth Road. (Courtesy of Hillingdon Local Studies, Archives and Museum Service)

councils of the importance of the collection of fruit stones and nutshells for war purposes. The surveyor at Uxbridge was instructed to write to the heads of all local schools and Boy Scouts in the district asking them to organise the collection of these. Scouts who carried out war service of one kind or another were awarded a little strip of red with a yellow date on it, which was worn on the right breast.

Already some Scout troops and groups of Girl Guides had been established and were still going strong. Some Scout groups had folded prior to hostilities breaking out. On 17 August 1914 at North House, Northwood, home of the Townsends, the 1st Northwood Scout troops came into being. The Townsends wanted to do something for the war effort, and boys from the National Schools in Rickmansworth Road were the first recruits. Miss Townsend, with the cooperation of the Pinner Troop, formed a Scout's Defence Corps. The boys were given training in drill and marksmanship and wore a red feather in their hats when they had passed proficiency tests. The Scouts had permission to make use of Northwood Rifle Range in November 1915. In March 1918 these Scouts approached Ruislip-Northwood UDC for permission to collect waste paper and dispose of it for the benefit of their funds for the 'contingent'. Permission was given on the undertaking that the Scouts would provide their own sacks. After two years the troop had thirty boys and also a Cub pack and Scout's Defence Corps had been formed. The 5th Northwood Company Girl Guides was formed at the end of 1915 by the girls at Northwood College, with its headquarters in a donkey stable. Towards the end of the spring term 1916 they launched a project to establish a recreation hut for the soldiers in France. £500 was needed and the money was to be earned by all kinds of tasks.

RECRUITMENT

IN THE beginning, Britain's forces were composed of regular soldiers, Territorials and Volunteers. In August 1914, Britain had only a small professional army of about 150,000 men. Britain alone relied entirely on volunteers. Lord Kitchener, Secretary of War, appealed three times for 100,000 volunteers in August and September 1914 and floods of volunteers came forward. Fathers, sons and husbands went off to the war, in many cases driven by unemployment. Before the war was six months old, more men from Britain and the British Empire were under arms than any time in history.

The Parliamentary Recruiting Committee for the Uxbridge Division was arranged in District Advisory Sub-Committees as follows: Uxbridge Urban; Uxbridge RDC (covering Hillingdon, Harefield, Cowley, West Drayton and Ickenham); Hayes Urban; Yiewsley Urban; Staines RDC (covering Harlington, Harmondsworth, Cranford, Ashford, Bedfont, Stanwell and Shepperton) and Ruislip-Northwood. Many men from the Ruislip-Northwood area enlisted at Harrow. Initial enlistments were carried out by the

Central London recruiting depot in August 1914. Thousands flocked to the call of the flag.

Left A typical recruitment poster from 1915. (Library of Congress, Prints & Photographs Division, WWI Posters, LC-USZC4-10918)

Right One of the best-known posters, 'forward to victory', printed in Middlesex. Other examples used more direct means of inspiring the reader: 'Have you any women-folk worth defending?' asked one. (Library of Congress, Prints & Photographs Division, WWI Posters, LC-USZC4-11027)

Army's own recruiting service, at the depots and the regular recruiting offices, council offices (as was the case at Northwood), or at a hastily opened temporary office, such as schools and business premises.

In mid–August 1914 the Uxbridge and District Emergency Committee issued an appeal in support of Lord Kitchener's second army of 100,000 men. A few days after war was declared the first recruiting appeal posters appeared in the district. Recruiting 'smoking concerts' began to be held and went on throughout hostilities. Other forms of recruitment also took place.

The Territorials came into being in 1908, formed from existing volunteer units – the 'weekend' soldiers so vitally important at a time when the regular Army had undergone such huge reductions. Territorials were only intended for home defence unless they personally volunteered to do otherwise, although by 1915 many Territorial battalions were at the front. There had been a surplus of volunteers who had sought to enlist, but the 8th Middlesex Regiment, with its full complement of men (along with other regiments

'Rally Round the Flag', an iconic poster designed in London in 1915. (Library of Congress, Prints & Photographs Division, WWI Posters, LC-USZC4-11310)

Above Royal Fusiliers, City of London Battalion, march to be sworn in.

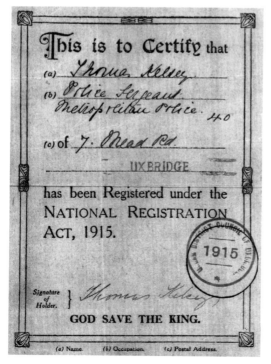

Left The National Registration form for local policeman Thomas Kelsey.

from the Regular and Territorial Army), had departed for war in early September 1914. In their place 1,000 West Middlesex men eagerly joined the new Territorial force, the 8th (Reserve) Battalion Middlesex Regiment. Recruiting for the Middlesex Territorial force took a very large number of men from the district as did the Royal Fusiliers. Between 12 August 1914 and October 11 1915, a total of 855 recruits had enlisted at Uxbridge. In March 1915 it was reported in the local paper that recruitment in the Uxbridge district was going smoothly, and that young men were still coming forward to enlist in both Kitchener's Army and the new Territorial Battalion, the 3/8th Middlesex. The 4/8th Middlesex (Territorial) Regiment was raised in July 1915. Many Cadet Corps were formed. By early 1915 a Boy's Junior Corps was formed at Northwood for drill, a preliminary to the Territorials. Rifle shooting practice was held in the church hall. A Ruislip platoon was also formed in May 1915.

There were numerous local men who were Reservists, former soldiers and sailors serving their seven years' reserve commitment.

By late 1914, recruitment numbers had fallen everywhere and continuing efforts were made to recruit more men, but as the lists of those killed in action or wounded grew ever longer there was, understandably, a lot of opposition. The National Register began in about August 1915, with certificates of registration issued by the end of the month. Every citizen aged between sixteen and sixty-five had to supply details of age, sex and occupation and whether or not they would perform work of national importance. It was not meant as an aid to recruitment but was ultimately used as such. In a final effort to save voluntary conscription, the Government introduced the Derby Scheme. Lord Derby was appointed National Director-General of Recruiting in October 1915, resulting in more systematic recruitment. On the basis of the National Register, every man between eighteen and forty-one was called up in groups as they were wanted, taking the younger single men first. In the north of the borough, in the same month, the Enlistment Committee of the Northwood and Ruislip Emergency Committee took over all the duties under Lord Derby's scheme. However, although there had been a huge number of volunteers this scheme was not successful, and by May 1916 conscription was brought in (although men could still enlist voluntarily). Britain was by now fighting in Western Europe, Turkey, the Middle East and Italy, and the losses on the Somme, the bloodiest day in the history of British warfare, put the pressure on for more recruits.

At the start of the war there had been four divisions at Mons; at the Aisne there were six; in the early days of the Battle of Ypres there were eight – and by the summer of 1915 the Army consisted of no less than 440,000 men in the line, with 120,000 more engaged in rear service – twenty-two divisions. Between 21 March 1918 and 20 April 1918, during the German spring offensive, fresh drafts, totalling almost 200,000 men had been sent to France, including – as a result of the emergency at that time – youths under the age of eighteen years.

Military tribunals were set up in every borough under the Military Service Act 1916. These were aimed at forcing unmarried men to do what they had hitherto failed to do at Lord Derby's invitation: to hear the appeals of men or local employers who could not – or would not – join up for reasons of occupation, religious belief, hardship or conscience. The military tribunals could grant temporary exemptions on condition that the applicant

Northwood Fire Brigade in around 1896, standing outside their original premises. (Courtesy of Hillingdon Local Studies, Archives and Museum Service)

joined the special constables, the VTC (where they were to undertake a specified number of drills), the Motor Volunteer Corps or went to work in munitions.

Also under Lord Derby's scheme of 1915, the basic principle for non-enlistment was that it was for the State to say whether or not a man was indispensable. Most exemption claims came from employers seeking immunity for their employees on the grounds of indispensability. A large number came from men engaged as market gardeners or in other forms of agriculture or those already working in munitions. Conscientious Objectors' groups sprang up all over the country.

The National Registration Act was passed on 15 July 1915, as by the spring of that year it had become clear that voluntary recruitment was not working. The Act was passed to help aid recruitment and to find out how many men aged between fifteen and sixty-five were engaged in each trade.

In the spring of 1916 Adam Priestley of Northwood, who had been out to the front with the Friends' Ambulance, had returned to England under the misapprehension that the corps was gradually becoming part of the regular Medical Corps. He was fined £2 at Uxbridge and handed over to the Harrow military authority. The various interested authorities, always with a military representative, were empowered to decide. Ruislip and Northwood held these tribunals (most petitions were unsuccessful) until they were abolished in October 1918.

In a desperate attempt to recruit more soldiers, a Military Service Act was passed in mid-April 1918 – hurriedly allowing the conscription of men up to the age of fifty-one, regardless of the effect on industrial output.

By January 1915, 353 men from the Ruislip-Northwood area had enlisted, including seventeen members of Northwood Rovers Football Club, and by June 1915, 236 men of the parish of Northwood (or those connected with the church) had joined up. Several councillors, council officials and council staff all went off to war. Amongst them were F.E. Baker, Assistant Overseer for Ruislip and Collector of General District Rate (killed); Dr Lionel Watson Hignett of Murray Road, Northwood, the MOH (RAMC); Councillor S. White, assistant in the Clerk's Office (RAMC); Councillor Dewhurst, Sanitary Inspector; (Peter) William Beckett, Captain of the Fire Brigade of Reginald Terrace, Reginald Road, into the Royal Engineers (POW), who already had over twenty years' service; Dr Douglas David Ritchie, Deputy MOH (RAMC); Frank W. Orr, a member of the council; firemen Arthur Maydon of New Farm Cottage, Pinner-Rickmansworth Road, and G. Stevens, who had served in the fire brigade for over ten years. These men joined up by 11 September 1916, a total of seven firemen from Northwood and two from Ruislip – out of a total of twelve men under Captain Beckett. Six other men also joined: H. Stimpson, W. Barclay and G. Ives; George Reuben Harding, superintendent caretaker at the Northwood cemetery, called up in September 1916; Thomas H. Bird, finance clerk, who was gazetted Lieutenant by mid-January 1918; H.J. King, who lived at Watford, and had been a surveyor's assistant for the Ruislip-Northwood UDC (killed). Towards the end of the war, the locum MOH was also thinking of giving his services to King and Country.

REFUGEES AND EVACUEES

DURING SEPTEMBER 1914 a constant stream of Belgian refugees poured into England. By direction of the authorities, the refugees were quarantined and vaccinated. At first they arrived at Folkestone, but in October, when it was seen that the German Army would soon reach the Belgian coast, many thousands arrived at Dover. On their arrival in London they were taken to a temporary haven in Aldwych. In the seven days beginning 10 October 1914, some 13,000 arrived, including 5,000 wounded Belgian soldiers. Within days of the outbreak of war preparations were being made to receive Belgian refugees, who in most cases were panic-stricken and had lost everything. Everywhere doors were flung wide open to receive the destitute refugees. Thousands of offers poured in from people willing to house and feed them. Local houses were rented for the refugee families from the early days of the war and furnished by contributions. Residents of Uxbridge, Denham and elsewhere loaned a great deal of furniture. Councils excused properties occupied by the refugees, who worked for their livelihood and supported themselves, from paying rates.

The difficulties of classifying and registering the thousands of offers, the fitting of the guests to the hosts in batches of twos and threes, the temporary housing, and the final dispatch of the refugees to country districts, all involved an immense labour. Local committees were formed, and there were soon 2,000 of them. Refugees were picked up from Aldwych, where the Belgium Consulate had, early in the war, opened an office in General Buildings; volunteer motorists conveyed many to their new homes. These volunteers became the Optimistic National Corps, Transport Section, then the Motor Squadron of the London Volunteer Rifles and eventually the National Motor Volunteers.

Many lantern lectures, charity concerts and other functions were held for the Belgian Relief Funds, to which many of the refugees came. For local residents these were times to join in and to forget, albeit briefly, their troubles and enjoy themselves. Schools also held fund-raising events and made clothes for the refugee children. The Belgian Relief Fund received more sympathetic support than fund raising for other causes.

The Ruislip-Northwood Belgian Refugee Committee undertook to find hospitality for fifty or more refugees, and a letter circulated in October 1914 stressed the need for hosts as well as funds towards the cost of housing families in rented accommodation. In Ruislip, Rosemead in Sharps Lane, No. 2 Park Way and No. 3 Manor Close were secured to house refugees for a short time.

The Rosery and Dean Cottage, looking north-east from Eastcote Road. (Courtesy of Hillingdon Local Studies, Archives and Museum Service)

Refugees were also billeted in houses in Northwood, at St Albans, and Melville, both in Chester Road, and for a time, Nos 1-2 Church Road and No. 2 Maxwell Road, the home of Edward Ryder, a hosier. Southill House, Eastcote High Road, now known as The Old Shooting Box, which had been lent by Mr R.H. Deane in November 1914, also housed nineteen Belgian refugees for a short time. Four refugees were housed at Eversholt; Mr Goschen of Sigers accommodated four more at Park Farm, Field End Road and at his own home, Sigers, at Eastcote; Mr Philips of Horn End had taken in some more, and further accommodation was provided at a house in Bridle Road. A spare room on the first floor of the council offices at Oaklands Gate was offered in October 1914 to the Northwood Belgian Refugees Committee as club rooms. Because of the cost of printing, no reports were issued regarding refugees in the Ruislip area, but one issued in July 1919 indicated that the first eighteen months was 'the most eventful'. Gradually the Belgian refugees found work to support themselves. A Belgian boy and his grandfather were amongst the refugees living in Northwood. The grandfather was employed as a temporary gardener at Northwood College while weekly contributions from the school maintained the boy. By the end of 1914, 133 refugees had been accommodated in Northwood and Eastcote. A family of five refugees were also guests of Mrs Tarleton and the employees of the Breakspeare estate at Wickham Cottage, Pinner Road.

Between 100,000 and 200,000 Belgians fled to England after Germany invaded their country. Many refugees did not establish new homes for themselves after the war but went back to Belgium. The last of them, two families – all women – remained in Ruislip-Northwood until they were repatriated in the spring of 1919.

PRISONERS OF WAR

PRISONERS OF war numbered into the millions and there were many charges, on both sides, that the rules, drawn up at an international conference at The Hague in 1899 and 1907, were not being observed. The exact number of local men taken prisoner is difficult to establish, although it is known that by August 1916, four Northwood men were prisoners. Civilians working abroad were also liable to be captured. Some POWs died from disease, starvation or dysentery.

In the spring of 1918, during the German spring offensive, many other local lads were captured. Among them was Corporal G. Woodman, son of Mr and Woodman of Hills Lane, Northwood, who was wounded and taken prisoner in March 1918. Privates Joe Wallace and Ted Lavender, and Sergeant Harry Berry, all of Ruislip, were prisoners in Germany for varying periods of time. Northwood postman Private F.M. Joyce of the Middlesex Regiment had been captured at Cambrai in a forceful counter-attack, which began on 20 November, and the second phase of which began shortly after dawn on 30 November 1917.

After the Armistice, those captured gradually returned home – Ted Lavender, Joe Wallace and Harry Berry arrived at the beginning of 1919. Mr William Beckett, formerly Captain of the fire brigade, and J. Stanley Chown, both from Northwood, were, in December, 1918 among the steady stream of Northwood men being repatriated from Germany. Celebrations were held everywhere to welcome them home.

Local prisoners of war funds were set up early in the war, affiliated to the British Red Cross Fund through its Central Prisoner of War Committee. It was agreed that properly selected food should be sent to each prisoner once a fortnight; each parcel should weigh 10lb, with 13lb of bread. Although food parcels were sent to the men, it is doubtful whether all of them were received. Unless a special label was affixed to the parcel, no post office would accept it and no individual could hand over a parcel there. In 1917 it was agreed that private parcels of food and clothing weighing up to 11lb from family and friends were allowed. The Northwood Fund, which was registered under the War Charities Act 1916, began in June 1915 and secured the responsibility of supplying parcels to prisoners in the Middlesex Regiment. It was the only centre for distribution in the whole of Middlesex. In the period beginning June 1915 and ending in December 1916 they had dispatched twelve large cases and 750 parcels of food to thirty-seven different prisoners, averaging one parcel per fortnight per prisoner. During

British prisoners returning from Germany at the end of the conflict.

1917, 864 parcels were sent. By June 1918, £1,170 had been collected, together with gifts in kind, and seventy-two parcels had been dispatched to twelve POWs in Germany that year. In early July 1915, Miss Wallis of Reservoir Cottage, Ruislip Common, whose brother Robert had joined the Royal Army Veterinary Corps early in the war, appealed for money in order to send Christmas parcels to English soldiers who were prisoners in Germany, for which she received several letters of thanks. She proposed to continue the next year. In May 1918 there was an appeal, signed by the Duke of Bedford, urging the claims of the Lord Lieutenant's County Fund for Middlesex Regiment's Prisoners of War (of which there were 1,400 by the beginning of 1918). £17,000 was needed to support them.

Captured German POWs were held at many places in Britain. For a period, during the latter part of the war, Eastcote Lodge, in the High Road, was used to house German officer prisoners of war, who were given half the pay of the corresponding ranks of infantry officers in the British Army and were messed free. Medical attendance and medicine was also free. The ration awarded to a German prisoner was actually larger than that given to a British citizen. They were, however, expected to clothe themselves. Officers lived comfortably but not luxuriously away from the rank and file. Denham Lodge and Eastcote, which was attached to Denham Lodge, were Agricultural Depots under Feltham. Other camps at The Needles, Northolt, Langley Park at Iver Heath and Stoke Green at Stoke Green, Bucks, were also Agricultural Depots attached to Denham Lodge under Feltham. Not surprisingly, many of the men were hired out to local farmers.

ALIEN INTERNEES AND SPY FEVER!

BRITAIN INTERNED between 29,000 and 30,000 foreigners during the 1914-18 period, most of whom were German Jews. Many had settled in this country long ago or had sought political refuge here. Unfortunately in some areas the policy was a disaster, with anti-civilian excesses. However, unlike some other districts, Ruislip-Northwood appears to have remained relatively unaffected.

Several local residents with German-sounding names changed them. These included Francis Zeppenfeld and G.A. Schultz (who changed his name to Sanford by deed poll in August 1917). Both lived at Northwood.

A large number of aliens had been interned on account of 'spy fever'. Twenty 'known spies' were arrested before war was declared on 4 August, with a further 200 people rounded up four days later. It was later claimed that this had broken up a German spy ring. The Aliens Restriction Act had come into force on 5 August 1914, which required all aliens to register with the police. Numerous aliens who had not registered were taken to court, where the fines were usually heavy. On 5 September the Home Office and War Office decided that it was necessary to intern all male Germans aged between seventeen and fifty-five. By 13 September this was suspended, as there was no more space to hold them!

In 1907 Josef Conn and his wife, Emily, a Dane who had pioneered physiotherapy in England, obtained a lease of the land in Northwood from King's College, Cambridge, to build a house, which they named Horsens. Mr Conn, who, it is thought, was of German extraction, was interned in 1914 suspected of having alien sympathies. There were rumours of spying and secret gun emplacements. Although he was released shortly afterwards, his business as an importer had been suspended by the war and it appears that the Conns moved into a smaller house in Ruislip, and then out of the district altogether. The house, which remained untenanted until 1916, was renamed Franklin House and eventually became known as the Battle of Britain House.

Anti-German feeling was whipped up by the press and politicians and further fuelled by the sinking of three British cruisers, the *Aboukir*, *Hogue* and *Cressy*, on 22 September 1914. In some cases Germans were interned for their own safety.

Although the problems of where to hold the aliens remained, by 20 October the internment of Germans, Austrians and Hungarians had started again. They were accommodated at a number of different camps – Beech Abbey, Hampshire; Douglas, Isle of Man and various old liners moored in the Thames estuary. The closest to home was at

Olympia, where conditions were rough and ready. By early November 1,500 men were held at Olympia, while the total throughout Britain had reached 10,000. The continued rise in internees prompted the Home Office to join the War Office in a search for other camp sites. By the spring of 1915 there were some 19,000 aliens in internment, some of whom had been taken to large camps such as that established at Alexandra Palace. A great many were also taking up valuable space in local prisons throughout the country. At the end of February 1915, Knockaloe, on the Isle of Man, was made available with accommodation for 2,000 men, which was increased to 5,000 men in November.

By 1915, 19,000 German aliens had been interned. The sinking of the *Lusitania* on 7 May 1915 further fuelled anti-German feeling and in less than one week the Prime Minister, Herbert Asquith, announced that all alien men of fighting age were to be interned. Knockaloe would have to be extended, as by the end of 1915 the 20,000 capacity of Knockaloe had been reached. In fact, there were almost 30,000 internees, internments having risen at a rate of 1,000 men per week. Although the largest camps remained on the Isle of Wight, other smaller ones were scattered throughout England and Scotland, including Reading gaol, Stratford, Islington, Alexandra Palace, Frimley in Surrey and Olympia.

Anti-German societies sprang up. The nearest seems to have been at Harrow, where the Anti-German Association was vehemently welcomed.

1918 saw a renewed public outcry for the internment of all enemy aliens, whether naturalised or not.

Authorisation for the release of wartime detainees came in the New Year of 1919 and arrangements were made for their repatriation. A few remained in England until the end of 1919, their personal particulars recorded as required by the Aliens Act.

PEOPLE

HUGH WARRENDER of Highgrove, Eastcote, rejoined his regiment in which he formerly held a commission. His sister, Eleanor Warrender, was commandant of the 2nd Middlesex Detachment of the Voluntary Aid Detachment, Uxbridge, and had served in the Balkan War for three months in 1913 nursing the wounded in Greek military hospitals. She arrived back in England in January 1913. She had also nursed on the South African hospital ship *Marne*, and for her good work then and at other times she was honoured by the distinction of being a Lady of Grace of the Order of St John. Between 1914 and 1919 she served with the French Red Cross, having qualified as a nurse in that country prior to 1914, after being judged as too old to qualify as a nurse in England. On 6 August 1915 she received the Croix de Guerre (1st Class) from General Hely d'Oiseul.

Christopher Addison was a British Labour politician who had qualified as a doctor at St Bartholomew's Hospital and became professor of Anatomy at Sheffield. In 1910 he was elected Liberal MP for Hoxton which he represented until 1922. During this time he had made his home with his wife and children at Garlands, situated at the junction of Sandy Lane and Watford Road in Northwood, which at that time was known as 'Pretty Corner'. He became parliamentary secretary to the Board of Education in 1914. When Lloyd George set up the Ministry of Munitions in May 1915, he was appointed parliamentary secretary to that instead. In July 1916, following Lloyd George's move to the Ministry of War, Addison became Minister of Munitions for a short time (1916-1917). In 1919 he became Britain's first Minister of Health.

The Distinguished Service Order, or DSO. This was for commissioned officers whose gallant actions in the face of the enemy had seen them distinguished with a mention in dispatches.

He remained in politics for most of the rest of his life, and was created a baron in 1937. In 1945 he became Viscount Addison of Stallingborough and in 1946 was awarded the Knighthood of the Garter. He died in 1951 in West Wycombe, Bucks.

Colonel Creighton Hutchinson Lindsay was born in 1877. He served with distinction, having taken part in the first landing at Gallipoli with the 29th Division. He remained there until the final evacuation. For his services he was awarded the CMG and mentioned in Sir Ian Hamilton's despatches. After the evacuation he served with the Canal Defence Forces in Egypt and subsequently in France, where he was appointed ADMS to the 59th Division. After the Armistice he was ADMS to the Rhine Garrison. He was mentioned in despatches eight times in all and also awarded the DSO. He later became Medical Officer to the Ministry of Health. He died early in 1941 at Wentworth, Dene Road, Northwood, but it is not known where he was buried or cremated. His only son served during the Second World War with the Royal Corps of Signals.

Edward George Honey, an Australian journalist, thought up the idea of a period of silence for the fallen of the First World War on the anniversary of the signing of the Armistice. His original idea of five minutes was deemed too long for crowds to have to remain still and silent, so two minutes was fixed upon. He was diagnosed with consumption in 1921 and died at Mount Vernon Hospital on 25 August 1922 and is buried in Northwood Cemetery. He was thirty-seven years old.

Brigadier-General S.V.P. Weston was, on the outbreak of war, a partner in the firm on the London stock exchange. A month later he joined the Epsom Public School Corps as a Private, shortly afterwards receiving his commission in the Royal Berkshire Regiment. In October 1915 he went to France in the Second Army and in February 1916 was gazetted Captain. In December 1916 he was awarded the Military Cross and, in April 1917, while acting in command of a battalion, won the DSO and the rank of Lieutenant Colonel. In November 1917, at Cambrai, he was awarded a bar to his DSO. In March 1918, during the British retreat, he won the second bar to his DSO. He had also been mentioned in despatches three times and in June 1918 was gazetted Brigadier-General – and also received in October the French Croix de Guerre and in December, the Belgian Croix de Guerre. He was a resident of Northwood and was invited to unveil the war memorial on 13 February 1921. Bishop Taylor-Smith, Chaplain-General to the Forces, himself also a resident of Northwood, was to dedicate the memorial but his duties compelled him to leave England for Egypt in early February 1921. The Revd D.F. Carey, DSO, one of his assistants took his place. The Bishop of Kensington unveiled and dedicated Ruislip's war memorial in the churchyard of the parish church of St Martin, Ruislip, in the spring of 1920. Eastcote War Memorial was unveiled on Sunday, 12 June 1921, by Col. Peel MP and dedicated by Prebend Vincent, RD, of Uxbridge.

ARMISTICE!
MONDAY, 11 NOVEMBER 1918

O N MONDAY, 11 November 1918, the day of the Armistice, it was dreary and wet. Hostilities in the west had ceased at 11 a.m. (French time), but the last four years, fourteen weeks and two days had taught everyone to be patient. Many false hopes and rumours had circulated before. Eleven o'clock came and went. A surprising silence had descended when suddenly guns, hooters, horns, etc, blared. Just before midday, as news of the Armistice spread, workmen downed tools and most schoolchildren were given a half-day holiday. Joyful crowds full of hysterical jubilation were cheering, whistling and singing and commandeered vehicles of every description. Drapers were besieged with people buying Union Jacks, which they hung from bedroom windows. All kinds of musical instruments appeared as if by magic. Patriotic songs were the order of the day, and his good-natured rowdyism lasted until the Saturday night. Perhaps the most striking thing was the lighted streets and no worry about special constables coming to knock at the door. Huge bonfires were lit after dark, but it started raining heavily and the fires were put out.

The scheduled meeting of the Ruislip-Northwood Urban District Council on 11 November 1918 was adjourned. In Ruislip the National School also closed for a half day. RAF lorries full of shouting servicemen from Northolt roared through the streets, and a line of flags could be seen across the street from the Post Office at Northwood. Streamers were still to be seen hanging across the High Street in Northwood just before Christmas.

The guns had fallen silent. The 'war to end all wars' was over and peace was here at long last – but the cost had been high. Death on such a scale had never been witnessed before. Almost 1 million Britons had lost their lives. Civilian losses, apart from those who perished in air raids, amounted to 15,000 deaths among the crews and passengers of merchant and shipping vessels.

Everywhere, things gradually began to turn back to normal, although some things that had been abandoned never returned and others took some time to return. Local clocks, in common with other timepieces throughout the country, including Big Ben, had all been stopped in the early days of the air raids; most of these were not to come on again until mid-1919. Various choirs had met annually for a festival service at Hillingdon on St John the Baptist day, 24 June: St Margaret's, Uxbridge; St Andrew's, Uxbridge; St John's, Uxbridge Moor; Cowley,; Yiewsley; West Drayton; Harmondsworth; Harlington Hayes; Ruislip; and Harefield. They had last met in 1913 and did not reconvene until 1923.

The King and Queen on the balcony of Buckingham Palace on Armistice Day, 11 November 1918.

Of the 7 million men who went to fight, a tenth of them never returned – almost a whole generation had been wiped out. It has been estimated that approximately 1,050,000 men from the Greater London area served during the war, and approximately 130,000 were killed or died of wounds. Britain lost a total of 750,000 soldiers, France 1.4 million and German 2 million. After four years of fighting, around 20 million soldiers, sailors, airmen and civilians had died. The war memorials show that sixteen men from Eastcote died (134 had answered the call of the flag); at Northwood 102 never returned, or returned home to die. Twenty-one names are on the Northwood Council Roll of Honour for having served during the war - one councillor, eleven firemen, four workmen and five officials. Two men never returned. Thirty-three residents of Ruislip never returned home, and eight men fell out of the sixty-nine who went off to war from Ruislip Common. Their names will live for evermore.

THE ROLL OF HONOUR

Abercrombie, Robert Henry Chester

Born at Stanley (or Standard) Lodge, Walm Lane, Willesden Green on 3 June 1890. When he was about six years old, his family moved to Southill House, Eastcote, and in 1905 to Sunnyside, Eastcote, removing to 'Ashberrie', Ickenham Road, Ruislip, in 1912. He joined the 2/9th Middlesex Regiment as a Private in October 1914 and was promoted Lance Corporal in November and Sergeant in December. He obtained his commission as 2nd Lieutenant with the 3/8th Middlesex in March 1915, and transferred to the 1/8th Middlesex Regiment the following month. He was killed in action at the Battle of St Julien at Frezenberg, near Ypres, on 3 May 1915, aged twenty-four. He was mortally wounded in the head by shell fire while in command – the officers all having been killed or disabled – while helping a wounded comrade to drink during close rifle fire, trench mortar fire and constant bombing. The only son of Chester and Ada Maria Abercrombie of 'Ashberrie', Ickenham Road, he was educated at Woodriding School, Pinner, and Elstow School, near Bedford. On leaving school he entered the London County and Westminster Bank and was successively in the St John's Wood, Hanover Square, Uxbridge and Hastings branches. He was a successful marksman in the Ruislip Rifle Club, which was affiliated to the National Rifle Association, the Society of Miniature Rifle Clubs and the North West Middlesex League in Ickenham Road. The club was situated within a comfortable walking distance from his home, and he had been their secretary – and, latterly their vice president. In 1913 he gained a place in the Middlesex Twenty for the Queen Alexandra Club and was awarded a certificate. Some of his sisters also belonged to the club, and his father was chairman. In early 1920 his family, who had lived in the district for many years, left Ruislip for Chelmsford, where they had taken a farm. He is commemorated on the St Martin's church, Ruislip, and Ruislip war memorials. He is buried at Poperinghe Old Military Cemetery, Belgium.

Abrahardt, E.

He enlisted in the 8th Middlesex before June 1915 and is commemorated on Northwood war memorial. He had been a member of Northwood Presbyterian church. Possibly Edwin ABRAHART, Driver 182221, RFA who died at the General Military Hospital, Edmonton, on 15 June 1920, aged thirty-nine. His home address was given as 38, Chedington Road, Edmonton. He left a widow, Laura, and was buried at Edmonton Cemetery, Church Street, on 22 June 1920.

Addis, Henry Dansey

Born in Bristol on 25 September 1898. Second Lieutenant, 43rd Squadron, RFC, Northolt Aerodrome. Henry died when his plane crashed while taking off from Northolt on 24 January 1917, aged twenty-three. His mechanic, Frederick Foott, died later in hospital. When between 40 and 50ft from the ground, Lt. Addis, an expert airman, made a very steep left-hand bank: not having enough speed to complete this manoeuvre, the machine side-slipped and nosedived to the earth. The machine had been tested prior to the flight. The son of the late Dr Philip Dansey Addis and Mrs W. Mansell Merry of 9, Linton Road, Oxford, he had emigrated to Canada. He is buried at Oxford (Wolvercote) Cemetery, Oxfordshire.

Aimer, George Edward Vernon

Born at Hokianga, New Zealand. 2nd Lieut., 11th Reserve Squadron RFC, Northolt Aerodrome. Died from terrible injuries received in a flying accident on 20 June 1916, aged thirty. He had taken off on a solo flight and was flying his machine (a Martynside SL696) at a height of between 1,000 and 4,000ft when he suddenly appeared to be in difficulties and crashed to the ground almost vertically. He was taken to the RFC Hospital in Bryanston Square, where he died later that same day. He was the son of Mr Edmond Baxter Aimer and Mrs Annie Elizabeth Aimer (née Feek) of Fairburn Road, Otahahu, Auckland, New Zealand. He had come to England long before the outbreak of war, suffering from blood poisoning, as his doctors had advised him to take a long voyage. He had been employed by the Bank of New Zealand. He is buried at Ruislip (St Martin) churchyard extension.

Allen, Job

Born at Ruislip, where he was baptised on 15 May 1880. Job was the son of William and Harriet Allen. Acting Corporal (Private), CH/8575, Chatham Battalion, RN Div., Royal Marine Light Infantry. He had enlisted on 20 August 1895 and received the China Medal in 1900 (without clasp) while on HMS *Dido*. On 26 November 1910, he received the RN Long Service and Good Conduct Medal, and was appointed Lance Corporal on 21 September 1914. He was in action at the defence of Antwerp in October 1914 and joined the Mediterranean Expeditionary Force on 6 February 1915. On 12 May 1915 he became Acting Corporal. He was killed in action or died of wounds on 12 July 1915, aged thirty-five. On 5 July 1915, Turkish counter-attacks took place: as soon as the artillery preparations by batteries were over, the Turkish advance began. The principal attack was made where the Royal Naval Division joined with the French. The battle continued until noon with heavy losses on our side. On 12 July the British and French made another furious assault on a forward system of trenches along a front of 2,000 yards from the mouth of the Kereves Dere to the main road from Krithia to Sedd-el-Bahr, and on the lines around Achi Baba (where the RND's armoured cars advanced over bridges constructed across the British trenches right up to the enemy's firing line). Amongst the losses for the French on this date was General Masnou, commander of the French 1st Division and General Ganeval from their 2nd Division. He was the son of Mr and Mrs Allen of Hayes and husband of Florence Anne Allen of Greenford, later Florence A. Shersby. He is not commemorated on the Ruislip or Hayes war memorials, but is commemorated on the Greenford war memorial. Buried: Skew Bridge Cemetery, Turkey.

Andrews, H.W.C.

He had been a postman at Northwood.

Annesley, James Ferguson St. John

Born in Belfast on 24 June 1864, he qualified as a doctor at the University of Ireland on 22 May 1888. He was a Captain in the Royal Army Medical Corps, serving with the Royal Navy on a hospital ship from June 1916. He was accidentally killed flying a biplane while on duty at Thetford Aerodrome in Norfolk – where there was a School of Navigation and Bomb Dropping – on 19 May 1917, aged fifty-two. He was a dispensary doctor, gazetted Lieutenant, RAMC in January 1916 and promoted to Captain in January 1917. He had married Geraldine Clara Carr in Dublin on 4 January 1898 and had four children. His widow, who lived at 6, Murray Road, Northwood, died on 12 February 1944 and is buried at Northwood. After her husband's death she threw herself wholeheartedly into numerous good causes locally and had been president of the Ladies' Guild of the Soldiers' and Sailors' Society. She was the sister of Ethel Culshaw, wife of the Revd George Culshaw, rector of Iver Heath, whose son, Ronald, was killed in action while 'gallantly leading his men' on 14 July 1918 after being at the front for only eighteen days. Captain Annesley is commemorated in Holy Trinity church, Northwood, and Northwood war memorial. He was the second son of the Revd J. B. Annesley, formerly rector of Drumkeeran, County Fermanagh. Buried: Euston (St Genevieve) churchyard, Suffolk.

Aplin, R.

He had been a postman at Northwood.

Murray Road, Northwood. (Courtesy of Hillingdon Local Studies, Archives and Museum Service)

Attwood, Arthur Charles

Native of St Albans, of Northwood, where he had been a postman. Royal Naval Volunteer Reserve, RMA/8077, Gunner, HMS *Good Hope,* RN. He went down with his ship, a Drake Class armoured cruiser, one of the fastest ships in the world, at around 7.50 p.m. on 1 November 1914. It was the flagship and had been hit by gunfire from the German armoured cruisers SMS *Scharnhorst* and SMS *Gneisenau* off the Chilean Coast during the battle of Coronel. The entire crew was lost. The *Good Hope* and the cruiser *Monmouth*, which also went down, were trying to prevent the return of the German China squadron to Europe. Both were sunk in the battle with the loss of over 900 men in each ship – almost all of whom were reservists. He was thirty-four years old, the husband of Kate Attwood of King's Langley. He is commemorated on the Emmanuel church, Northwood, and Northwood war memorials. His family was helped financially by the Soldiers' and Sailors' Families Associations (Uxbridge Division of Middlesex). Commemorated: Portsmouth Naval memorial.

Avery, George

Born at Ruislip and baptised there on 5 June 1892, son of Robert William and Sarah Ann Avery. The family later moved to Palmers Farm, Heathrow. He enlisted at Mill Hill, and lived at Hounslow. L/9797, Sergeant, 1st Royal West Kent Regiment. In January 1915 he was wounded by shrapnel which fractured his thumb and spent some time in Fort Pitt Hospital at Chatham. On 10 February 1917, the morning had passed relatively quietly. Zero hour had been fixed for 3 p.m. for a daylight raid against the German lines just north-east of Givenchy. He was killed in action during this raid, which became known as 'The Royal West Kents' Givenchy Raid', aged twenty-six. He had enlisted in the 1st Royal West Kent Regiment at Maidstone in January 1912, after being employed as a factory hand (a pipe repairer) at the Imperial Tobacco Co., Fulham Palace Road, living at that time at Stonebridge Park. He was appointed Lance Corporal on 18 March 1915; promoted to Corporal on 22 November 1915; appointed Lance Sergeant on 2 January 1916; Acting Sergeant from 22 June 1916 and promoted to Sergeant on 11 December 1916. He is not commemorated locally but is commemorated on the Harlington war memorial. Buried: Gorre British and Indian Cemetery, Pas de Calais, France.

Backer, Eugene

He lived at 29, Cathcart Street, Kentish Town, and was a motor mechanic (ex Private, Royal Marines) from No. 4 Stores, RAF. Died of influenza and pneumonia at No. 4 Stores, RAF Depot, Ickenham Road, on 26 February 1919, aged twenty-five. Buried: Ruislip.

Bailey, John Winkworth

Second-Lieutenant, RFC 19 RA Squadron, Northolt Aerodrome. Killed on the night of 31 March 1916 when his plane, a B.E.2c, crashed at Northolt. He was thirty-three years old. He had taken off at 21.05 hours during a slight haze, the only sortie from Northolt to intercept Zeppelins, although in all, eight naval and nine military airmen went up. At first he seemed to climb normally, and passed the last flare: then, suddenly, his machine crashed, as if he had lost control, probably killing him instantly. He was dead when picked up. He was the son of the Revd John Bailey and Penelope Ann Bailey of New Road House, Rochester, Kent. Old Harrovian and M.A. Exeter College, Oxford. Buried: St Martin's churchyard, Ruislip.

Baker, Francis Edgar

Born at Acton, where he was baptised at All Saints, South Acton, on 21 October 1888. The son of Samuel, an accountant, and Letitia Baker of Acton Vale, he enlisted at Harrow in November 1915, of Snaefell, Roy Road, Northwood. 88123, Gunner, 147th Heavy Battery, Royal Garrison Artillery (Royal Regiment of Artillery (RGA) Corps). He was mobilised on 25 May 1916, arriving in France later that year on 29 September. Reports from spies, deserters and other sources clearly indicated that an attack might be expected any time after 17 March 1918, but it was only on 19 March that aeroplane reconnaissance and photographs showed large numbers of fresh German batteries, including trained storm troopers, in the vicinity. At 5 a.m. on the very misty morning of Thursday, 21 March 1918 troops were awakened by heavy artillery fire along a 50-60 mile front from the Oise to south-east of Arras. Sometime on this day he was killed in action at the Battle of Bapaume, amidst a deluge of minenwerfers, cannons of unknown calibre, and toxic gas shells. The British troops had been overpowered by an enemy who outnumbered the defenders by three to one. The prisoners and guns captured by the Germans in this (and in the attack on 27 May) exceeded the highest record of the Allies in any of their great offensives. He had been appointed assistant overseer for Ruislip and Collector of General District Rate and Assessor of Taxes at Northwood on 13 October 1913, previous to which he had been assistant rate collector for Harrow Council. His salary at the time of his appointment was £60 per annum as assistant overseer and £60 per annum as collector, with annual salary reviews each January. He also received £2 10s per annum for the upkeep of his bike. The council had appealed to the tribunal for his exemption. He left a wife, Lena Evelyn (née Reed) of Brighton, whom he had married at St Phillip's church, Aldrington, on 21 March 1914, and daughter, Phyllis Dorothy, who had been born at Northwood on 28 November 1914. His widow appealed to the Ruislip-Northwood Urban District Council for financial aid after her husband's untimely death – and was turned down. His brother, Second Lieutenant F. Gerald Baker of Butler Road, Harrow, was killed in action on 17 April 1918. Francis is commemorated on the Emmanuel church, Northwood, and Northwood war memorials. Commemorated: Arras memorial, Pas de Calais, France.

Baldwin, G.E.

He had been a postman at Northwood and is commemorated on Northwood war memorial. Possibly George Edwin Baldwin, who enlisted in London and lived with his wife at 28, Holywell Road, Watford. Private 738040, 24th London Regiment, formerly 3871, 1/8th London Regiment, he was killed in the failed action to keep possession of Metz on Thursday, 21 March 1918 and buried at Metz-en-Couture Communal Cemetery British Extension, Pas de Calais. He had been slightly wounded by gunshot in the left leg at the beginning of 1916. His daughter was born posthumously on 18 October 1918.

Barrett, George Charles

Born at Tonkers, USA. He had been a painter and enlisted at Mill Hill in the 15th Middlesex Regiment on 22 January 1915. George lived at Brinscombe, Hilliard Road, Northwood. On 20 April 1917 he was posted to the 4th Middlesex Regiment, serving as G/11994, Private. Killed in action near Zero Wood during the Third Battle of Ypres, on 29 July 1917, aged twenty-two. He was the son of Elizabeth Barrett of 159, High Street, Northwood, and the late William Barrett, who had been a painter, grainer and house decorator of Hallowell Road. George is commemorated on the Emmanuel church, Northwood, and Ruislip war memorials. Commemorated: Ypres (Menin Gate) memorial, Belgium.

Barrett, George William

Born at Ruislip or Harefield and baptised at Ruislip on 7 November 1897, son of George James and Ellen Barrett, enlisted at Harrow, lived at Northolt. G/61595, Private, 23rd (Service) Royal Fusiliers. Formerly 21196, East Surrey Regiment. Killed in action at Arras on 3 January 1918, aged nineteen. The son of George and Ellen Barrett of 3 Bourne Cottages, Long Mile, Harrow, he is commemorated on the Eastcote, St Lawrence's church, Eastcote, and St Martin's church, Ruislip's war memorials. Buried: Hermies Hill British Cemetery, Pas de Calais, France.

Barrett, Herbert Robert

Born at Northwood on 14 August 1892, Private 718025, 16th Canadian Infantry (Manitoba Regiment), Canadian Scottish Regiment. In March 1918 raiding activity increased on both sides until the whole Canadian Front seethed with continuous minor fighting; he was killed in action here on 4 March 1918. He was the younger son of the late Mr William Barrett, a builder, and Mrs Barrett of 2 Warwick Villas, Hallowell Road, Northwood. He was educated at Northwood Council Schools and later became a butcher. He was 5ft 10ins tall, with black hair and brown eyes. He had married Miss S. Fletcher of Great Missenden on Christmas morning 1917. He is commemorated on the Emmanuel church memorial, Northwood. Buried: Bully-Grenay Communal British Cemetery Extension, Pas de Calais, France.

Bayetto, Tone Hyppolite

Of the Old House, Lime Grove, Eastcote. He had not lived there for long, but was there by 1915/1916. Captain Bayetto, RFC was accidentally killed while flying near Beaulieu on 28 July 1918, aged twenty-six. He died as a result of a 'fall whilst flying in an aeroplane', a Sopwith Dolphin E 4449. He was the son of H. and Rosalie Lemair Bayetto of The Stag, Eastcote. He was educated at Battersea Polytechnic, after which he went to India – where he soon became a director and secretary in the works of Maraja Mucargi in Calcutta. He returned to England shortly before war was declared. He enlisted in April 1915, promoted on 12 March 1916 and received his Captaincy in June 1917; he was wounded in September 1917. On 30 September 1917, while with 66 Squadron, he had destroyed an enemy aircraft while at a disadvantage. He is commemorated on the Eastcote, St Lawrence's church, Eastcote, St Martin's, Ruislip, and Ruislip war memorials. Buried: Ruislip (St Martin) churchyard extension, I.72.

Bell, Callum Gray Munro

Northolt Aerodrome. Second Lieutenant, RAF. Killed instantly on 16 August 1918 when his plane fell from a height of 2,000ft locally. He had started descending when the machine spun and nosedived. He was nineteen years old. Buried: Halewood (St Nicholas) churchyard, Lancashire.

Bennett, John Blake

Second Lieutenant. General List and 1st Aircraft Supply Depot, Royal Flying Corps. He had joined the London Scottish on 28 January 1917, when he was eighteen years old, and after six months' training he was transferred to the RFC. He was killed in action on Thursday, 21 March 1918, 'on the first day of the great battle' – the German spring offensive known as 'The Great Battle of France' – while flying. He was nineteen. The weather was very misty but much fighting had taken place during the day. However, on this day co-operation between the artillery and the RFC failed completely from the very start. He had worked at Wealdstone Hyposol Ltd., surgical and medical instrument makers of Northwood. He was the only son of John H. Bennett and Emma Bennett of the Ironmonger's Shop, 4 Church Road, Northwood. Buried: Boulogne Eastern Cemetery, Pas de Calais, France.

Bennett, Reginald Harry

Born in London, enlisted at Guildford. 55629, Private, 10th Northumberland Fusiliers. Formerly 9379, The Queen's. Killed in action in heavy fighting near Reutel, east of Ypres, on 10 October 1917. He had joined the Forces in about 1907 and had been a Staff Sergeant in the Army Service Corps, later transferring to the Northumberland Fusiliers. He was the second son of Mr Harry Bennett, a fruiterer and grocer, of 5, The Pavement, Northwood, and was shortly to be married. His mother, Emily, who was born on 4 February 1865, died on 10 November 1917. His father had been the Hon. Sec. of the Northwood Traders' Association. Reginald is commemorated on Northwood war memorial. Commemorated: Tyne Cot memorial, Zonnebeke, Ypes, Belgium.

Bentley, George Henry

Born at Northwood, enlisted at Willesden, resided at Wembley. T.F.265411, Lance-Corporal, 1/9th Middlesex Regiment. In October 1914, the 9th Middlesex went out to India with the 44th Division to replace the regular battalions being sent to France and remained there, sending drafts to fighting units in the Middle East. He died here on 23 August 1917. Commemorated: Kirkee 1914-1918 memorial, India.

Bentley, William Douglas

Born at Hanley, Staffs, enlisted Longton, Staffs, lived at Northwood, Middx. 60530, Private, 17th Royal Welsh Fusiliers. Formerly 285117, Royal Army Service Corps. During the whole month of July, the British Army knew an attack was pending. All roads north of Armentieres were thick with troops moving up day after day. Our front was at that time about 11 miles long around the Ypres salient, and north of Ypres it was around the Yser Canal. He was killed in action at the Battle of the Ridges, part of the Third Battle of Ypres, on 31 July 1917, the day the great ill-fated offensive at Ypres was opened on a front of 15 miles from La Basse Ville on the River Lys to Steenstraat on the Yser Canal, the main object being an arc of small hills in front of the British valley positions around Ypres. Twelve divisions advanced on an 11-mile front in pouring rain. Two divisions of the XIV Corps on either side of the Ypres-Staden railway had another 1,800 yards to reach the Steeneek. The 38th (Welsh) Division (which included the 17th R/Welch Fusiliers who had been slipped into the front line as fresh troops sometime on this day and who were making for the Steenbeek stream) were faced with a fresh German garrison and were held up at the start by machine-gun fire from the left flank. Without artillery support it gallantly fought a strong counter-attack until it reached the stream at 12.30 p.m. with its strength reduced to four officers and 200 other ranks. He was aged thirty-two, the son of Mrs A.E. Bentley of 78 Bold Street, Hanley. Buried: Poelcapelle British Cemetery, Langemark-Poelkapelle, West Vlaanderen, Belgium.

Berkeley, Christopher

2nd Lieut., 30th TDS, RAF and 2nd Btn Coldstream Guards, formerly a Private in the 28th London Regiment, Northolt Aerodrome. He died at an RAF hospital on 30 January 1919, aged twenty-two, after his plane nosedived from 1,200ft. He had swerved to avoid a collision with another plane and cut off the engine. He was rendered unconscious. He was an instructor with the RAF at Northolt and was instructing a pupil at the time of the accident. The pupil survived. He had also served in France and was wounded in action. He was the son of the late Revd S. and Mrs E.M. Berkeley of Abbots Bromley Vicarage, Stafford. Buried: Hendon (St Mary) churchyard.

Billingham, J.

He had been a postman at Northwood.

Birch, Sydney James

Born at Hatfield, he enlisted at Marylebone on 2 September 1914 in the 3rd King's Own Hussars, of Northwood. He was transferred to the 8th Royal Fusiliers as Private, 16618, in June 1915 and served with the Expedition Force. He had been one of his company's covering party, and was employed in digging a trench between Hulluch and Vermelles when a shell burst over his head, badly wounding him. He died in a dressing station on 2 October 1915, aged twenty-three. He was the only son of James William and Jane Birch of 28 Primrose Cottage, Hatfield. He was educated at Hatfield, after which he became a telegraph boy at Hatfield post office. He later became a grocer's assistant at Northwood. He is commemorated on the Emmanuel church, Northwood, and Northwood war memorials, as well as the Loos memorial, Pas de Calais, France.

Bishop, Basil Frederick, MC

Born at Swansea in 1880, of Northwood. Lieutenant Colonel, 9th South Lancashire Regiment. The Regiment had landed in France on 7 September 1915 and sailed from Marseilles 29 October, landing at Salonika on 5 November 1915. Early in the morning of 18 September 1918, the British attacked the positions of the Bulgarian 2nd Army, on the front west and east of Lake Doiran. The Division had to attack what was thought to be the strongest point in the whole line in a hill of slopes, which were so steep that to get to their objective they had to go on hands and knees to the top of a height of 3,000ft. He had been wounded when the attack commenced, but went missing; eventually he was reported as killed on that date, aged thirty-nine. The 22nd Division had been nailed down by heavy machine-gun fire, and no advance made. The principal fighting had been borne by the 22nd Division, the 77th infantry brigade and a Greek division. Awarded the Military Cross, he was the elder son of the late Frederic Sillery Bishop, who had died on 17 July 1913, aged sixty-five, and Amy Bishop (who died on 14 February 1917, aged sixty-seven), of Welwyn, Eastbury Avenue, Northwood. He had been educated at Repton and joined the Army in September 1914. In December 1914 he was Temporary Captain, 9th South Lancashires, serving in France and Salonika. He is commemorated on the Emmanuel church, Northwood, and Northwood war memorials. Commemorated: Doiran memorial, Greece.

Blackford, Henry James

Born on 28 July 1889 and baptised at Ruislip on 1 September 1889, Henry lived at Raisons Hill, Eastcote. He had attended Pinner Road School, after which he became a farm carter. He had married at St Martin's church, Ruislip, on 27 April 1913. His wife, Agnes, died on 12 February 1915, aged twenty-two. On 11 April 1916, by now a widower with two children, Emily and James (who were both born at Eastcote), he enlisted in the Middlesex Regiment at Mill Hill. He was later transferred to the Royal Engineers and embarked with the British Expeditionary Force for France on 12 June 1917 as 280046 Pioneer, Royal Engineers, 332 Coy. In July 1917 he was wounded by gas while on active service and transferred to the Royal Engineers Road Troops Depot at Aldershot. He was discharged on 20 December 1917. He died of pleurisy to the left lung on 3 January 1919, aged twenty-nine. He was the son of Mr Simeon and Mrs Emily Blackford of Raisons Hill, Eastcote. He is commemorated on the Eastcote and St Martin's church, Ruislip, war memorials. There is also a J. Blackford commemorated on the St Lawrence's church, Eastcote memorial. Buried: St Martin's churchyard, Ruislip.

Blathwayt, Gerald Wynter

Born at Belevdere, Kent, on 30 June 1879. Captain, 56th Battery, 44th Brigade, Royal Field Artillery. On Sunday, 13 September 1914, the British had forced the passage of the Aisne. It was a hazardous crossing, about 15 miles in length. The following morning a general advance began but our men soon came under very heavy shell and machine-gun fire. Captain Blathwayt was killed in action by the bursting of a shell on this, the first day of the Battle of the Aisne on 14 September 1914, near Verneuil, aged thirty-five; he is 'buried in the garden of the chateau', his body later being removed. Younger son of Arthur Pennington Blathwayt, a stockbroker, and Mary Constantia Blathwayt, who died on 12 February 1919 and is buried at Northwood, of Northwood Grange, Green Lane, Northwood; husband of Margaret Aline Blathwayt, daughter of the late C. Pickersgill-Cunliffe, of Red Oaks, Haywards Heath, Sussex, whom he had married in 1911. They had two daughters. He was educated at Aldenham School, Herts. On 22 December 1896,

Green Lane, Northwood, in around 1910. (Courtesy of Hillingdon Local Studies, Archives and Museum Service)

he received his commission in the RFA from the Kent Artillery Militia. He served in the South African War and received the Queen's Medal with three clasps. On his return to England, he was gazetted Captain on 18 July 1906 and Adjutant of the 49th Brigade Royal Field Artillery from December 1906 to December 1909. He was garrison adjutant, Eastern Command, from February 1910 until 31 January 1914. On expiration of his Staff appointment in February 1914, he joined the 56th Battery, 44th (Howitzer) Brigade at Brighton. He is commemorated Northwood war memorial and on Holy Trinity church memorial, Northwood. Buried: Vendresse British Cemetery, Aisne, France.

Boag, Alfred

Born at Newcastle-upon-Tyne, of Cape Town. Lieutenant 3/7th London Regiment/RFC Northolt Aerodrome. Killed flying between Dorney and Windsor on 29 April 1916, aged thirty-one (or thirty-two) years. He had only been attached to the Flying Corps for about a fortnight and this was his fourth flight. At an inquest at Eton Wick it was found that the machine was struck by a sudden gust of wind at about 100ft from the ground and the pilot lost control. Verdict: accidental death. He was the son of Mr A. and Mrs J. Boag of 255 Victoria Road, Salt River, Cape Town. Buried: St Martin's churchyard, Ruislip.

Bonny, Gerald C.

He is commemorated on the Eastcote St Lawrence's church, Ruislip and St Martin's church, Ruislip war memorials, and also on the Pinner and Harrow war memorial. Probably Gerald Charles Bonny, son of Edwin and Julia Bonny of Amersham, who was born in Highgate. He served as Air Mechanic 2nd Class, 49214, 58th Training Sqdn., RFC, which was based in Suez and died on 25 June 1917, aged eighteen. Buried: Alexandria (Hadra) War Cemetery, Egypt.

Boreham, Harry Pendry

Born at Pinner, where he was baptised on 26 January 1890, the only son of Mr Harry White Boreham (a railway clerk at the time of his birth) and Emma Boreham of Balvaig, Green Lane, Northwood, and later of Hastings. Harry lived at Northwood, renting one furnished room on the first floor of his parent's house for 6s a week. He enlisted in the QVR in September 1914. He was a Corporal by 1915 and given a commission in the 1/8th Middlesex Regiment in November 1916. At the time of his death he was serving as Lieutenant with the 18th Middlesex Regiment (Pioneers). The 33rd Division arrived upon the scene of action, the Battle of the Lys, on 11 April 1918, taking their position covering Neuve Eglise after dusk, which was captured by the enemy early on 13 April. The morning of 16 April 1918 was very misty but around 10 a.m. this cleared and it turned to rain. The west of Meteren was by now held by the 18th Middlesex. During the morning, the enemy had made several strong local attacks on the Meteren-Wytschaete Front and after penetrating the line as far as 20km inside had established themselves in both villages. The switch line on that morning was held by the 18th Middlesex who made an unsuccessful attempt to check the enemy at Meteren. He met his death when leading his men in a counter-attack near there at about 8 a.m. of 16 April 1918 at the First Battle of Kemmel. He had been shot through the head by a German machine-gunner. On this day, in the fog on a 15km front from Wytschaete to Merville, all sides were trying different ways to attack, the Germans attacking with enthusiasm. Meteren, Zillebeke and Wytschaete were lost, retaken and lost again. For both sides, nothing was gained. He was educated at Northwood church schools and at John Lyon School in Harrow, after which he had a post in the Chief Accountant's office at Euston station. Hubert Cram was a great friend of his. Together they had organised and run the Church Lads Brigade and Junior Corps connected with Emmanuel church. They both died on the same day. He is commemorated on Northwood and Emmanuel church, Northwood, war memorials. Commemorated: Ploegsteert memorial, Comines-Warneton, Belgium.

Borns, Frank Fairfield

Born at Wimbledon, enlisted at Hampton Court in May 1915. 40533, Lance Corporal, King Edward's Horse, with the 'B' Coy, 2nd Lancashire Fusiliers. Formerly 1336, King Edward's Horse in which he had served from 1914. He was killed in action at the Third Battle of Ypres in action near Houthulst Forest in an advance along the Ypres-Staden railway, on 9 October 1917, aged twenty-nine. The troops were ready in their assembly positions and the advance went forward at 5.20 a.m. Reinforced by the 1st Rifle Brigade, the advance went swiftly forward over dreadful ground until it reached its limits at Landing Farm, about 0.5 miles north-east of Poelcapelle. He was the son of Marion Ewer Borns (née Thomas), of Primrose Hill, Ruislip, and the late George Max Borns, MIME. Margaret, his only sister, had died after a painful illness on 25 January 1902, aged sixteen. She is buried at Ruislip. His father was already dead when his sister died; his mother died on 18 June 1927. Lance Corporal Borns is commemorated on the St Martin's, Ruislip, and Ruislip war memorials. Commemorated: Tyne Cot memorial, Zonnebeke, West Vlaanderen, Belgium.

Bowden, John

Born at Ruislip, where he was baptised on 2nd June 1889, son of John and Sarah Ann Bowden, John enlisted at Wembley and lived at Alperton. 51578, Private, 1st Royal Fusiliers, formerly PW/6915, 25th Middlesex Regiment. Killed in action on 31 July 1917, in the great opening attack in the Battle of the Ridges, part of the Third Battle of Ypres, the day the Ypres offensive was opened on a front of 15 miles from La Basse Ville on the River Lys to Steenstraat on the Yser Canal, the main object being an arc of small hills in front of the British valley positions around Ypres. Twelve divisions advanced on an 11-mile front in pouring rain. The 24th Division, which included the 1st RF, with the 30th and 8th Divisions were on a 3-mile frontage from Klein Zillebeke to the Ypres-Roulers railway. Their task was to capture the entire Gheluvelt plateau and form a defensive flank across the south-western corner of the plateau, astride the Basse-villebeek re-entrant. The heaviest fighting took place east of Ypres where the Menin road crosses the Wytschaete-Passchendaele ridge and the attacking troops, which included the 1st Royal Fusiliers,

Mount Pleasant, Eastcote (at the junction of Field End Road and Bridle Road). (Courtesy of Hillingdon Local Studies, Archives and Museum Service)

suffered very severe casualties before succeeding to penetrate. He was forty. He was the brother of William, below, and brother-in-law of Ernest Puddefoot. John does not appear to be commemorated locally. Commemorated:Ypres (Menin Gate) memorial, Belgium.

Bowden, William

Born at Ruislip, where he was baptised on 2 July 1893, he was the son of John and Sarah Bowden of No. 5 St John's Villas, Hallowell Road, Northwood, and enlisted in London before June 1915. 81304, Private (or Driver or Gunner), 146th Bty, Royal Horse and Royal Field Artillery. He died at the front in one of the hospitals around Wimereux from enteric fever on 19 June 1915, aged twenty-two. He had only been at the front for about six months. Brother of John, above. He is commemorated on the Emmanuel church, Northwood, and Northwood war memorials. Buried: Wimereux Communal Cemetery, Pas de Calais, France.

Bray, William Ernest (Ewer?)

Born in about 1894, son of James and Mary, and lived at 3 Coteford Close, Fore Street, Eastcote, enlisted at Northwood. 57694, Lance-Corporal, 'E' Coy, 5th Royal Fusiliers. Formerly 28171, 14th Royal Fusiliers. He had attended Pinner Road School. He had married Evelyn May, only daughter of Mr and Mrs J. Neal of Bury Street, in 1916 and enlisted the same week. He was, at first, sent to Dover where he contracted bronchitis. After he had recovered he was sent to German East Africa in July 1917, where he contracted malaria. He was in hospital for some time, after which he was invalided home and stayed at his parent's house, The Glen, Howlett's Lane, for five weeks, very ill. From there he was taken to a military hospital in Hounslow, and on to the Fever Hospital in Epsom. From there he went back to France, spending most of the time in a French hospital. He was sent back to Denmark Hill, London, and was later discharged. He afterwards went to Aldershot for a course of lessons as a musketry instructor. While there, he had a slight attack of fever and contracted influenza. He died of pneumonia in the Military Hospital at Aldershot on 2 November 1918, aged twenty-five. He is commemorated on the Ruislip Common, Ruislip and St Martin's church, Ruislip's war memorials. Buried: St Martin's churchyard, Ruislip.

Brill, Arthur

Born at Northwood, where he was baptised at Holy Trinity church on 11 January 1880, the son of Edward and Amy Brill of 6 Norfolk Terrace, Church Road, Northwood. He had attended Pinner Road School, after which he had been working as a labourer when he enlisted at Mill Hill as G/34930 in the North West Kent Regiment in September 1914. He transferred to the Loyal North Lancashire Regiment as a Private in December 1916. After two years and eight months' service he was discharged from the Army as unfit, having a congenital deformity to one of his feet. He was taken ill on 5 December and died on 26 December 1917 from pleuro-pneumonia at home in the presence of his mother; he was buried on 31 December 1917, aged thirty-nine. He is commemorated on Northwood and Emmanuel church, Northwood war memorials. Buried: Northwood Cemetery.

Brill, Harold Gilbert

Born at Northwood on 27 February 1893, where he was baptised at Holy Trinity church on 2 October 1893. Enlisted at Shepherds Bush on 30 November 1914. 52471, Gunner, 26th Siege Battery, Royal Garrison Artillery (Royal Regiment of Artillery (RGA) Corps). Killed in action on 7 March 1917, aged twenty-four. Son of Mrs Alice Brill, by now a widow, of 84, St Albans Avenue, Bedford Park, London, formerly of Northwood. He had attended Pinner Road School and was a grocer. He is commemorated on the Northwood war memorial. Buried: Vlamertinghe Military Cemetery, Belgium.

Brooks, Godfrey

Born at Tottenham, where he lived at 97, Manor Park Lane, and where he enlisted. TF 203924, Private, 1/7th Middlesex Regiment. Died from cellulitis of the arm and pyaemia at the Voluntary Aid Hospital, Northwood, on 14 April 1917, aged thirty-three. Buried: Northwood Cemetery.

Bruce, Gilbert Ross

Born at Salisbury in about 1892, enlisted in London, of Northwood. 7798, Lance-Corporal, 1st Scots Guards. Part of the 1st Infantry Brigade, the Guards went to France between 12 and 17 August 1914. On 22 August they took up a position extending from the fortress at Conde, a few miles to the north of Valenciennes, through Mons to Binche in the east. They took part in the Battle of Mons and during the retreat took up a supporting position in the neighbourhood of Peissant. He was later wounded and taken prisoner and died from lockjaw at the Military Hospital, Roulers, on 10 November 1914, while a POW. He was the son of George Ross Bruce and Helena Bruce of Oakdene, 7, Reginald Road, Northwood. He had at some time worked for the Metropolitan Railway. He is commemorated on the Emmanuel church, Northwood, and Northwood war memorials. Buried: Roeselare Communal Cemetery, Roeselare, West Vlaanderen, Belgium.

Burrows, William James

Born on 2 March 1879 and baptised at St John the Baptist church, Uxbridge Moor, on 22 June 1879; he was the son of William and Mary. He was working as a gardener when he enlisted at Harrow in July 1916, of 5 Woodview Terrace, Hilliard Road, Northwood. 5557, Private, 2nd/5th Durham Light Infantry. The 2/5th Durhams had embarked at Southampton on 1 November 1916, arriving at Salonika on 17 November. For some months they were engaged on guard duties on the road from Salonika to Seres, until, on 1 March 1917, although only classed as fit for garrison duties, it was brigaded in the 228th Brigade and brought into the line. William died in hospital in Salonika on 8 March 1917, aged thirty-eight. He was the son of Mr William Burrows and Mrs Mary Burrows of 8 Mill's Cottages, Wood End Green, Hayes; husband of C.K. Burrows of 141 Hilliard Road, Northwood. He is commemorated on the Emmanuel church, Northwood, and Northwood war memorials. Buried: Struma Military Cemetery, Kalocastron, Greece.

Burton, Henry

Born at Symondsbury, Dorset, enlisted at Harrow, of Northwood. G/33943, Private, 1st Middlesex Regiment. On 26 September 1918 the Battalion moved back to support positions west of Chapel Crossing and on the night of 28/29 September 1918, the 1st Middlesex were in place for the operations, having relieved the 5th Scottish Rifles – the Battle of the St Quentin Canal – the following day. Their objectives were from Derby Post to the eastern end of Villers Hill, in an attack supported by the French in the direction of Busigny. At 3.30 a.m. the attack was launched, and he was killed in action in intense artillery barrage near Villers-Guislain on the Advance to Victory. The centre Company of the Middlesex had met with strong opposition at Gloster Road. He was married to Mrs Susan Burton of 128 Hilliard Road, Northwood, and is commemorated on the Northwood war memorial. Buried: Villers Hill British Cemetery, Nord, France.

Bushell, Harry George

Enlisted at Handel St, before the end of June 1915 of 109 High Street, Northwood. Corporal (or Private), 200545 'A' Coy, 1st London Regiment. The 56th Division had relieved the 18th Division in the Glencorse Wood–Stirling Castle line when a renewed attack took place; he was killed in action in an attack at Langemarck in the fight for the German stronghold on the Gheluvelt Plateau on 16 August 1917, aged twenty-one, on the German Passchendaele Ridge. At 4.45 a.m. the barrage opened and the assaulting troops clambered out of their mud holes. The 1st London Regiment, part of the 56th Division, entrusted with the desperate task of carrying Nonneboschen and Glencorse, had been heavily shelled from the start from a strong-point at the north-west corner of Inverness Copse, and snipers too were a hazard. The 167th Brigade got well forward to Nonneboschen, but were stopped by bogs and fell behind the barrage. On the left they reached Albert Redoubt but were driven in by strong counter-attacks. The 56th Division suffered very serious losses. He was the son of Harry and Emily Bushell of 109 High Street, Northwood. He is commemorated on the Emmanuel church, Northwood, and the Northwood war memorials. Commemorated: Ypres (Menin Gate) memorial, Belgium.

Butler, Desmond George

Captain, Leinster Regiment and RFC Northolt Aerodrome. Killed while flying on Thursday, 21 March 1918, aged twenty-three. Elder son of the late Captain G.J. Butler, RE. He was educated at Plymouth College and had enlisted in the Army Service Corps the day war broke out. A few months later he received a commission in the Leinster Regiment and was wounded at the Battle of Ypres at Hill 60 in April 1915. He was promoted to Lieutenant in February 1916 and Captain in March 1918. He had been in action at the battles of the Somme, Arras and Vimy Ridge and was mentioned in dispatches. In August 1917 he applied for a transfer to the RFC and came to England for his training; he had acted as adjutant to the 86th Squadron at Northolt since Christmas 1917. Buried: St Martin's churchyard, Ruislip.

Butler, Roland

Born at Ruislip in about 1892, enlisted at Willesden, of Eastcote. T.F. 265488, Private, 1/9th Middlesex Regiment. The Regiment had gone out to India in October 1914 and remained there, sending drafts to fighting units in the Middle East, where he died in the Persian Gulf on 29 August 1916. Son of Charles and Hannah Butler of New Cottages, Eastcote. He is commemorated on the Eastcote, St Lawrence's church, Eastcote, Ruislip and St Martin's church, Ruislip war memorials. Buried: Baghdad (North Gate) War Cemetery, Iraq.

Campbell, Kenneth Preston

Born on 27 October 1897, son of Mr K. and Mrs A.M.P. Campbell of 709, Lorne Avenue, Brandon, Manitoba. Lieutenant Overseas Military Forces of Canada, attd. 210 Sqdn., RAF Northolt Aerodrome. He enlisted in March 1916 and died from influenza at Ruislip Aerodrome on 28 November 1918, aged twenty-one. Buried: St Martin's churchyard, Ruislip.

Carey, Frederick

Born at Godstone, Surrey, enlisted at Harrow on 17 May 1916, lived at Northwood. 81429, Gunner, 196th Siege Battery, Royal Garrison Artillery (Royal Regiment of Artillery (RGA) Corps). Injured by shrapnel in his right chest and shoulder. Realizing that his wounds were serious, his father and mother were sent for. He died two days later in No. 24 general hospital at Étaples on 2 November 1917, aged thirty-four. He had been a butcher at Harrow, prior to which he had worked as a salesman in a Watford shop. Son of Frederick William and Jane Carey of Hilbre, Halliwell Road, later of Felday, 20 Roy Road, Northwood. He is commemorated on the Emmanuel church, Northwood, and Northwood war memorials. Buried: Étaples Military Cemetery, Pas de Calais, France, J.3.

Carpenter, Cedric Theodore Arundel

Lieutenant, 7th Cheshire Regiment attd. King's Shropshire Light Infantry. Died, probably in one of the 38th, 45th or 59th casualty clearing stations at Awoignt, on 6 November 1918 from wounds received the previous day. He was twenty-nine. Youngest son of Captain William Sidney and Marion Carpenter of 15 Murray Road, Northwood. He does not appear to be commemorated locally. Buried: Awoingt British Cemetery, Nord, France, C.18.

Carter, Alfred Sidney

Born on 7 May 1896 and baptised at Holy Trinity church on 7 June 1896; enlisted at Willesden in September 1914; resided at Club Cottage, Barrow Point Lane, Pinner. T/1803, Private, 1st/9th Middlesex Regiment. On 29 October 1914, the 9th Middlesex went out to India with the 44th Division to replace the regular battalions being sent to France and remained there sending drafts to fighting units in the Middle East. He was taken ill and was admitted to the Barian Hospital, Barian Muree Hills, India, on 2 August 1916, where he died of pyrexia fever at about 3.20 p.m. on 7 September 1916, aged twenty-one. Son of Edwin and Kate Carter of Northwood. He does not appear to be commemorated locally but is commemorated on the Pinner war memorial. Commemorated: Karachi 1914-1918 war memorial, Pakistan.

Carter, Leonard

Born at Rickmansworth, son of Leonard, a window cleaner, and Jane Carter of Ranmore, 12, Reginald Road, Northwood, enlisted in London, of the same Northwood address as his parents. DM2/179544, Private, Royal Army Service Corps. Died in the 3rd general hospital, St Peter-in-the-East, Oxford, of *Carcinomatisis Mesenterica* on 3 June 1917, aged forty-one. He had been a postman at Northwood. He is commemorated on the Emmanuel church, Northwood, and the Northwood war memorials. Buried: Northwood Cemetery.

Champion, Cecil

Born at Brixton in about 1881. He was a Reservist and had been an insurance clerk when enlisted at the Tower of London on 31 August 1914. 200539, Rifleman, 18th Rifle Brigade. He left Devonport on 25 November 1915, arriving in Rangoon on 5 January 1916. He was admitted to hospital in Rangoon on 8 April 1919, transferring to the Station Hospital at Myanmar on 10 May where he died of malaria at 2.20 p.m. on 11 June 1919, aged thirty-eight. His body was moved in the 1950s to the newly constructed Taukkyan War Cemetery. Son of Charles Frederick and Sarah Champion; husband of Bessie Marguerite Champion of 'Oakford', Larne Road, Ruislip, whom he had married at St Luke church, Peckham, on 15 August 1908. He does not appear to be commemorated locally. Buried: Taukkyan War Cemetery, Myanmar, (Burma) J.12.

Chapman, Cecil Sutton

Born at Ballycastle, Co. Antrim; enlisted at Northwood on 19 October 1914 as 15924, Royal Dublin Fusiliers; lived with his wife, Constance, and children at Hazeldene, Hallowell Road, Northwood. He had been a surveyor (civil engineer) and had served in the Royal Navy, from which he resigned in 1901, and the RGA, from which he resigned in 1912. He was appointed Lance Corporal on 3 November 1914; promoted to Corporal on 5 December 1914, appointed Lance Sergeant on 4 January 1915 and Sergeant on 23 January 1915. For absence of half-an-hour on 5 December 1915 he was reduced to the rank of Corporal on 8 December 1915 but promoted to Sergeant again on 7 January 1916. He was transferred to the MGC on 18 July 1916 and posted to the 48th Coy on 2 August 1916. He was lastly serving as 22877, Sergeant, 48th Coy, Machine Gun Corps (Infantry). He was killed in action in the fighting in the area of Delville and High Woods on 5 September 1916, aged thirty-four. He is commemorated on the Emmanuel church, Northwood, and Northwood war memorials. Commemorated: Thiepval memorial, Somme, France.

Chapman, H. S.

Private, East Surrey Regiment. He is commemorated on Emmanuel church, Northwood, and Northwood war memorials.

Probably Henry Sewell Chapman, who was born at Willesden and lived at Pinner. He was the son of Mrs Amelia Smith, formerly Chapman, of Haringey. 3548, Private, 8th East Surrey Regiment. Killed in action in some hard fighting at Montauban on the first day of the Battle of the Somme, 1 July 1916, aged thirty-one. Previously the 8th East Surreys had been in the trenches near Carnoy, with all preparations completed for the battle. At 4.30 a.m. on 1st July 1916 they had breakfasted. Two hours later, after the mist had lifted, the enemy opened a barrage on our trenches for a number of hours, causing several casualties. The objectives had been Breslau Trench to 300 yards of the road from the west end of Montauban, running along the ridge to Mametz. It was on this day that the now infamous act occurred when, at 7.27 a.m., Captain Nevill (8th East Surreys) climbed out of his trench and kicked off a football to begin the advance. Henry is commemorated on the Pinner war memorial. Commemorated: Thiepval memorial, Somme, France.

Clapton, George

Born at West Ham, enlisted at Northwood, where he lived. He had been a grocer. 50076, Corporal, 14th Middlesex Regiment, transferred to 350076, 613th Area Employment Coy, Labour Corps (24th Recruit Distribution Battalion Training Reserve). Formerly 12831, Middlesex Regiment. He was taken ill on 24 October 1918 and died at Frensham Hill Military Hospital, Farnham, from influenza and bronchopneumonia on 30 October 1918, aged thirty. He was the son of Walter and Annie Clapton, and the husband of A.M. Clapton of St Mary's School House, Hendon. He is commemorated on Northwood war memorial. Buried: Bordon Military Cemetery, Hampshire.

Clough, Thomas

Born in Fulham. Lieutenant attd. 1st/72nd Battalion Punjabis Indian Army Reserve of Officers attd. Inf. During hostilities, the 72nd Punjabis had been deployed along the North West Frontier to prevent incursions by Afghan tribes and for the greater part of the war remained comparatively quiet, but trouble was brewing. In 1918 they served in the Middle East where, between 19 September and 1 October 1918, they were involved in the Battle of Megiddo. After the end of hostilities in Europe, the Turks still held a large amount of land in Mesopotamia and they were still in the war, supported by the Germans. An attempt was made to overthrow the Turks, and Jerusalem fell on 9 December 1918. In order to ensure the fulfilment by the Turks of the Armistice terms, and in preparation for the establishment of a British mandate over Mesopotamia, troops remained in the region. He was reported as missing on 2 February 1919, aged thirty-two. He was the son of Thomas and Elizabeth Clough of Talland, Kingsend, Ruislip and brother of Vernon and Dorothy. He is commemorated on the St Martins', Ruislip, and Ruislip war memorials. Commemorated: Jerusalem memorial, Israel.

Collins, Albert Edward Edge

Private, 1st Dorsetshire Regiment. Born at St Pancras, enlisted in London, and lived at Cricklewood. He had enlisted in the 2nd Dorsetshire Regiment at Dorchester in 1903, transferring to the 1st Battalion on 17 December 1904. From 17 December 1904 until 8 December 1906 he was stationed in India. After transferring to the Army Reserve he had been a labourer. He served with the Expeditionary Force from 16 August 1914. During the 'race to the sea', when the Allies were trying to prevent the enemy from capturing English Channel ports, he was wounded and died on 17 October 1914, aged twenty-nine, the day after the 1st Dorsets had helped take Givenchy during severe fighting. Between 12 and 15 October the 1st Dorsets had distinguished themselves: on one day (13 October) at Pont Fixe, near La Bassee, they held onto their position amidst devastating fire. 130 men were killed and 270 wounded. He was the foster son of Mr John Mezen of 18 Manor

Cottages, Pinner Road, Northwood. He is not commemorated locally. Buried: Bethune Town Cemetery, Pas de Calais, France, C.27.

Comper, William

Born St Marylebone, London. G/68017, Private, 'A' Coy, 1V Platoon, 7th Royal Fusiliers. Killed in action in hard fighting during the German offensive in Picardy, north-west of Albert, on 5 April 1918, aged thirty-five. He had at first been reported as missing on that date. The German Supreme Command had given the 18th, 2nd and 17th Armies a rest from 1-3 April 1918. On the two following days, with all seventeen divisions (six of them fresh), they made one last effort to reach Amiens, by attacks south of the Somme on 4th and astride and north of the Somme on 5th. Son of Alfred and Emma Comper of Inverness, Hilliard Road, Northwood, formerly of Lilly Villas, Northwood; husband of Nellie Comper of 54, Eskdale Avenue, Chesham. His father at some time had been a policeman at Northwood, where most of his siblings had been baptised. William is not commemorated locally but is commemorated on the Chesham war memorial. Buried: Aveluy Wood Cemetery, Mesnil-Martinsart, Somme, France, E.15.

Cook, Horace George

Enlisted at Willesden on 7 September 1914, lived at Northwood. T.F. 2143, Lance-Corporal, 'A' Coy, 2/10th Middlesex Regiment attd. from 2/9th Middlesex. On the morning of 18 July 1915, the 2/10th Middlesex sailed from Devonport for an unknown destination on the *Huntsgreen*. They landed at Imbros on 8 August. At 6 a.m. on 10 August 1915 the attack began in an attempt to force Turkey out of the war and open a supply route to Russia. Their objectives lay roughly between Scimitar Hill and Baka Baba, and as they advanced on Salt Lake they came under terrible shrapnel fire. Further along they came under machine-gun and rifle fire. Once they were on Chocolate Hill, they came into the firing line. In the evening the dry bush caught alight and many wounded men were unable to get away from the flames. Lance Corporal Cook was reported as missing, presumed killed in action, sometime on this day or after, aged twenty-three. Son of George and Mary Cook of Church View, Northwood; husband of Amy Cook of the same address. He is commemorated on the Emmanuel church, Northwood, and Northwood war memorials. Commemorated: Helles memorial, Turkey.

Corbett, Frederick St John, MA

Chaplain 3rd Class attd. London Regiment (Royal Fusiliers). Died on 14 March 1919, aged fifty-six. Of the Rectory, St George in the East, London. Buried: Ruislip churchyard extension.

Corfield, Thomas

From Northampton. 1898, Sergeant, 86th Squadron, RAF, Northolt Aerodrome. Accidentally killed while flying at Northolt in late 27 September 1918. He was in formation with six other planes when the order came to break away. He died instantly when his plane crashed with another. The inquest verdict was that he died from a fractured skull. Buried: Northampton (Billing Road) Cemetery.

Cox, R.T.

He had been a postman at Northwood and played for Northwood Rovers Football Club.

Cram, Hubert Arthur

Born at Eastcote on 11 August 1889 and baptised at Ruislip on 3 November 1889. He was educated at University College School, London, where he joined the OTC. On leaving school he obtained a position at the Stock Exchange as a clerk. On 3 September 1914, he enlisted. It is known that he was a promoted to Corporal in the 19th Royal Fusiliers by the end of December 1914, and on 28 May 1915, became a Sergeant. On 4 December 1915 he was wounded in the left thigh and sent back to a hospital in 'Blighty', returning to duty when he was fit enough. On 27 March 1917 he was commissioned to Second Lieutenant, 16th King's Royal Rifle Corps. On 15 April 1918, 2nd Lieutenant Cram and three other officers, and 150 other ranks, received orders to form a Composite Battalion at Keersebrom Farm and go to the railway cutting to clear up 'the situation at the Crucifix'. At 12.20 a.m. on the 16th, orders came that no attack would take place on the Crucifix but they would move back, taking over the line held by the North Lancs. He was wounded at Ravelsberg during this move after fierce fighting and heavy shelling. Enemy machine guns were sweeping the front on 16 April 1918, and he died the same day in the 101st field ambulance, aged twenty-seven. He was buried 1.5 miles south-east of Boeschepe, but was later reinterred in Klein-Vierstraat. The enemy had nudged 20km inside the British positions on Mount Kemmel, Mont Rouge, Mont Noir, the Mont des Cats and Nieppe forest. In the fog, on a 15km front from Wytschaete to Merville, all sides were desperately trying different ways to attack. Meteren, Zillebeke and Wytschaete were lost, retaken and lost again. Nothing was gained for either side.

He was the son of Joseph Oliver Cram, a shipping accountant, and Margaret Cram of Laurel Cottages, Eastcote, later of 56 Hindes Road, Harrow. Hubert's father retired as churchwarden at St Martin's church, Ruislip, in the spring of 1920 after twenty-four years' service. Hubert was a great friend of Harry Boreham, who also died on the same day. He is commemorated on the Eastcote, St Lawrence's church, Eastcote, St Martin's church, Ruislip, Ruislip, Emmanuel church, Northwood, and the Pinner war memorials. Buried: Klein-Vierstraat British Cemetery, A.22, Belgium.

Crittall, Holroyd Berrington (or Berrington Holroyd Crittall)

Born at Oswestry, Salop, enlisted Park Royal, lived at Ruislip. 38812, Lance-Corporal, 2nd/7th Lancashire Fusiliers. Formerly 186226, RASC. Killed in action during the Third Battle of Ypres, on 11 October 1917, aged twenty-seven. The muddy and sodden battlefield was strewn with the wounded, who lay amongst the dead for two days and nights – since 10 October. The pillbox shelters were piled high with unattended wounded while the dead lay heaped outside. Son of the late D. P. Crittall of 149 Victoria Street, London and Mrs Crittall of Seaways, Langdale Road, Hove, Sussex, and husband of Ethel Lily Crittall of 'Bryn Hafod', St Catherine's Road, Ruislip. He is commemorated on the St Martin's church, Ruislip, Ruislip and Ruislip Common war memorials. Commemorated: Tyne Cot memorial, Zonnebeke, West Vlaanderen, Belgium.

Cudmore, Herbert Victor

Born at Hackney, son of Henry and Mary Cudmore, enlisted at Hackney. Private, 533692, 15th London Regiment (Civil Service Rifles). Died of wounds, probably received in one of the German counter-attacks at Bourlon Wood where gas was released before, during and after that date, and probably in one of either the 21st or 48th casualty clearing stations at Ytres on 1 December 1917. His father lived at Fowey, Hilliard Road, Northwood. Herbert is commemorated on Emmanuel church, Northwood, Roll of Honour. Buried: Rocquigny-Equancourt Road British Cemetery, Manacourt, Somme, France.

Curl, James

Born at Northwood, and baptised at Holy Trinity church on 11 January 1885, he was the son of James and Jane Curl, enlisted at Watford. 50197, Private, 2nd Suffolk Regiment. Formerly, 35162 Suffolk Regiment. On 12 June 1917, the 2nd Suffolks took over trenches near Monchy-le-Preux, moving on the following night to their assembly position for an attack on Infantry Hill. At 2 a.m. on the 18th, the enemy, which included the 26th Reserve Infantry Division (Wurtembergers) north and south of Bois de Vert attacked in force, causing heavy casualties in Hook, Tool and Long trenches; it was in this action that he was killed in action on 18 June 1917. He does not appear to be commemorated locally. Commemorated: Arras memorial, Pas de Calais, France.

Curzon, Frank Alfred Leveson

Born at Ruislip, where he was baptised on 30 July 1893, Frank was the son of Frank Joseph and Florence (née Stringer, later Hynes); he enlisted at Wembley, and lived at Preston. Middx. 250251, Sapper, 47th Heavy Artillery G.A.A.G. Brigade. Signal Section, RE. (Corps of Royal Engineers). Formerly 74298, Royal Garrison Artillery. Died of wounds, probably in the casualty clearing station at Roye, on 23 March 1918, aged twenty-four. Husband of the late Margaret. He is not commemorated locally. He was originally buried in Roye Old British Cemetery. In 1920 he was reburied in Roye New British Cemetery, Plot No. 1, Row E.

Dawson, Frederick Charles Blakeman

Second Lieutenant, 11th Battalion Royal Fusiliers, (City of London Regiment), attd. Honourable Artillery Company. Killed in action on 3 May 1917, at the Third Battle of the Scarpe, on the first day of the third and last stage of the Battles of Arras, aged twenty-seven. At 3.45 p.m on 3 May 1917, the British attacked from the Acheville-Vimy Road, north of Arleux, to Bullecourt, on a 12-mile front. He was the elder son of William and Ellen Mary Blakeman Dawson of Westcliffe-on-Sea; husband of Gladys Blakeman-Dawson (née Peck) of Jackets Lane, Northwood. He joined the University and Public Schools Brigade in August 1914 and obtained a Commission in the Royal Fusiliers in October 1915. He does not appear to be commemorated locally. Commemorated: Arras memorial, Pas de Calais, France.

Day, G.W.

He is commemorated on Northwood and Emmanuel church, Northwood, war memorials. He was a Private in the Royal Warwickshire Regiment.

Possibly George William Day, who was born at Denham, enlisted in London, of Pinner. 28752, Private, 'Z' Coy, XV Platoon, 2/7th Btn, Royal Warwickshire Regiment, he was reported as missing near St Quentin on 22 March 1918. The battle zone ran, in the main, along the eastern edge of the Bois d'Holnon and was desperately defended from morning to night. It was not until the later afternoon of 22 March that the 61st Division retired, still fighting, to a prepared position north of Vaux. He is commemorated on the Pozieres memorial.

Dixon, William Charles

Born and enlisted at Walthamstow. 235214, Private, 'C' Coy, XI Platoon, 2nd/5th East Lancashire Regiment, formerly 201691 Essex Regiment. Reported missing in action between 21 and 31 March 1918, aged twenty-seven. For official purposes he was declared as having died on the latter date. The great German spring offensive to end the war in victory began on the Western Front on 21 March 1918, the Battle of St Quentin, with the 2/5th East Lancs (amongst others) defending from Le Verguier to the Cologne Valley amidst very heavy enemy machine-gun fire all afternoon and evening. The battle had taken place over a 50-mile front and lengthened on the following days, the regiment taking part in the ongoing attacks continually until 27 March, the Battle of Rosieres, when they retired. At the Actions of the Somme Crossings, on the 24 to the 25 March, they had been strongly attacked, and those that remained had to find cover in some houses at Biaches. He was the son of Mr and Mrs W. Dixon of 16 Shepperd Road, Bow; husband of I.L. Hewitt (formerly Dixon) of 46, Acre Way, Northwood. He is not commemorated locally. Commemorated: Pozieres memorial, Somme, France.

Doe, John

Born at Great Dunmow, Essex, enlisted at Harrow before mid-1916, of Home Cottages, Ruislip. 3/3011, Private, 1st Essex Regiment. As a diversion to distract the enemy's attention from movements further north at Anzac and Suvla, which were to take place on 7 August, an attack was ordered towards Krithia on a broad front. The 88th Brigade came up from reserve on the night of 5th. He was killed in action at the Battle of Gully Ravine on 6 August 1915, aged forty. The first objective of the 88th Brigade was a series of H trenches – H12, H13 and a front of over 1,000 yards. The 1st Essex men managed to gain the enemy's front trench, meeting with very little hostile fire. The trench was found to be very deep. Some men got in and a bombing fight took place where the men outside were fired upon. Husband of Mrs A. Doe of No. 3 Home Cottages, Ruislip, he had served in the South African Campaign. He is commemorated on the St Martin's church, Ruislip, and Ruislip war memorials. Buried/commemorated: Twelve Tree Copse Cemetery, special memorial B85, Turkey.

Dolwin, Charles Joseph

Born at Muswell Hill, enlisted at Chenies Street in September 1914 as 2478, 12th London Regiment. He was appointed Rifleman; attached as a Lance Corporal in January 1915 and transferred as a Private to the HAC. He was appointed Lance Corporal on 22 April or 22 July 1916. 7042, Lance-Corporal, 2nd Battalion Honourable Artillery Company. The 2nd HAC, which had been formed in 1914 of raw recruits, had landed in France in October 1916. He was probably wounded in trench warfare at Ploegsteert and died of wounds, in

21st field ambulance, on 13 October 1916, aged twenty-four, and buried in the 'English plot, Rue de Romarin Cemetery, Belgium'. Son of William Walter Dolwin of Yaxley Cottage, Sharps Lane, Ruislip, formerly of Muswell Hill, Charles is not commemorated locally, as his widowed father did not move into the area until after his son's death. Buried: Nieppe Communal Cemetery, Nord, France, A.1

Douglas, Ernest A.

Commemorated on Northwood war memorial and on Holy Trinity church memorial, Northwood. It is known Douglas joined the Army before about mid-1916 and was serving as a Private when he died.

Probably Ernest Arthur Douglas, who lived at Rickmansworth. 266225, Private, 1st Hertfordshire Regt, who died on 22 March 1918. On the day he died, the 1st Herts were heavily engaged and suffered many casualties in strengthening the line of defence in the rear zone with a switch line from Saulcourt to Tincourt Wood and in the defence of Epehy. One of the companies of the Hertfordshires and a heavy gun on a railway mounting, which could not be moved as the line was broken, were cut off in Ste Emilie, which was not taken until between 1 p.m. and 2 p.m., after very strong opposition. He is commemorated on the Villers-Faucon Communal Cemetery Extension Special Memorial 5, Somme, France.

Draper, Marcus D.

2nd Lieut. Northolt Aerodrome. Accidentally killed while flying at Northolt on 7 February 1917. When about 90ft from the ground something went wrong with the engine and the machine, a Shorthorn, came down in a nosedive around noon. The machine was a total wreck and both occupants were killed – Capt. Farrow, the pilot, and 2nd Lieut. Draper, the observer, who 'belongs to Bloomsbury' (this was possibly his very first trial flight). The inquest verdict was that he died from a fractured skull. Eldest son of the Revd William Henry Draper, MA, rector of Adel, and the late Mrs C. Edith Draper. Educated at Repton School, he took up the dramatic profession. In 1915 he joined the Artists' Rifles, after which he obtained a commission in the Royal Flying Corps. His brother, Capt. R.F. Draper, York and Lancaster Regt was killed at Suvla Bay in August 1915. Buried: Alfeston (St Martin) churchyard, Derbyshire.

Earle, George Bertram

38962, Corporal, Royal Engineers. Died of pulmonary tuberculosis on 5 April 1920 at Mount Vernon Hospital, aged thirty-five. He is commemorated by the CWGC. He lived at Manor Lane, SE and was a stationer's traveller (ex-Army). Buried: Northwood Cemetery.

Easy, R. B.

He had been a postman at Northwood.

Ebling, William George

C/6709, Rifleman, 'C' Coy, 18th King's Royal Rifle Corps. Born at Peterborough (or at Watford), enlisted in London, and lived at Watford. He had been a postman at Northwood.

Killed in action on the Menin Road Ridge during the Third Battle of Ypres on 21 September 1917, aged twenty. Snipers and machine guns were very active on this and the next couple of days. Buried: Larch Wood (Railway Cutting) Cemetery, Ypres Belgium.

Elgood, Reginald Lloyd

Baptised at Holy Trinity church, Northwood on 1 March 1896, 'Rex', was the younger son of Frank Minshule Elgood (later Sir Frank) – an architect and sometime member of the Ruislip-Northwood UDC, chairman of the National Housing and Town Planning Council, chairman of the Church Army Housing and Vice-President of the Town Planning Institute – and Frances Isabel Lloyd Elgood of The Close, Pinner Road, Northwood. A road in Northwood was named after Sir Frank, who at some time was President of the Northwood Rifle Club. On the outbreak of war, Reginald was serving on HMS *St Vincent* and later served as Lieutenant on HMS *Vanguard*. He was killed by the internal explosion of the vessel, a dreadnought, while lying at Scapa Flow on 9 July 1917, aged twenty-one. Only two seamen survived. Sacks of coal had been stored around the handling rooms of the aft turrets, cutting off air to the magazine. The rising temperature of the magazine spontaneously ignited the cordite. He is commemorated on Northwood war memorial and on Holy Trinity church memorial, Northwood. Commemorated: Chatham memorial, Kent.

Elliott, Philip Frederick

Only son of Frederick and Clara H. Elliott of 'Haven', 60 Reginald Road, Northwood, he was Aircraftsman 2nd Class, 326121, Royal Air Force, School of Artillery Co-operation. Killed while flying on 15 April 1921, aged twenty. Air Mechanic Elliott and his Flight Officer, Bernard Deane, were killed in an aeroplane smash near Andover. They had come from Old Sarum and had landed at Andover to pick something up. Shortly before 1.30 p.m. they left and had climbed to an altitude of about 600ft when, it is believed, the engine failed. He was educated at Roy House School, Northwood, and the Harrow Boys' School. He started his business career with Messrs Handley Page. He is not commemorated locally but is commemorated by the CWGC. Buried: Salisbury (London Road) Cemetery, Wiltshire.

Evans, Tim Evelyn

Born on 2 February 1895 and was baptised at Ruislip on 4 August 1895, he was the son of Albert John (an actor) and Constance Rosalind Evans of Kirby Cottage, Northwood. Sub-Lieutenant, S/M 'C29', Royal Navy. He was killed by a mine explosion in North Sea on 29 August 1915, aged 21. HMS 'C29' and the trawler *Ariande* were carrying out anti-U-boat duties off the Outer Dowsing Light Vessel off the Humber. The submarine was under tow and in telephone contact with the trawler when the mine exploded. The entire crew of twenty all perished. He is commemorated on Northwood war memorial and on Holy Trinity church memorial, Northwood. Commemorated: Plymouth memorial, Devon.

Ewers, Thomas Herbert

7576, Company Quartermaster Sergeant (WO.11), King's Shropshire Light Infantry Labour Corps. Born in Meerut, India, he enlisted at Shrewsbury in the Shropshire Light

Infantry on 1 January 1904 when he was fifteen, almost sixteen years old. His occupation was listed as 'clerk'. He had worked his way up from Boy, and by 7 September 1914 had been promoted to Sergeant. He became QMS on 23 July 1915. He died from influenza and pneumonia on 18 October 1918, aged twenty-eight. Tom was the son of Thomas Henry and Kate Florence Ewers of Rosegarth, Ruislip. He does not appear to be commemorated locally. Buried: Shrewsbury General Cemetery, Shropshire, I.B.

Fairbairns, Arnold H.

T/Lt, (A/Capt) Alexandra, Princess of Wales's Own (Yorkshire Regiment) 10th Battalion (at 13th West Riding Regiment). Born at Harlesden, but resided at Saxonhurst, Murray Road, Northwood. Killed instantly on 14 October 1918, aged thirty-seven. After extricating his company from a very critical position when they were almost surrounded, he was killed while carrying in a wounded man from another regiment. He had heard the wounded man cry out and had returned to pick him up. He, a keen antiquarian, was the youngest son of Mr and Mrs W.H. Fairbairns of Radlett, Herts, and husband of Ethel, the elder daughter of Mr and Mrs F.W. Fletcher of Enfield, whom he had married in 1911. They had one son. Arnold was educated at Priory House School, Upper Clapton, at University College School and at Lincoln College, Oxford. He had joined the Bedfordshire Regiment in April 1916, subsequently receiving a commission in the Yorkshire Regiment. Shortly after arriving in France he was attached to the Duke of Wellington's Regiment. He is commemorated on Northwood war memorial and on Holy Trinity church memorial, Northwood. Buried: Rue-David Military Cemetery, Fleurbaix, France.

Fairweather, Herbert Harry

Born at Northwood, enlisted in London. 20962, Sapper, Corps of Royal Engineers (23rd Field Coy, RE). Died of wounds on 16 August 1916. He does not appear to be commemorated locally. Buried: Albert Communal Cemetery Extension, Somme, France.

Farrow, Eric Tony

Born in Brisbane, Australia. Captain 15th Middlesex Regiment, attached RFC Northolt Aerodrome. He was accidentally killed while flying at Northolt on 7 February 1917, aged nineteen. When about 90ft from the ground something went wrong with the engine and the machine came down in a nosedive. The machine was a total wreck and both occupants were killed – Capt. Farrow, the pilot, and 2nd Lieut. Draper, the observer. The inquest verdict was that he died from a fractured skull. Eric was the only son of Mrs Thomas Finney of Brisbane, Australia. He had lived in Ruislip for only a few months, at the Old House, Lime Grove. He had been educated at Mill Hill and Lausanne and on 19 November 1914 joined the Inns of Court OTC, and obtained a commission in the Middlesex Regiment. In October 1915 he transferred to the RFC in which he secured a commission in January 1916. He served for eight months at the front where he obtained his Captaincy. He was on duty with a reserve squadron and was about to return to France when he was killed. Buried: St Martin's churchyard, Ruislip.

Featherstone, Walter

2nd Lieut., RFC and General List, Northolt Aerodrome. Died from awful burns at Eaton Square RAF Hospital on 3 October 1917, aged twenty-seven. Buried: Beaconsfield Cemetery.

Finch, James

Born at Northwood, where he was baptised at Holy Trinity church on 4 August 1895. He was employed as a porter at Paddington station by the London, Brighton & South Coast Railway and had enlisted at Lewisham on 3 September 1914. 12928, Lance-Corporal, 8th Norfolk Regiment. He had been wounded by gunshot several times, mostly to his arms, and had spent time in casualty clearing stations. Prior to the Battle of the Somme, the 18th Division had rehearsed every move to the finest detail on ground in the Picquigny area – a replica of the battlefield itself. On the day of the battle, every man knew the exact spot he was to make for and what to do once he got there. On the first day of the Battle of the Somme, 1 July 1916, the Picardy front was to be attacked between the region of Hebuterne and the region of Lassigny (about 70km) in the general direction of the Bapaume-Peronne-Ham line. The British sector had been between about Arras and Albert on the Bapaume Front. The 18th Division had assembled just north of Carnoy for an attack south-west of Montauban. They were ready in position by 2 a.m. for the assault on Pommiers Redoubt, near where he was killed in action on 2 July 1916, aged twenty-one. On this day, Fricourt was taken and shelters of 40ft deep found. He was the son of Henry and Elizabeth Finch of 36 Willow Walk, Sydenham. He is not commemorated locally. Commemorated: Thiepval memorial, Somme, France.

Fincher, William Arthur

Born at Tring, he enlisted at Harrow; of Northwood. Rifleman, 472392, 2nd/12th London Regiment (The Rangers). The Regiment had landed in France on 9 February 1917. Killed in action near Ypres during the Third Battle of Ypres, on 14 August 1917, aged twenty-three. Son of Sarah Jane Fincher, a confectioner, of The Bee Hive, 68, Church Road, Northwood, and the late Arthur Edward Fincher. He is commemorated on the Emmanuel church, Northwood, and Northwood war memorials. Commemorated: Ypres (Menin Gate) memorial, Belgium.

Fisher, Frederick Thomas

Born at Northwood on 21 July 1895 and baptised there at Holy Trinity church on Easter Day, 2 April, 1899, with his brother and sister, the children of Joseph Thomas and Augusta Fisher, enlisted in September 1914. Private, 7th Canadian Infantry (British Columbia Regiment). He had come over with the first contingent of Canadians and was killed in action at St Julien (Hill 60), about 5 miles north of Ypres, on 24/25 April 1915, aged nineteen or twenty, during the Second Battle of Ypres. At about 4.30 a.m. on 24th the enemy let loose a fresh emission of gas on the trenches of the 2nd and 3rd Brigades. Immediately afterwards the Germans attacked. Towards noon, the pressure on the 2nd Brigade became unbearable and at around 1 p.m. the enemy was gathering new masses north of St Julien, which completely outflanked the 2nd Brigade but could not surround them owing to spirited supporting fire. On the following afternoon there was a last attempt to save St Julien. At 5.15 p.m. the 2nd Brigade was compelled at last to fall back. At sometime on these dates Frederick had been shot through the head by a German bullet. Shortly before he was killed it was reported that he was 'waving his cap at the enemy, daring them to come on'. Hill 60 had been taken from the French in December 1914. It was of considerable tactical importance, since from its summit the enemy were able to observe the British movements. Son of Mr Joseph Thomas and Augusta Fisher, formerly of Mount View, Pinner Road, Northwood, where they had lived for a number of years, and grandson of Mr W. Fisher of Cowley Road, Uxbridge. He emigrated with his parents to Canada to Kelowna, British Columbia, in about 1913 and was a bricklayer. He was 5ft 8ins tall, with light brown hair and blue eyes. He is commemorated on Northwood war memorial. Commemorated: Ypres (Menin Gate) memorial, Belgium.

Fisher, John Walter

Born at Northwood on 15 May 1894 and lived at Northwood, enlisted on 14 August 1914. Private, CH/18663, Royal Marine Light Infantry, Chatham Battalion. He had served in the Defence of Antwerp from 3 to 9 October 1914 with the Deal Battalion after which he transferred to the Chatham Battalion on 2 or 3 February 1915 and served with the MEF. He was killed in action by shrapnel while going up to the trenches on 7 (or 15) June 1915, previous to which he had been helping the wounded get out of the trenches. He is officially listed as having been killed in action on 6 June 1915. Jack, as he was known, was the son of Mr John Courtney Fisher and Lillian Fisher of 6, White Cottages, Hilliard Road, Northwood, and is commemorated on Emmanuel church, Northwood, and Northwood war memorials. Commemorated: Helles memorial, Turkey.

Foott, Frederick

Born in 1884, enlisted on 27 June 1916. 1st Air Mechanic, 29686, RFC, Northolt Aerodrome. Died at Southall Auxiliary Hospital on 29 January 1917 from injuries sustained in an aeroplane accident on 24 January 1917 in which Lt. Addis was killed. He was thirty-three years old. His death certificate states that he 'died from concussion and congestion of the brain and shock from fractured thighs caused by the aeroplane in which he was a passenger accidentally nosediving to the ground'. Husband of Rosina Foott of 14, Brownlow Gardens, Dalston, London. He was buried privately in Abney Park Cemetery.

Fountain, John Alfred Arnott

Born at Chiswick on 30 January 1893 and baptised at Christ church, Turnham Green on 5 March 1893, the son of Edward and Isabella Fountain of Gunnersbury. 2nd Lieutenant, 10th King's Own Yorkshire Light Infantry. The 10th Yorkshires were leading one of its brigades, and as he was leading his men at Fricourt at the battle of the Somme 1st July 1916, he was wounded as he was leaving the trenches south of the Bapaume Road. The Germans got their machine guns in action and fired at his battalion, and he fell 10 yards from the British trench, wounded in the thigh. An orderly came to his assistance but while bandaging the wounded man he was shot at. He then called upon some stretcher-bearers of the East Yorkshire Regiment to give 2nd Lieutenant Fountain some assistance, but he was found to be dead. He was twenty-three years old, the grandson of the late Mr Edward Fountain of Hillingdon and second son of Dr Edward Osborne and Isabella Maria Fountain of Crossley House, King Edward's Road, Ruislip. The family had lived at Ruislip for over three years. While at Bradfield College he was in the OTC as a Private from September 1908 until he left in December 1911. Before joining the Army as a Private in the Royal Sussex Regiment on 19 November 1914, he was articled to a firm of solicitors in Bedford Row, London, and had been there for three years. On 5 February 1915 he was recommended for a commission, transferring to the Royal Fusiliers on 22 February until 1 March 1915 when he was granted a commission in the 10th King's Own Yorkshire Light Infantry. He is commemorated on the St Martin's church, Ruislip, and Ruislip war memorials. Buried: Gordon Dump Cemetery, Somme, France.

Fowler, Cecil James

Born at Dudley, Worcs., lived at Ealing. Lieutenant., 30th Training Depot Squadron, RAF, Northolt Aerodrome. Accidentally killed while test-flying at Northolt on 25 July 1918, aged twenty: his machine crashed from a height of 200ft, and he died instantly. Son of James Adolphus and Elizabeth Wilkinson Fowler, of 11 Hart Grove, Ealing. Buried: Hanwell Cemetery.

Fowler, Charles Thomas

143976, Airman 2nd Class, RAF, No. 4 Store Depot (Ruislip). Died from concussion at the Uxbridge Armament School on 10 August 1919. He was thirty-four years old and had been involved in a car accident at Norton's Hill, Northwood, when the car he was in veered to avoid pedestrians. He was in the back seat. Buried: St Martin's, Ruislip, church extension.

Franklin, Leslie Willoughby

Born at Kobe, Japan. Lieutenant, 10th Battery, 147th Brigade, Royal Field Artillery. Died of wounds on 16 October 1918, aged twenty. Younger son of J.W. and S.A. Franklin of 'Minato', 5, Dene Road, Northwood. The family came to England when their younger son was eight years old. Lieutenant Franklin was educated at Dulwich College, and at the age of eighteen he left for the OTC and obtained his commission in January 1917. He had also had served as a Gunner (175149) in the Royal Horse Artillery. He went to the front at the end of March 1917. He does not appear to be commemorated locally. Buried: Queant Communal Cemetery British Extension, Pas de Calais, France, E.15.

Frayne, S.

He is commemorated on the Northwood and Emmanuel church, Northwood, war memorials. He was a Corporal in the Middlesex Regiment and was a member of the Northwood Rovers Football Club.

Possibly Sidney Frayne, who enlisted at Willesden. Corporal 6042, 2/7th (or 17th) London Regiment, formerly 2339, 9th Middlesex Regiment, who was killed in action on 9 August 1916, aged twenty-six. The 17th Middlesex had gone to France in November 1915. On 5 August 1918, the Regiment had moved to Agenvillers. He was the son of

William Henry and Eliza Frayne of Barnstable. Buried: Ecoivres Military Cemetery, Mont–St Eloi, Pas de Calais, France.

Frazier, Donald Refah

Private, United States Army 369th Aero Squadron, attached to 86th Squadron RAF. On 19 April 1918, while assisting to start an aeroplane at Northolt, his head was hit by a propeller. He died from a fractured skull and fracture and dislocation of the spinal column, aged twenty-one. No other details are known.

Gibson, R.B.

He is commemorated on St John's, Uxbridge Moor Roll of Honour. There is also an R.B. Gibson commemorated on the Ruislip and St Martin's church, Ruislip, war memorials.

Possibly Robert Bowness Gibson, Lieut., 'B' Coy, 2nd Bedfordshire Regiment who was killed as he entered Trones Wood on 11 July 1916, aged twenty-one, and was buried in Maricourt Cemetery, near Napiers Redoubt, which later became known as Peronne Road Cemetery, Maricourt, Somme, France. This attack began on 7 July 1916 and ended on 15 July with the taking of Contalmaison (defended by the 3rd Prussian Guards), Bazentin, Bazentin-le-Grand, the most part of Ovillers, Trones Wood, Longueval and Delville Wood. He was born on 8 January 1895 at Hampstead and educated at Winchester College and New College, Oxford. On 1 November 1914 he joined the 28th London Regiment (Artists Rifles) as a Private. On 26 October 1914 he was appointed to a commission, and on 1 November 1914 joined the 3rd attd. 2nd Bedfords. Son of Revd Thomas William Gibson and his wife, née Currey.

Gilbert, Arthur

265918, Private, 21st Middlesex Regiment. Died on 24 November 1917, aged twenty-four. He had probably been wounded near Cambrai the previous day when the 40th Division was in action at Bourlon Wood where they cleared the greater portion of the wood and occupied a position within it, clinging on to the hard-won ridge within the wood. During the night of 23/24 November, the 21st Middlesex were withdrawn into reserve amidst continuous artillery and gas shells. On 24th, between 8.30 a.m. and 9 a.m., the Germans attacked in considerable force, both from Fontaine on the right and Bourlon on the left. By 11 a.m. things had eased a bit, although German guns were still very busy putting down a heavy barrage on all the sunken roads leading from Graincourt and Anneux. At around 1 p.m. a heavy attack was made from the direction of Fontaine. The attackers, who had fresh troops, pressed on and drove in the right of the weary 119th Brigade. A counter-attack succeeded in stemming this advance and all through the afternoon sporadic attacks and counter-attacks took place in Bourlon Wood, mainly on the 119th Brigade. The approaches to the wood were heavily shelled and the wood itself reeked with gas. At 8 o'clock the 119th Brigade was still holding the northern slope of the ridge within the wood, together with part of the southern outskirts of Bourlon village and with patrols pushed out north of it. Half an hour later reinforcements arrived. On this day the whole of Bourlon was captured. The next day, the Germans retook it. Arthur was the son of Robert and Annie Gilbert of 153 High Street, Northwood, and he is commemorated on the Emmanuel church, Northwood, and Northwood war memorials and well as the Cambrai memorial, Louveral, Nord, France.

Gill, Samuel George

He lived at Knole Terrace, Northwood. 157712, Private, Labour Corps. Died of pneumonia after a very short illness at Ripon Camp at Thetford on 1 December 1918, aged nineteen. He had enlisted in the 29th Middlesex Regiment in May 1917 but was found unfit for foreign service. He was transferred to the Labour Corps for agricultural work at various places. He had been transferred to an overseas company at Ripon when he became ill. Samuel was the son of PC Samuel and Elizabeth Ann Gill of 110 Hallowell Road, Northwood. He is commemorated on the Emmanuel church, Northwood, and Northwood war memorials. Buried: Northwood Cemetery.

Glyn, Guy Godfrey

Born on 4 March 1879, of Northwood. Lieutenant, 109th Railway Company, Royal Engineers. Accidentally fractured his skull on 16 August 1915 and admitted to 'B' Section, No. 5 stationary hospital, Abbeville, where he died at 2.30 p.m. the same day. The youngest son of the late Richard Henry Glyn and Mrs Glyn of Northwood, he trained as a civil engineer and was elected as Associate Member of the Institute of Civil Engineers on 6 December 1904. After finishing his training, he worked as an engineer's assistant, engaged on the construction of Victoria station, electrification of suburban lines, etc, for the London, Brighton & South Coast Railway until the outbreak of war. He is commemorated on the Northwood war memorial and on Holy Trinity church memorial, Northwood. Buried: Abbeville Communal Cemetery, Somme, France.

Gooden, Bertie Levi

See Hildred, Bertie Levi.

Gray, Geoffrey Thomas

2nd Lieutenant Royal Engineers, attached to 8th Squadron, Royal Flying Corps. Killed in action on 24 March 1917. On that day, in cooperation with the Army, thirty-five targets had been engaged. Second son of Mr and Mrs J. Gray of Red House, Kings End Avenue, Ruislip. He had received his commission in the Royal Engineers in December 1915. He is commemorated on the St Martin's church, Ruislip, and Ruislip war memorials. Buried: Warlincourt Halte British Cemetery, Saulty, Pas de Calais, France.

Gribble, John Charles

Born at Hounslow, enlisted at Northwood, of Northwood. 881961 Gunner, 'C' Bty, 121st Bde, RFA (Territorial Force). Killed in action on 23 April 1918, aged thirty. He was helping unload shells when a shell from the German lines burst, killing him instantly. Son of Henry and Emily Gribble of Sunninghill; husband of E. Gribble of 3 Duke Cottage, Nursery Lane, Brookside, Ascot, Berks. He had been a postman at Northwood. He is commemorated on the Emmanuel church, Northwood, and Northwood war memorials. Buried: Harponville Communal Cemetery Extension, Somme, France.

Kings End Avenue, Ruislip. (Courtesy of Hillingdon Local Studies, Archives and Museum Service)

Haines, Albert Victor

Born at Hinton St George, Somerset, enlisted at Mill Hill, of Northwood. P.W. 5271, Private, 26th Middlesex Regiment. In 1916 the 26th Middlesex had gone to Salonica, where he died of malaria on 28 September 1918, aged thirty-one. Son of Edwin and Jane Haines of Hinton-St-George, Somerset; husband of Cecilia Marie Haines of 149 Hilliard Road, Northwood, whom he had married at Emmanuel church on 26 February 1916. He is commemorated on the Emmanuel church, Northwood, and Northwood war memorials. Buried: Karasouli Military Cemetery, Polycastron, Greece.

Halsey, Robert Henry

Born at Edgware, and baptised at St Lawrence's church, Little Stanmore, on 30 September 1883, he was the son of Robert and Adelaide, and enlisted in London (Mill Hill) in late October 1916. Like his father before him, he was a butcher; he lived with his wife, Rosina, whom he had married at Emmanuel church on 14 July 1909, and their daughter at Church Road, Northwood. 535033, Private, 15th London Regiment (PWO Civil Service Rifles), posted to 8th Kings Royal Rifle Corps on 13 June 1917. He had been wounded – on 24 August 1917 and possibly again at Rouen on 26 August 1917. On 7 September 1917 he was posted to the 12th KRRC. At 3.10 p.m. on 19 November 1917, the 12th KRRC had marched out of their camp at Heudicourt, through Gouzeaucourt to Station Quarry at Villers-Plouich. As they moved up, they led their respective platoons into their places. At 6.20 a.m. the following morning, the attack was launched. On the first day of the battle the Germans had surprised the British forces holding the southern base of the Cambrai salient, the very first time tanks were used en masse. The ground was favourable for an attack, but the weather was miserable and had impeded the action of a large force of British flying machines secretly collected, at the expense of the Canadian soldiers holding Passchendaele Ridge, for ensuring the local command of the air in this new theatre of war. As the tanks came into the open, the guns of the Third Army began a huge bombardment, and Private Halsey was amongst those killed. He is commemorated on the Emmanuel church, Northwood, and Northwood war memorials. Commemorated: Cambrai memorial, Louveral, Nord, France.

Hamber, Harold Balleny (Bellamy)

Born at Winnipeg on 29 December 1885. Enlisted at Toronto in February 1915 and signed further attestation papers 'in the Field' in July 1916. Captain, Canadian Army Pay Corps and RFC, Northolt Aerodrome. Killed on 22 June 1917, while flying near Hounslow, aged thirty-two. He had gone to the assistance of another pilot who had come down. After seeing him safely off, Hamber reascended. The machine was seen to turn sharply and fall for some distance, resume a level course and finally crash to the earth from a height of between 300 and 400ft into a field at Cherry Lane, Harlington. His Air Mechanic, Peter Stanescu, was also killed. Husband of Norah Elizabeth Hamber. Buried: Brookwood Military Cemetery, Surrey.

Hammond, Reginald Ernest

All that is known that he was a Lance Corporal in the Royal Fusiliers (City of London) Regiment, of Northwood. He is commemorated on the Emmanuel church, Northwood, and Northwood war memorials. Son of Thomas Hammond, a farmer of Northwood. Twenty-five-year-old Reginald had married Charlotte Norton at Emmanuel church on 13 February 1917.

Probably Reginald Ernest Hammond from Walthamstow who enlisted and lived at Ealing. Private 25837, 11th Royal Fusiliers who died on 10 August 1917, aged twenty-six. On about 4 August, the 18th Brigade heard they were going to take part in an assault six days later, 10 August 1917, on the German strong points in and about Glencorse Wood and Inverness Copse – positions of momentous value to the enemy for observation purposes. The 11th Royal Fusiliers had formed up near the Hooge-Menin Road. They were caught early in difficulties, and by 6 a.m. all the officers had fallen. They had been caught by a heavy enfilade of machine-gun fire. The enemy then launched a counter-attack from Inverness Copse, forcing the Fusiliers back from their advanced posts and a line was established 200 yards east of Clapham Junction. He is commemorated on the Ypres memorial, Belgium.

Hancock, John Mervyn

Of Australia. Lieutenant RAF, Training Squadron (Northolt). Formerly 2063, Driver, AASC, Australian Imperial Force. Killed while flying at 2,000ft on 1 March 1919, aged twenty-five, when he jumped or fell from the plane, which was on fire, into Sidmouth plantation at Richmond Park. His plane continued flying upside down and dived into the Thames. It took an hour to find his terribly injured body. He had enlisted when he was about twenty-one years old and was a motor mechanic. He had embarked for service abroad as an Army Medical Corps driver at Sydney on 13 April 1915, sailing on HMAT *Kyarra*. Son of Mr A. and Mrs C.M. Hancock of Prince of Wales Hotel, 25 Fitzroy Street, St Kilda, Victoria, Australia. He had 296 hours experience and was on his way to Croydon where he was to leave the machine, a Sopwith 'Snake'. An inquest was held at Richmond where the jury returned a verdict of accidental death. Buried: St Martin's churchyard, Ruislip.

Hardman, Frederick Harcourt

Born at Northwood, where he was baptised at Holy Trinity church on 10 July 1887, he was the son of Rose and Harcourt Hardman of 7, St James Square, Pall Mall, London; enlisted at Slough, and lived at Piccadilly, London. 18312, Private, 15th Royal Warwickshire Regiment. Formerly 22959 (or 22590), Somerset Light Infantry. At noon on 3 September 1916, the Allies made a combined assault on a front extending from the right bank of the Ancre, north of Hamel, as far south as Chilly. As the 5th Division were making a successful advance on the German Second Position, he was killed in action at Angle Wood in support of a failed attack at Falfemont Farm on this date, aged twenty-nine. The 5th Division did pursue its victorious way up the Leuze Wood and to the lower corner of Bouleaux Wood, always in close touch with the French 20 and 35 Corps d'Armee and one of their colonial regiments upon their right. He is commemorated on the Eastcote, St Lawrence's church, Eastcote, and Northwood war memorials, and the Thiepval memorial, Somme, France.

Harley, Arthur Darent

Captain, 'C' Coy, 1st/6th South Staffordshire Regiment. During the evening of 30 June 1916, the 6th South Staffs moved forward from Souastre to positions facing Gommecourt. On 1 July, on the first day of the Battle of the Somme, they had attacked at 7.30 a.m. He was killed in action at the front at Gommecourt on this day, aged twenty-one. Son of Mr and Mrs Percy Harley of Rathlin, Northwood. His regiment, part of the 46th division, was the first division composed entirely of Territorials to go to the front. They had left from Southampton on 5 March 1915. He is commemorated on the Emmanuel church, Northwood, and Northwood war memorials and the Thiepval memorial, Somme, France.

Harris, Alfred George

Born at Aylesbury, enlisted at Northwood in June 1916, lived at 11 Church Road, Northwood. 32424, Private, 7th Wiltshire Regiment. Formerly 23348 Middlesex Regiment. He had been wounded while in Salonika in April 1917. In July 1918 the 7th Wilts sailed across the Adriatic, disembarked at Taranto, travelled across Italy by train and reached France at the beginning of July 1918. They detrained at Forges, north-east of Rouen. On 3 October they relieved the 1st Yorkshire Light Infantry at Epehy to take part in the final Allied offensive, where he was killed in action at Le Cateau in the final advance in Picardy at the battle of the Selle River; this took place between 16 and 18 October 1918, though he was officially declared as killed on 16 October 1918. The 50th Division held the right sector near Le Cateau with St Souplet as its southern limit. The enemy's position by now was growing more hopeless. News of his death was received after the Armistice. Husband of Annie O'Dell (formerly Harris) of 11 Church Road, Northwood; brother-in-law of the late Joseph Rackstraw. Alfred had been employed for some years by Mr J. Whittle, a local builder. He is commemorated on the Emmanuel church, Northwood, and Northwood war memorials. Buried: Highland Cemetery, Le Cateau, Nord, France, E.9.

Harris, George Alexander
RNR. He died on 26 March 1916, aged twenty-eight. He was the son of George and Mary Harris of Ruislip. He does not appear to be commemorated locally.

Possibly Lieutenant George Alexander Harris, RNR, HM Submarine E24 who died on 27 March 1916, after the sub was mined on 24 March 1916, aged twenty-two. He is commemorated on the Portsmouth Naval memorial.

Harris, Robert Charles
Of High Street, Ruislip. 75588, 3rd Class Air Mechanic, Royal Flying Corps. For six years he had been manager at a butcher's shop and had been a special constable. He joined the RFC in about April 1917 after being summoned for a medical re-examination at Mill Hill. Although he had already been in hospital after being ill with gastric trouble for at least one year, the authorities decided he was well enough to enlist. After joining up he underwent two more operations, but he never recovered from his complaint and died at Aldershot on 26 May 1917, aged forty. He is commemorated on the St Martin's church, Ruislip, and Ruislip war memorials. Buried: St Martin's churchyard, Ruislip.

Hart-Davies, Ivan Beauclerk
Born at Huntingdon Vicarage on 21 April 1878, fourth son of the late Revd John and Emily Rachel Florence Hart-Davies. Educated at Clifton College and King's College, Canterbury. Lieutenant, 48th Squadron RFC. He was accidentally killed at Northolt during a flying accident on 27 July 1917, aged thirty-nine (or forty-one). As he was about to land the machine too sharply it suddenly nosedived and crashed. He died of 'shock due to the fall'. He was a well-known amateur motorist, having broken the 'End to End' record in 1909. Buried: Southam (St James) churchyard, Warwickshire.

Haythornthwaite, Rycharde Mead
Born at Agra, India, on 4 January 1894, of St Helen's Northwood. Second Lieutenant, Special Reserve, 3rd attd. 2nd Buffs (East Kent Regiment). The German aim was to capture Ypres, and between 4 May and 13 May 1915 the second phase – the new Battle of Ypres – took place, consisting of violent attacks pushed chiefly by poison and artillery against the 27th and 28th Divisions of the Fifth British Army Corps and the 4th Division. The fight broke out again on Monday, 24 May. The attack, the battle of Bellewaarde Ridge, had begun before dawn, preceded by signal rockets flared up from behind the German lines, and at 2.45 a.m. a violent bombardment of gas shells, which the British were expecting, was opened against our lines which ran from Wieltje, north-east of Ypres, to Hooge, on the Menin road – a total frontage of 4½ miles – followed by a terrific barrage of artillery fire, shrapnel and high explosives – the largest yet experienced. This torrent of gas and other shells poured into the trenches from a farm called 'Shell-trap', between Poelcapelle and Langemarck. The main force of the chlorine struck the extreme right of the 4th

Division and the whole of the 28th Division. A company of the 2nd Buffs, on the front between Verlorenhoek and the Ypres-Roulers railway, despite a brilliant resistance, were overwhelmed and wiped out almost to a man. Sometime on this day Richard was killed in action 'in the field' at the Second Battle of Ypres, aged twenty-one, and 'buried outside the garden gate of a ruined cottage on the right-hand side of the Menin Road, about 1,000 yards beyond the level crossing of the Ypres-Roulers Railway in one of three graves'.

Elder son of Revd John Parker Haythornthwaite and Iszet Mead Haythornthwaite of Agra Lodge, Green Lane, Northwood, later of King's Langley Vicarage, Herts. He was educated at Haileybury College and Sidney Sussex College, Cambridge where he was a Private in the OTC, rising to Colour Sergeant by the time he left in August 1914. He was gazetted 2nd Lieut. with the 3rd Buffs on 15 August 1914, trained at Dover from September 1914-May 1915 and went to the front on 5 May 1915. He is commemorated on the Emmanuel church, Northwood, and Northwood war memorials. Commemorated: Ypres (Menin Gate) memorial, (Addenda), Belgium.

Heath, John Alfred

Enlisted at Handel Street in August 1914. 200564, Sergeant, 1st London Regiment (Royal Fusiliers). Died of wounds in 1st Australian general hospital, Rouen, on 23 May 1917, aged twenty. He may have been injured in action at Bullecourt, which was fought between 3 and 17 May 1917, and taken to the hospital at Rouen. He was the son of the late John and Ida Heath of Holmewood, Dane Road, Northwood. He was educated at the Church Schools and afterwards entered the GWR Goods Department at Paddington as a clerk. He is commemorated on the Emmanuel church, Northwood, and Northwood war memorials. Buried: St Sever Cemetery Extension, Rouen- Seine-Maritime, France, G.135.

Hedges, Harry

Born at Marylebone and enlisted in London. 392798, Rifleman, 'A' Coy, 9th London Regiment (Queen Victoria's Rifles). According to the Red Cross enquiry list of wounded and missing, he died of wounds on 8 September 1918. He may have been wounded in action while occupying the trench system north and east of St Emilie on that date. He was thirty-two years of age. He was the son of Harry and Mary Hedges, and husband of Alice E.E. Hedges of Ruislip. He does not appear to be commemorated locally. Commemorated: Vis-en-Artois memorial, Haucourt, Pas de Calais, France.

Heywood, Herbert

Of Eastcote. Captain, 5th Middlesex Regiment, attd. 'C' Battalion Tank Corps, to which he was gazetted to be Acting Captain, dating from 21 August 1917. He had been an articled clerk when he enlisted. Badly wounded on 22 August 1917 and died in one of the hospitals close to where he was wounded the same day, aged twenty-seven, and buried in Dozinghem British Cemetery, Proven, north-west of Ypres. He had already been wounded in the second week of 1915. Son of Mr John Heywood of Devonshire Lodge, Eastcote, formerly of Pinner Place, Pinner, who died at his home after a long illness in the spring of 1921 and was buried at Kensal Green. He was aged sixty-seven when he died. Captain Heywood, who was married, is commemorated on the Ruislip, Eastcote,

St Lawrence's church, Eastcote, and St Martin's church, Ruislip war memorials. The Tank Corps Roll of Honour records 879 killed, 5,302 wounded and 935 men missing.

Higgs, Edwin

Born at Northwood, where he was baptised at Holy Trinity church on 13 March 1884, the son of William and Mary. He enlisted at Hounslow, but resided at Staines. G/23257, Private, 1st Royal West Kent Regiment. Formerly G/11940 the Buffs (East Kent Regiment). Died of wounds on 27 October 1917. He may have been wounded on the previous day's fighting at Gheluvelt. The 1st West Kents had been in action on 3-4 October at the Third Ypres. They did not return to the firing line until 24 October and found themselves almost in the same point from which they had advanced on 4 October. He is not commemorated locally. Buried: Longuenesse (St Omer) Souvenir Cemetery, Pas de Calais, France.

Hildred, Bertie Levi

Born Upton-on-Severn on 21 September 1900. He joined the Navy on 5 July 1915; was appointed to HMS *Cyclops*; served in the Battle of Jutland and was twice torpedoed while escorting convoys on HMS *Antrim*. He was appointed to HMS *Vindictive* in April 1918. CH/19730, Private, 4th Royal Marine Light Infantry. On St George's Day, 1918, the Dover Patrol carried out one of the most audacious and brilliantly conceived operations; it was in this attack that he was seriously injured, during one of a series of raids against the destroyer, mine-layer, U-boat and naval aviation bases at Zeebrugge, the point from which Germany could launch air-attacks on the British coast, the eastern entrance to the Channel which had fallen into enemy hands in 1914 when Belgium was overrun. He died at the Royal Naval Hospital, Chatham, on 20 May 1918, aged seventeen. The enemy had been forewarned that an attack was about to take place after one of our boats was captured. On the night of 22-23 April 1918, Zeebrugge and Ostend were to be simultaneously attacked at midnight – a feint attack to draw the German fire. Under cover of darkness and a large smoke-screen the assaulting troops would be landed on the Mole and attack the heavy guns guarding the harbour as well as the enemy stationed there. The main object was to block the two ports – which were connected by canal with the inland port of Bruges, the main naval base for smaller vessels operating in the North Sea – by sinking three ships, the *Thesis*, *Intrepid* and *Iphigenia*, filled with concrete in the bay. The *Vindictive* was to be withdrawn when the aforementioned ships had manoeuvred into position. It worked up full speed to dash into Zeebrugge Mole through choppy seas and German mine-fields. A searchlight at Zeebrugge disclosed the *Vindictive* as the fog cleared. Every hostile weapon opened on her. On reaching the Mole, gangways were dropped, and laden with machine guns, flame-throwers, bombs, helmets and gas-masks, seamen and the Marines reached the tip of the gangway and dropped down to the parapet swept by hostile machine guns. The men dropped down another 16 to 20ft to the surface of the Mole, where grievous losses were suffered. A fierce struggle took place as the British surged forward. A huge explosion was heard and a gap of between 60 and 80ft had been blown in the Mole. Once the object had been attained, Zeebrugge was sealed up and the ships withdrawn. *Vindictive's* siren sounded repeatedly. Her decks were chocked with the dead and the wounded. Back over the battered gangways came the survivors with a large number of wounded; as she was leaving a tornado of shells were fired on her and about a quarter of a ton of masonry from the Mole crashed down on her. It was a brilliant naval attack, but it was probably in this terrible fighting that Bertie was wounded, as it seems that the *Vindictive's* next venue, on the night of 9-10 May, was when she was used as a blockship at Ostend.

He was the son of Harold and Elizabeth Hildred of White Cottage, Reginald Road, Northwood. He was educated at Spicer's School, Upton-on-Severn, after which he worked as a clerk in a solicitor's office. He is commemorated in Holy Trinity church, Northwood, and also commemorated at Northwood as Bertie Gooden. Buried: Gillingham (Woodlands) Cemetery, Kent.

Hill, Cuthbert Alexander

Born in Scotland, the son of Alexander (a mining engineer) and May Hill. Midshipman, HMS *Invincible*, RN. He died at the Battle of Jutland when the ship was hit by a German shell on 31 May 1916, aged eighteen. At approximately 6.20 p.m. the 3rd Battle Cruiser Squadron, of which the *Invincible* was flagship, opened fire on German battle cruisers. At 6.32 p.m. a heavy shell from the *Derfflinger* hit the *Invincible's* 'Q' turret and blew the turret roof off. The flash that followed shot down to the magazines and the ship blew up, but not before helping to inflict fatal damage on *Lützow* – Germany's most serious loss of the war. The Rear Admiral the Hon. Horace Hood was lost with his flagship, and of 1,026 officers and men only six survived. He is commemorated on Holy Trinity church, Northwood war memorial. Commemorated: Portsmouth Naval memorial, Hampshire.

Hill, Mark Carr

Born in Córdoba, Spain, on 11 April 1894, son of Alexander and May (or Mary) Margaret Hill and brother of Cuthbert (above). Lieutenant, 6th Leicestershire Regiment (21st Division). He matriculated in 1913, studied at Magdalene College, University of Cambridge. While at Rossall School he spent four years in the school corps as a Corporal, playing occasionally in the cricket XI. On 8 or 9 October 1915 he was wounded by gunshot in his right leg: the rifle bullet entered below the knee, traversing the joint. He was admitted to the Red Cross hospital at Le Touquet on 12 October. On 9 November 1915 he was taken aboard the hospital ship, *Munich*, at Boulogne – bound for Southampton, where he arrived later the same day. He was granted two months leave due to disability. He later rejoined his unit, who were in action at Bazentin-le-Petit, on 14 July 1916, having moved forward at 3.25 a.m. from their assembly positions in front of Mametz Wood. He died (or was killed in action) on 14 July 1916, aged twenty-two, at the Battle of the Somme. A large-scale night attack on that date, the first day of the second stage of the Battle of the Somme, heralded another long struggle for the German second position on the main Ginchy ridge, where the 6th Leicestershires were in the most desperate fighting at Contalmaison. The attack, which had began on 7 July 1916, continued until 15 July; on that day Contalmaison, defended by the 3rd Prussian Guards, as well as Bazentin, Bazentin-le-Grand, the most part of Ovillers (which had been defended by the 26th Wurtembergers), Trones Wood, Longueval and Delville Wood were all successfully seized. He is commemorated on Holy Trinity church, Northwood war memorial, and at Thiepval memorial, Somme, France.

Hill, Reginald

Born at Ruislip, he enlisted at Whitehall at the end of August 1914, and lived at Ruislip Common. 11293, Private, 1st Coldstream Guards. First posted as missing after the engagement at Givenchy during the unsatisfactory Battle of Cuinchy, on 22 December 1914, but later declared 'died of wounds' on that date, aged twenty-one. He had only been at the front since 8 December 1914. The son of Mr and Mrs George Hill of Kendall Cottages, Ruislip, he is commemorated on the Ruislip Common, Ruislip and St Martin's church, Ruislip war memorials. Commemorated: Le Touret memorial, Pas de Calais, France.

Hillier, Frederick John

Born at Balham, enlisted at Hendon, and lived at Child's Hill. G/2979, Private, 'D' Coy, 8th East Kent Regiment. The 8th Buffs had landed in France between 1 June and 1 September 1915. They began their march to the battle area on 21 September. Early on 25th they reached Bethune after a long march, mostly over bad roads. The attack had already started but on the next day, wet through and without sleep, they attacked on the German second position between Bois Hugo and Hulluch at 10.30 a.m., heading downhill to Hulluch and grappling with wire entanglements – under heavy fire from either side. Later that night, the Germans counter-attacked. At 11.55 p.m. an order came to withdraw and from that moment hostile fire became even hotter. Sometime on 26 September 1915, Frederick was killed in action, aged twenty-two, on the second day of the Battle of Loos. He was the son of Henry and Ruth Hillier of The Cottages, Wood Lane, Ruislip, and brother of Henry. He does not appear to be commemorated locally. Commemorated: Loos memorial, Pas de Calais, France.

Hillier, Henry

Born at Child's Hill, Hendon. He enlisted at East Narrogin, Western Australia on 1 March 1916 and embarked for the Western Front on HMAT *Miltiades* at Fremantle on 7 August 1916. 5375, Private, 28th Australian Infantry, AIF. Missing, believed killed in action on or after 3 May 1917, aged twenty-six. He was the son of Henry and Ruth Hillier of Kings End Cottages, Wood Lane, Ruislip and brother of Frederick. He does not appear to be commemorated locally. Commemorated: Villers-Bretonneux memorial, Somme, France.

Hiscock, Frederick

Born at Pinner, enlisted at Mill Hill, of Northwood. 34103, Private, 2/8th Worcester Regiment. Died 'in France on 16th August 1918, aged 26, when his battalion was in the Lys Valley'. He was almost certainly a POW. On 1 August 1918 while at Liettres (in the Lys valley), three 'boys' from the 2/8th Worcesters had been taken prisoner. He is commemorated on the Emmanuel church, Northwood, and Northwood war memorials. He was the son of the late Thomas and Emma Hiscock of Pinner. Buried: Hamburg Cemetery, Germany.

Hodson, Ernest Thomas Pickering

Born in London. Pensioner Petty Officer, 223756, HMS *Sarpedon* (a shore establishment), RN. Died of tuberculosis of the lungs and influenza at Vista Linda, Exton, Woodbury, in the presence of his father on 17 February 1919, aged thirty-one. He was the son of Thomas Pickering Hodson (born on 13 November 1857, died 1 November 1936) and Fanny Louisa Hodson (born on 3 December 1857, died 19 July 193–?), of 64 Reginald Road, Northwood. He is commemorated on the Emmanuel church, Northwood, and Northwood war memorials. Buried: Woodbury (St Swithin) churchyard, Devon.

Hogg, Arthur Mcgarel

Born at Kensal Rise, enlisted at Staines. 30600, Guardsman, 4th Grenadier Guards. On 13 April 1918, the Intelligence Branch reported that four more German divisions had reached the Western Front from Russia, three of which had gone to the British sector. He was killed in action on this day in an attack which began at 6.30 a.m. in the fog; it involved more than four German divisions (part of the 8th, the 35th, 12th Reserve, 42nd and part of the 81st Reserve) – the day the 'enemy attacked heavily all along the front' in their efforts to reach the channel ports, in an attempt to obstruct the vital British lines of communication. He was thirty-two years old. The 31st Division, of which the 4th Grenadiers were a part, was holding the sector directly covering Hazebrouck between the Bourre and Merris, south-east of Strazeele, on a front of some 9,000 yards, east of the Forest of Nieppe. The division was greatly reduced in strength as a result of earlier fighting. The troops were informed that their line had to be held to the last to cover the detaining of reinforcements. Furious assaults were carried out by the enemy, who menaced Mont Kemmel, Mont Noir and Mont-des-Cats – splendid observation stations dominating all the surrounding area, the possession of which would assure a considerable advantage to whoever held control. He was the son of William Alexander and Gertrude Hogg of 'Alwyn', Sharps Lane, Ruislip. He is not commemorated locally. Buried: Merville Communal Cemetery Extension, Nord, France, F.3.

Holden, Robert Edwin

Born at Great Malvern, Worcs, enlisted Mill Hill, and lived at Northwood. 20443, Private, 7th East Surrey Regiment. On 5 August 1917, the battalion was to have been relieved as support in the Monchy trenches, but was not withdrawn from its position owing to the inclement weather. On 8 August, the bombardment had been postponed for 24 hours. It commenced at 6.30 a.m. on 9 August, the raiding parties moving out of Hill and Shrapnel Trenches, and continued with varying intensity until 7.45 p.m., when the infantry advanced under a creeping barrage. Sometime on this day Robert was killed in action, aged twenty-one. He was the son of Fanny E.S. Holden of St Alban's Golf Common, Malvern, Worcs, and the late William Holden. He is not commemorated locally. Commemorated: Arras memorial, Pas de Calais, France.

Holland, A.B.

He had been a postman at Northwood.

Hone, Edward John

Born at Harefield on 27 March 1885 and baptised at St Mary's church on 31 March 1885, he enlisted in London within weeks of the outbreak of war; of Northwood. 5/3948, Rifleman

(Private), 1st King's Royal Rifle Corps. He had joined the Army in London on 30 July 1910 and was mobilised on 8 August 1914. On 24 January 1916 he was wounded in action by a bullet and was treated in the 5th field ambulance, transferring to 1st casualty clearing station at Chocques on 29th. On 30th he was sent to Argues, then to a stationary hospital at St Omer, transferring to the 10th stationary hospital at St Omer. On 23 February he transferred to Base, and on the following day was admitted to the 23rd general hospital at Étaples, being moved on following days. He rejoined his regiment on about 8 April 1916. He was wounded by gas in the fighting at Delville Wood on 27 July 1916 and admitted to 36th casualty clearing station at Heilly, where he died on 1 August 1916 (or 29 July 1916). He is buried in the Cimetiere du Bois Hareng, Heilly. He was aged thirty-one. Edward was the son of Charles Henry and Harriet Hone of The Laurels, 46 Roy Road, Northwood, formerly of Hanover Cottage, Reginald Road. His father died in July 1953, aged ninety-nine, and his mother in April 1927, aged seventy-two. Both are buried at Harefield. Edward had been a fishmonger. He is commemorated on the Emmanuel church, Northwood, and Northwood war memorials, but not on the Harefield war memorial.

Hopkins, Arthur Martyn

Second Lieutenant, 11th King's Royal Rifle Corps. He was killed in action on 28 March 1918. On the previous day, at noon, the 11th KRRC, which had been in reserve behind Folies, was sent up to relieve another battalion in front of Erches. There they beat off an attack. They were relieved late morning owing to an attack on Arvillers. During its withdrawal from Arvillers they were subjected to heavy shell fire before reaching their bivouacs near Domart. His parents lived at Denmark, No. 33 Roy Road, Northwood. He is commemorated on the Emmanuel church, Northwood, and Northwood war memorials. Commemorated: Pozieres memorial, Somme.

Hughes, Robert

Born and lived at Ealing, enlisted at Hounslow. Lance-Corporal, L/9521, 'A' Coy, 1 Platoon, 12th Middlesex Regiment. From 1 May 1917, the 12th Middlesex had been bivouacked in the front line near Cherisy Village, which was to be captured on 3 May, at the Third Battle of the Scarpe, on the first day of the third and last stage of the Battles of Arras. At 3.45 p.m. on 3 May 1917, the British attacked from the Acheville-Vimy Road, north of Arleux, to Bullecourt, on a 12-mile front. Five minutes later, the enemy put down a very heavy HE barrage. He was reported missing on this day, aged thirty-one. He was the son of William and Mary Hughes; husband of Louisa Ann Ayres (formerly Hughes) of Manor Cottages, Ruislip. He does not appear to be commemorated locally or even on the Ealing war memorial. Commemorated: Arras memorial, Pas de Calais, France.

Imber, Mark

Born at Shaftesbury, he lived at Northwood – where he enlisted in September 1914. 10814, Private (or Trooper), (Old) 6th Reserve Cavalry Regiment (5th and 12th Lancers). Died at Dublin on 11 June 1915, aged thirty-two. He was of the Church of England and is commemorated on the Emmanuel church, Northwood, and Northwood war memorials.

Buried: Grangegorman Military Cemetery, County Dublin, Republic of Ireland, where he was interred on 14 June 1915 in Plot No. 600.

Jackson, Alfred Walter George

Born Forest Hill, Kent, enlisted at Redhill, Surrey, on 28 September 1914, as Private, 2646, 8th West Surrey Regiment. On 20 November 1914 he was discharged as medically unfit. He later served as 56495, (Acting Bombardier) or Gunner, 78th Coy, Royal Garrison Artillery (Royal Regiment of Artillery (RGA) Corps). He died in India on 6 May 1918. The son of Walter James Jackson of Church Road, Northwood, Alfred, who had been a gardener, is commemorated on the Northwood war memorial. Buried: Colombo (Kanatte) General Cemetery, Sri Lanka.

Jackson, Robert Cameron

Lived at 40, 43 or 45, Ickenham Road, Ruislip. Second Lieutenant, 233rd Coy, Machine Gun Corps. He was killed in action near Zonnebeke at the battle of Menin on 24 September 1917, aged thirty-five. The son of Catherine Theodora Jackson of Northwood and the late Thomas Jackson, he was a partner in the firm of Messrs Sidgwick & Jackson, publishers of London. He was a publisher of poetry: although no poet himself, he appreciated and encouraged those who were. He had already served time in the Army with the Royal Scots and had attested in London on 10 December 1915 as Private 1356 (or 7356) with the London Scottish. He was mobilised on 31 March 1916, and on 4 August 1916 was attached to the No. 1 Officers Cadet Battalion and Denham. After October 1916 he was given a Temporary Commission in the MGC. Commemorated: Tyne Cot memorial, Zonnebeke, West Vlaanderen, Belgium.

Jackson, W.A.G.

He is commemorated on Emmanuel church, Northwood, and Northwood war memorials. He was as a Bombardier. Probably a mistake for A.W.G Jackson.

Jackson, W.H.

He is commemorated on Emmanuel church, Northwood, and Northwood war memorials. He was a Private serving with the Royal Fusiliers (City of London) Regiment.

Jenkins, Frederick

Born at Shanklin, Isle of Wight, enlisted at Harrow, of Northwood. G/21585, Private (Signaller), 7th West Kent Regiment. Formerly 21007 East Surrey Regiment. The 18th Division had had a fortnight's rest before 18 September 1918. On the morning of 19th, the 7th West Kents assembled behind Ronssoy. At 11 a.m. they set off from just east of Ste Emilie, attacking under a creeping barrage – although in the fog they failed to keep up with it – in an attempt to get through to the northern portion of Lempire and on to Braeton. Frederick was killed in action near Epehy in the battles to break the German Hindenburg Line, on this date, aged twenty. They were met with very heavy machine-gun fire, not only from Lempire but also from the three copses nearby. From 18 September to 24 September, the 18th Divisional troops, by this time a very great proportion of them youngsters and with no battalion at full strength, gained ground only by heavy hand-to-hand fighting against machine-gun fire more murderous than at any period of the war, and against the ceaseless efforts of the enemy artillery to defend the vital points of the Hindenburg Line. He was the son of Harry and Margaret Jenkins of 94 Hallowell Road, Northwood, and is commemorated on the Emmanuel church, Northwood, and Northwood war memorials. Buried: Unicorn Cemetery, Aisne, France, G.21.

Jennings, A.G.
He had been a postman at Northwood.

Jewell, John Belmont
Lieutenant, RAF and General List, Northolt Aerodrome. Killed on 6 April 1918 when his plane nosedived in a field near Northolt Junction, aged eighteen. Buried: St Martin's churchyard, Ruislip.

Johnson, Lawrence Samuel
Born at Horsepath, Oxon, and enlisted at Marylebone on 8 August 1914; of 15, The Lynch, Uxbridge. He proceeded to the Expeditionary Force on 30 August 1914. T2/016739, Driver, Royal Army Service Corps. Died of enteric fever at Nancy (probably a mistake for Nantes) on 21 October 1914, aged twenty-one. Lawrence was the son of Thomas and Harriet Johnson of Crown Road, Wheatley, Oxon. He had been a packer or plate-layer in the Engineering Department at Ruislip station for two years. He is not commemorated locally. Buried: Nantes (La Bouteillerie) Cemetery, Loire-Atlantique, France.

Jones, C.
He had been a postman at Northwood.

Jones, George Charles
Born at Dalston, Middlesex, enlisted at Harrow, of Northwood. G/41010, Lance-Corporal, 21st Middlesex Regiment. Killed instantly in action by a bursting shell over the trench near Cherisy in which he was stationed on 1 May 1917, aged twenty-two. They were in the front line at La Vacquerie, just off the Cambrai road, which was practically the only village in the immediate front still in German hands. George was the eldest son of Mr and Mrs Percival Jesse Jones of Church Road, Northwood. He had been educated under Mr Fenwick of the Northwood Council Schools and on leaving joined his father's fishmonger's business. He joined the 9th Middlesex Territorials in 1912. When war broke out his battalion was mobilised, and he rose to the rank of Acting Sergeant. In October 1915 he was drafted to France with the 21st Middlesex as Corporal due to the reorganisation of units of the force. He was an extremely good cyclist and had joined the Uxbridge Cycling Club; at the Northwood annual sports day he rode first in the bicycle handicap for three years in succession, so that in 1913 the prize silver cup became his. The same year he won the silver cup at the bicycle handicap at the Ruislip sports in the mile-flat race. He had also been a keen and regular member of the Northwood Men's Discussion Class. He is commemorated on the Emmanuel church, Northwood, and Northwood war memorials. Commemorated: Thiepval memorial, Somme, France.

Joscelyne, Clement Percy

Born on 8 July 1885 at Bishop Stortford, he attended Bishop Stortford College where he had joined the OTC, afterwards becoming an auctioneer. He was living in Buenos Aires and volunteered for duty. On 18 July 1917 he embarked at Folkestone for Calais and joined the battalion in the field, having been made a Second Lieutenant in the Suffolk Regiment on 16 June. Second Lieutenant, 3rd, attd. 11th Suffolk Regiment. On the night of 8/9 October 1917, the battalion had concentrated around Proven. Very soon afterwards they moved north and for the next few days were engaged on repairing roads in the forward area close to the front line. This was carried out in daylight in awful weather and under constant shell and machine-gun fire. It was in this action that 2nd Lieutenant Joscelyne was injured, on 10th; he died of wounds in No. 47 CCS on 11 October 1917, aged thirty-two. He was the son of Fanny and the late Clement Joscelyne, of Bishop's Stortford, Herts; husband of Rosamund Joscelyne of The Old House, Ruislip, whom he had married at Colchester on 1 June 1911. They had two sons, one born at Ruislip and the other born on 21 August 1917, and one daughter, born at Colchester. He is commemorated on the St Martin's church, Ruislip, and Ruislip war memorials. Buried: Dozinghem Military Cemetery, Belgium.

Keevil, Cecil Horace Case

Captain, RFC and 18th Btn, West Yorkshire Regt, Northolt Aerodrome. Killed in action when approaching Southend. Whilst trying to intercept a formation of 3 Gotha aeroplanes over Ilford, on 13 June 1917, he was shot in the neck. He was aged thirty-six and was the observer, flying in a Bristol Fighter. He was the son of Richard and Georgina Keevil of Clitter House Farm, Cricklewood, London. Buried: Hampstead Cemetery.

Killen, Edward Osborne Brice

Born on 26 September 1893, of Ravenswood, Northwood. He was educated at Bedford Grammar School, where he was a Sergeant in the OTC. He went on to study mechanical science at the Trinity College, Cambridge. On 9 January 1915 he was appointed temporary 2nd Lieutenant in the Royal Engineers and went for training at the School of Military Engineering. In the late summer of 1916 he went with his unit to Basra, where he suffered from dysentery and was sent to England. For a time, while he was recovering, he was put on light duties at home. Lieutenant (TP), Corps of Royal Engineers (71st Field Co.); Trinity Hall Cambridge. Killed in action on 15 January 1917, he was the only son of (Edward) Brice and Genevieve Killen of Bedford. He is commemorated on the Northwood war memorial and on Holy Trinity church memorial, Northwood. Buried: Amara War Cemetery, Iraq.

King, Albert

Born at Ruislip, possibly the Albert King, son of Margaret King, who was baptised at Ruislip on 6 December 1892, enlisted in London, and lived at Plumstead. 14723, Lance-Corporal, 2nd Worcester Regiment. On 16 July 1916, the 33rd Division was withdrawn to near Bazentin-le-Petit, the 100th Brigade in Divisional Reserve. They had been in support at Bazentin. As the pressure grew at Deville Wood it was deemed advisable to attack strongly by the Fifteenth Corps – the 33rd Division and the depleted 7th Division on their right. The objectives to be attacked were High Wood, the strongly held Switch Trench and the connecting trench between them. He was killed in action in the first day of the Second Phase of the Battle of the Somme near High Wood (Bois des Foureaux) on 20 July 1916, probably in the big attack on that day in the region of Pozieres and Vermandovillers. At one time the wood was clear of the enemy, but a counter-attack recaptured the northern half. He does not appear to be commemorated locally. Commemorated: Thiepval memorial, Somme, France.

King, Frank Benjamin
Enlisted at Westminster, of Northwood. 550661 (or 550664) Sergeant, 2nd/16th (County of London) Battalion (Queen's Westminster Rifles). On 7 December 1917, the 60th Brigade, of which the 2/16th Londoners formed a part, concentrated near Soba in the rain, almost 3 miles north-west of Ain Karim, during the afternoon. Killed in action on 8 December 1917, aged twenty-five. He was serving with the EEF, and on that date the British line ran from Neby Samwil, to the east of Beit Iksa, through Lifta, to a point about 1.5 miles away from Jerusalem; Wadi el Hesi had fallen. Rain was still falling when the 60th Division carried out a surprise attack on the Turkish works on a front of 4.5 miles from south-east of Ain Karim to south of Nabi Samweil. The first objective, a particularly difficult one, included the defences east of Ain Karim, the village of Deir Yesin and its redoubts, the 'Heart' and 'Liver Redoubts', covering the Jaffa-Jerusalem road and the trenches west of Beit Iksa, most of which was captured by 7 a.m. Frank was the son of Alfred William and Agnes Eliza King of 4421 Pine St, Central Park, New Westminster, British Columbia. He is commemorated on the Emmanuel church, Northwood, and Northwood war memorials. Buried: Jerusalem War Cemetery, Israel.

King, H.J.
Born Watford, enlisted at Willesden, lived at Watford. T.F. 204005, Corporal, 1/7th Middlesex Regiment. By 30 March 1917, the British Army was north of Amiens. Vast preparations were being made for an attack at Arras. The 56th Division was assigned the capture of Neuville Vitasse and the strong works which surrounded it, the advance to be carried out on 9 April 1917, Easter Monday, at 7.45 a.m., although further along the line the British forces had attacked at 5.30 a.m. on a front of 40km from Arras to Lens and Havrincourt wood on the banks of the Ancre and had great success north of Arras. It was not until 1 o'clock that the Battalion had assembled in four lines on the sunken road leading down to St Martin-sur-Cojeul. The 7th Middlesex, with the 1st London Regiment, captured Cojeul Switch Trench and then stormed forward against the powerful Ibex Trench. By 3 o'clock they were in complete possession of the first line of the Cojeul Switch, known as Telegraph Hill Trench, having worked their way forward through thick mud. The 167th Brigade then turned south and their depleted ranks were strengthened by the 9th London Regiment (Victorias) from their reserve brigade.

The enemy was only 40 yards off but the mud was so awful that some men who got in could hardly be brought out again alive. In spite of all the difficulties, they swept triumphantly down Ibex and Zoo Trenches, clearing the whole position and capturing

Commissioned officers in the 9th London Regiment.

almost 200 prisoners of the 31st Prussian Regiment and several machine guns. King was killed in action on this Easter Monday in horrendous machine-gun fire near Neuville-Vitasse in an attack which ultimately failed, mainly due to the thick mud which clogged the trenches. He had been a surveyor's assistant for the Ruislip-Northwood UDC. Buried: London Cemetery, Neuville-Vitasse, Pas de Calais, France.

King, J.H.
He is commemorated on the Emmanuel church, Northwood, and Northwood war memorials. He served as a 'Corporal with the Middlesex Regiment'. Almost certainly H.J. King above.

King, Maurice Edmund
Born on 14 April 1896. 2nd Lieutenant (TP), 13th Middlesex Regiment. In the middle of March 1916 the pressure upon the French at Verdun had become severe, and it was determined to take over a fresh section of line so as to relieve troops for the north-east frontier. In March 1916, the 13th Middlesex went back into Sanctuary Wood, close to Ypres, where, on 14 March 1916, the 13th Middlesex were subjected to a particularly violent bombardment between midday and 3 p.m. Maurice was killed in action, shot dead by a sniper, at dusk on 15 March 1916, aged just eighteen (or nineteen). He was buried at Sanctuary Wood, 4,500 yards south east of Ypres, but his body must have 'gone missing'. Third son of the late Henry William King, MD,VD, and of Annie Sarah King, of Carlton Vicarage, Nr Barnsley, Yorks, formerly of Kilmun, Northwood. He is commemorated on

the Holy Trinity church, Northwood, and Northwood war memorials. Commemorated: Ypres (Menin Gate) memorial, Belgium.

King, Ronald Welby

Of Northwood, Leading Seaman, London/9/1340. HMS *Clan McNaughton*, Royal Navy Volunteer Reserve. HMS *Clan McNaughton,* a merchant ship formerly of the Clan steamship line, had been requisitioned for war service and patrol duties in November 1914. It had been missing since 3 February 1915 and no further news of her was received. An unsuccessful search was made and it was thought that the ship foundered in a storm off the north coast of Ireland, possibly mined, on 3 February 1915. Ronald was twenty-eight and had been a clerk for the Metropolitan Railway. Second son of George Welby King, who was suddenly taken ill on Easter Monday 1919 and died in April 1919 – and was buried at Ruislip, aged seventy-three – and Mary King of Ellerslie, Carew Road, Northwood. They had lived in the area for twenty years or so. Ronald is commemorated on the Emmanuel church, Northwood, and Northwood war memorials. Commemorated: Chatham memorial, Kent.

King, Sidney

Born at Ruislip on 6 November 1899, where he was baptised on the 10 December that same year; the son of George and Mary King, he lived at Ruislip, and enlisted Mill Hill. 41363, Private, 7th Bedfordshire Regiment, 'D' Coy, XV Platoon. On 22 March 1918, soon after 10 a.m., as the fog thinned, the enemy swept the front of the 54th Brigade with trench-mortar and machine-gun fire, under cover of which his infantry crept up to the banks of the Crozat canal. No attempt was made to cross until 6 p.m., when, under a heavy bombardment, a number of Germans rushed the undamaged Montagne railway bridge. The defending company of the 7th Bedfordshires was driven back but, with reinforcements, it counter-attacked, and by 7.30 p.m. the situation was completely established. At midnight, the 54th Brigade was transferred from the 14th Division to the 18th Division. Before dawn on 23 March 1918, heavy attacks were resumed. At 9 a.m. the 54th Brigade pushed out into the fog and found that the enemy was over the canal at Jussy. The 54th Brigade was still covering the crossing at Jussy and Montagne, but the pressure was rapidly increasing as fresh German divisions made their presence felt. At 10 a.m. on that date, the 7th Bedfordshires, during bitter fighting, were ordered to retire to a ridge in front of Faillouel. Later they had to abandon this, as the left flank had fallen into German hands. They therefore fell back to the Tombelle Ridge – high ground west of the village. In early evening they were instructed to march back to Caillouel. Some heavy fighting broke out near Rouez Camp, before they fell back on Villequier Aumont. Sidney was wounded and went missing on this day – a disastrous day, as the passage over the Somme at Peronne, and the whole line of that river with it, was lost. There now lay no natural barrier to thwart the enemy's path to Amiens. He is commemorated on the St Martin's church, Ruislip, and Ruislip war memorials. Commemorated: Pozieres memorial, Somme, France.

Kirby, A.

He is commemorated on the Emmanuel church, Northwood, and Northwood war memorials. It is known that he was a Corporal who enlisted in September 1914 and when he died (after 1915) he was a 'Lance Sergeant, Scots Guards'. An Arthur Kirby, son of Henry and Emma, of 146 Hallowell Road, Northwood, was travelling to Marylebone to undergo treatment in a London hospital in the autumn of 1918 when he was suddenly taken ill just as the train was leaving Pinner; he died before reaching Harrow on the Hill. The cause was given as syncope; he was aged forty-seven, and is buried at Northwood Cemetery. An A. Kirby's family was amongst those from the Uxbridge Division of Middlesex who were helped by the Soldiers' and Sailors' Families Association sometime between 1914 and the end of 1915.

Knox, William

Second Lieutenant, 30th training depot station (RAF Northolt). On 31 October 1918, while flying over Ruislip, his machine suddenly nosedived to the ground. He was crushed and burnt to death. He was almost nineteen years old. William was the son of George Wallace Knox of 17 Hunters Terrace, South Shields. His sister Jane, who was serving with the Queen Mary's Army Auxiliary Corps, died on 11 November 1918. They are both buried in the same graveyard. Buried: South Shields (Harton) Cemetery, Durham.

Kopyloff

A Russian cadet stationed at Northolt Aerodrome. It is not known when he died or where he is buried.

Lacey, Albert John

Baptised on 5 April 1891 at Ruislip, Albert was the son of Albert and Elizabeth Lacey (née Lavender) of Eastcote, who had married at Ruislip on 21 September 1890; he enlisted at Mill Hill. Of Eastcote. G/12347, Private, 26th Middlesex Regiment. The regiment had gone to Salonika in 1916, joining the 27th Division as Pioneers on 28 August 1916. It was here that he died of wounds, possibly in the No. 1 Canadian stationary hospital, Salonika, on 28 September 1918. On 18 September the Battle of Doiran began, the 26th Middlesex providing guards for the Gumendje and Bohemitza bridges. After Doiran and Bulgar trenches to the west of Doiran had fallen into the Allies' hands, the 27th Division, on the western bank of the River Varder, pursued the enemy in a northerly direction. It may have been in this action that he had been wounded, as on 24th the fit men had marched to Artillery Berg and on 25th to Pardovica, where they remained for one day; then, on 27th, they began three days' hard marching. The Nos 37 general hospital at Veryekop and 38 general hospital at Samlis were both within a few miles of Salonika. They were there by the autumn of 1916, as was the No. 1 Canadian stationary hospital at Salonika, although some hospitals may have come later. He is commemorated on the Eastcote, St Lawrence's church, Eastcote, and St Martin's church, Ruislip (as J. Lacey, although this may refer to his brother, who predeceased him), and Ruislip war memorials. Buried: Salonika, (Lembet Road) Military Cemetery, Greece.

Lavender, Arthur William

Born at Ruislip, where he was baptised at St Martin's on 3rd December 1896, he was the son of John and Hannah Lavender; he enlisted at Harrow, but lived at Eastcote. 201429, Private, Royal West Surrey Regiment, Area Employment Coy, Labour Corps, formerly 52569, 22nd Labour Coy. He probably died in one of the many hospitals at Étaples on 25 January 1918, aged thirty-seven. The cemetery at Étaples is the largest in the whole of France and contains the graves of English servicemen, the Non Combatants Corps, Chinese Labour Corps, one British West Indies serviceman and others, with a very small part of the cemetery devoted to German servicemen who died in hospitals at Étaples sur Mer. Arthur was the son of Mrs Lacey of Coteford Close, Eastcote. He is commemorated on the Eastcote and Ruislip war memorials. Buried: Étaples Military Cemetery, Pas de Calais, F.13, France.

Lavender, Thomas

Born at Ruislip, where he was baptised on 3 May 1896, Thomas was the son of Walter and Emily; he lived at Ruislip, and enlisted at Uxbridge in August 1914. 5502, Private, 3rd Royal Fusiliers. The 28th Division had left Winchester by route march for Southampton, arriving there at noon on 17 January 1915. They immediately embarked on the SS *Maidan* and sailed at 6.30 p.m. for France. They had just arrived from England when, by late April 1915, the 28th (which included the 3rd Royal Fusiliers) and 27th Divisions formed a line which passed a mile north of Zonnebeke, curling around south outside the Polygon Wood to close to Hill 60. Two attacks were made on enemy trenches in the early morning of

October 1914. New recruits marching down Uxbridge High Street. Thomas Lavender, like many of Ruislip's and Northwood's men, joined the Army here. (Courtesy of Hillingdon Local Studies, Archives and Museum Service)

26 April 1915. In their first battle he was killed near Zonnebeke in action on Hill 60, an artificial hillock made of the earth excavated in cutting the Comines–Ypres railway, in the Ypres salient, during the Second Battle of Ypres, the Battle of St Julien, on this day, aged nineteen. The 28th Division had been severely attacked. During that one afternoon, the 366th Battery of the 28th Division had fired 1,740 rounds. It was a day of heavy losses and very little gains. He was the youngest of three sons of Mr and Mrs Walter Lavender of Old Workhouse Cottages, Ruislip Common. He is commemorated on the Ruislip Common, St Martin's church, Ruislip, and Ruislip war memorials. Commemorated: Ypres (Menin Gate) memorial, Belgium.

Lavender, William J.

He had been a labourer and had enlisted in London or Halifax as 6712, Private, West Riding Regiment on 6 May 1901 when he was nineteen years and three months old, for the duration of seven years' Army Service and five years' Reserve Service. He served in India from 13 February 1901 to 23 April 1906 and his Reserve Service ended just as war began. In 1907 he had been convicted of being absent without leave and neglecting to obey an order. He rejoined soon after the outbreak of war and was discharged on 26 December 1914 as physically unfit suffering from rheumatic fever. He and his wife, Eleanor (née Wright), and their three children lived at Hilliard Road, Northwood. The family of a W.J. Lavender was helped by the Soldiers' and Sailors' Families Association sometime between 1914 and the end of 1915. He is commemorated on the Emmanuel church, Northwood war memorial, but it is not known when he died or where he is buried.

Leach, G.

Of Northwood. He was a Corporal in the West Riding Regiment when he died. Possibly an alias for Arthur Teale, Private 5900, 1/4th West Riding Regiment who enlisted at Masham, Yorkshire. He was killed in action near Crucifix Corner, near High Wood, on 17 September 1916, aged twenty-two, and is commemorated on the Thiepval memorial, Somme, France.

Le Rossignol, Leonard F.

Enlisted Westminster, lived at Wallington. 3021, Rifleman, 1/16th London Regiment (Queen's Westminster Rifles) (56th Division). On the night of 30 June 1916 the Westminsters moved up from St Amand and assembled in trenches at Hebuterne. At Gommecourt, on 1 July 1916, the first day of the Battle of the Somme, when the English sector was between about Arras and Albert and the fighting at the most bitter between Hebuterne and Noyon, he was killed in action, aged twenty-nine. The men, who had been given the task of attacking the bulge on the German line and cutting off the Gommecourt salient, had advanced, six paces between each with smoke clouds in front and with splendid steadiness reached enemy trenches, with the 168th Brigade and the Westminsters and Victorias leading the 169th Brigade. The first, second and third German lines of trench were successively carried and it was not until they, or those who were left, had reached the fourth line that they were held. It was powerfully manned and bravely defended – and well provided with bombs. It was a terrific obstacle for a scattered line of weary and often wounded men. For hours on end the struggle went on and when over, few of the advanced line ever got back. In the late afternoon the remains of the two brigades went back in the British front line. Losses were very heavy. Never in one day had London sustained so grievous a loss. This attack on the southern side of the Gommecourt peninsula had no more success than the fighting in the north. In trying to divert the VII Corps enemy artillery and infantry, which otherwise might have been used against the left flank of the Fourth Army at Serres, the 56th Division induced the enemy to shoot at them with as many guns as could be gathered together and prevent the Germans from moving troops. Leonard was the son of Pauline E. Le Rossignol, of 'Pendower', Oxhey Drive, Northwood, and the late F. Le Rossignol. He is commemorated on the Northwood war memorial and on Holy Trinity church memorial, Northwood. Commemorated: Thiepval memorial, Somme, France.

Lewington, Henry George

Able Seaman, J/13825. HMS *Invincible*, Royal Navy. Killed in action at the Battle of Jutland at 6.32 on 31 May 1916. He and Midshipman Cuthbert Hill (se p. 132) were amongst the crew of 1038. Only six survived. The vessel was the flagship of the 3rd Battle Cruiser Squadron on the day, and she is said to have sunk after an explosion. At the time she was engaging the Battle Cruiser *Defflinger* or a ship of that class. He was the husband of Ellen Lewington of Wincot, Church Road, Northwood, whom he had married at Holy Trinity church on 2 May 1916. He is commemorated on the Emmanuel church, Northwood, and Northwood war memorials. Commemorated: Portsmouth Naval memorial, Hampshire.

Lewis, George Hardy, LLB

Of Northwood. Captain 4th attd. 'A' Coy, 2nd East Surrey Regiment. The 28th Division had reached Vermelles in the early hours of 27 September 1915. The whole of the Hohenzollern Redoubt was on the point of recapture by the enemy – Fosse 8 had been captured, the Quarries had been wrested from the 7th Division by the enemy and a very strong German attack was surging in from the north. The 28th Division had arrived just in time. In an effort to recapture Fosse 8 (behind the German front line near La Bassee) the 85th Brigade, which included the 2nd East Surreys, were hurriedly ordered in the early morning of 28 September 1915 to take part in the attack. They were on the way up to relieve the 9th Division in the Hohenzollern area. The attack began at 2.30 a.m. and desperate struggles to advance lasted all day. Whilst leading his men in a short advance, both of George's legs were broken by a bomb which had fallen at his feet. He was taken to hospital but died after a few hours. Only son of Mr George Francis Lewis and Elsie Lewis of 118 Oakwood Court, Kensington, formerly of Northwood. He had joined the Inns of Court Officers Training Corps on 27 March 1914 as Private 779 and on the outbreak of war was given a commission in the 4th East Surrey Regiment on 15 August. In November 1914 he went through a musketry course at Hayling Island and obtained a certificate. He proceeded to France in May 1915 and was gazetted Lieutenant in July and was given command of a company on 25 September. His sister, the only daughter, died on 31 January 1916 aged twenty-five, as the result of an accident. He is commemorated on Northwood war memorial and on Holy Trinity church memorial, Northwood. Buried: Chocques Military Cemetery, Pas de Calais, France.

Liddiard, George

Born at Henley, enlisted at Mill Hill in July 1916, of Ruislip. 30766, Private, 1st East Surrey Regiment. Died in hospital on 5 December 1916 as a result of serious wounds received in action in the Cuinchy sector on 25 November, aged thirty-seven. Around 14 October 1916, the 1st East Surreys had moved back into support in the village of Cuinchy and until 26 November the 1st East Surreys and 1st Devons held the right sub-sector of Cuinchy alternately, relieving each other every four days. He was the eldest son of George and Charlotte Liddiard of Dedworth, Windsor; husband of Ellen Liddiard of Ruislip. He had been butler at Ruislip Vicarage for five years before enlisting. He is commemorated on the St Martin's church, Ruislip, Ruislip, and Ruislip Common war memorials. Buried: Longuenesse (St Omer) Souvenir Cemetery, Pas de Calais, France, B.2.

Lilico, Percy

Lieut, RFC. He died when his plane nosedived and crashed at Northolt, close to the north side of the railway, on 16 February 1918. He was aged twenty-three and it was his second solo flight. Son of Mrs E. Lilico of West Terrace, Wooler and the late Mr C.G. Lilico. Buried: Wooler (St Mary) church burial ground, Northumberland.

Lord, Reginald

Born at Northwood on 21 August 1890 and baptised at Holy Trinity church on 5 October of that same year, he lived at 'Belmont', 16, Reginald Road, and enlisted at Willesden on 1 November 1914 in the 9th Middlesex Regiment, with which he had already served a term of four years. He served with the 1/7th, 4/7th, 1/7th until March 1917 when he became T.F.201120, Private, 1st Middlesex Regiment. Died from influenza and broncho-pneumonia in No. 13 general hospital at Dunney, Cambrai, after a short illness on 27 October 1918, aged twenty-eight. He had been a postman. Son of Charles and Mary Lord of Hoxon House, Church Road, Northwood; husband of Ella May Lord of Hillingdon Heath, whom he had married at Emmanuel church, Northwood, on 29 December 1915. He was the Hon. Sec. of the Northwood Rovers Football Club at the time of his enlistment. He is commemorated on the Emmanuel church, Northwood, and Northwood war memorials. Buried: Étaples Military Cemetery, Pas de Calais L.18

Love, James Ellis

Born at Winnipeg, Canada. Second Lieutenant, 18th Manchester Regiment. Killed in action at Bapaume on 2 September 1918, aged twenty. Son of John and Florence Selina Love of The Gables, Northwood. He was educated at Mostyn House, Parkgate, and Fetter College, Edinburgh. He is not commemorated locally as his parents moved to Northwood shortly after his death, but there is a commemorative window to him in Holy Trinity church, Northwood. On the 19 February 1918 the battalion was disbanded and amalgamation with the 17th Entrenching Battalion took place at Haute Allaines on the following day. Buried: Manchester Cemetery, Riencourt-les-Bapaume, Pas de Calais, France, B.21.

Lovett, Albert Charles

Born at Pinner where he was baptised with his two brothers on 5 December 1886, sons of John and Eliza Lovett. He enlisted at Pinner, and lived at Northwood. G/2915, Private, 2nd Royal Fusiliers. On the first day of the Battle of the Somme, 1 July 1916, the Picardy front was to be attacked between the region of Hebuterne and the region of Lassigny (about 70km) in the general direction of the Bapaume-Peronne-Ham line. The British sector had been between about Arras and Albert on the Bapaume Front. On the first day of the battle, the 29th Division on the right of the sector, facing Beaumont-Hamel, were to advance, the 86th and 87th Brigades forming the first line, due east across the Beaucourt spur to the German second position. They had moved forward from assembly positions in Mailly-Maillet Wood for an attack towards Hawthorne Ridge. Hostile machine-gun fire in front of Beaumont Hamel swept across the leading waves soon after they had left the front trenches. Two platoons of the 2nd Royal Fusiliers rushed forward to hold the Hawthorn Redoubt and were held up through horrendous cross machine-gun fire. Some men managed to fight their way to Hawthorn Ridge mine crater, while others, including Albert, entered the German front line, but all were killed. He is not commemorated locally. Commemorated: Thiepval memorial, Somme, France.

Lukyn, Stanley Edward, MC

Captain, RFC and 1st Battn, Royal West Surrey Regiment, Northolt Aerodrome. 'Pom', as he was familiarly known, was the second son of Herbert and Edith Lukyn of Sunbury-on-Thames. He died from injuries received in a flying accident on 10 April 1917, at the age of twenty-two. He had been awarded the Military Cross in early 1916 for courage and initiative in the reconnaissance of enemy wire and trenches prior to a raid. Buried: New Sunbury Cemetery, Middlesex.

Macfarlane, Harold Embleton

Second Lieutenant, 55th Squadron Royal Flying Corps, and General List. An air offensive had begun on 11 July 1917 in order to gain air supremacy over an area of the German front line back to the enemy observation-balloon line, a depth of about 5 miles on the entire front from the Lys to the coast. He was killed in action on 14 July 1917, aged eighteen. On this day, ninety-three targets were dealt with by aeroplane observation. He was born at Harrow on the Hill on 11 September 1890, the eldest son of Harold (who died, on 14 December 1919, from pneumonia at the age of fifty) and Elizabeth McFarlane (died 17 October 1939) of 'Baysgarth', 21 Eastbury Road, Northwood. Harold's father had been an active worker at Emmanuel church, and chief inspector of the special constabulary in the district. His parents came to live in Northwood when he was six months old and he was educated at The Briary, Northwood, and afterwards at Mr J. Douglas Gould's Preparatory School, The Briary, Westgate-on-Sea. In September 1911 he was transferred to Westminster School, where he played football, cricket and fives for his house and had taken part in the drill competition of the OTC. His friends called him 'Peter'. On leaving school at the end of the summer term of 1916 he joined the Army and received his commission in February 1917 and his 'wings' in May. He went to France in June 1917. He is commemorated on the Emmanuel church, Northwood, and Northwood war memorials. Buried: Longuenesse (St Omer) Souvenir Cemetery, Pas de Calais, France, C.55.

Maddox, John Anslow

Lieutenant, 15th Royal Warwickshire Regiment. Killed in action on 4 June 1916, aged nineteen. He had previously been reported as missing. Eldest son of Sir Henry Maddox, K.C., and Lady Maddox of Wytheford, Sandy Lodge, Northwood. He was educated at University College School where he was in the cricket XI 1912-1914. He had been captain in his final year. He had joined the Artists' Rifles before obtaining a commission in the Warwickshire Regiment. He is not commemorated locally. Buried: Faubourg D'Amiens Cemetery, Arras, Pas de Calais, France, D.29.

Maidlow, John

Born in London on 26 June 1875. Major 49th Battery Royal Field Artillery. On his first day in France, 23 August 1914, he was riding forward to take up a new position for his guns when he was shot in the head on the opening day of the Battle of Mons, aged thirty-nine. He was taken to hospital near Mons without gaining consciousness, and died there. The hospital was afterwards set on fire by a shell but his remains were recovered and buried in the grounds of Mr C. Gendebien, near Mons. Although the British had held their ground all day, the collapse of the Fifth French Army and its forced retirement, on the very next day, 24 August, the great retreat from Mons commenced. Son of John Mott Maidlow, Barrister-at-Law; husband of Amy Maidlow of the Corner Cottage, Eastcote, Middlesex, whom he had married in November 1897. They had a son. He had been educated at St Paul's School and Woolwich and joined the Royal Artillery and 2nd Lieutenant in June 1895 and served in Egypt and India. He is not commemorated locally. Buried: Mons (Bergen) Communal Cemetery, A.1A, Belgium.

Main, Percy Rowland

2nd Lieut., Hampshire Regt, attd. RFC, Northolt Aerodrome. Killed while flying on 23 September 1916. Son of Charles and Edith Main of Harrow, Portsdown Avenue, Cosham, Hampshire. He was twenty-four years old. Buried: Portsmouth (Kingston) Cemetery, Hampshire.

Mansell, William

Born at Tunbridge Wells, enlisted at Harrow before the end of June 1915, of Northwood. G/1480, Private, 7th Royal West Kent Regiment. The 18th Division had rested after being in action at Cherisy and on 3 July 1917 the regiment, who had been out of the line for most of June training at Coigneux, entrained at Doullens for Dickebusch where William was killed in action in a ghastly effort to capture the Passchendaele Ridge on 23 July 1917 at the Third Battle of Ypres (or Passchendaele). He had served from the commencement of the war, two years of which he spent in France, crossing from Southampton to Le Havre on 25 or 26 July 1915 in pouring rain. For nine years he had lived in Northwood, at the home of Mrs Prince of Giffard Villas, Hallowell Road. Mrs Prince had already lost one of her sons on 9 April 1917. William had previously been employed for Mr Jones, fishmonger, of Church Road and also Mr Rickards, a Northwood cab proprietor. He is commemorated on the Emmanuel church, Northwood, and Northwood war memorials. Commemorated: Ypres (Menin Gate) memorial, Ypres, West Vlaanderen, Belgium.

Marrian, Arthur Wilfred

Born at Birmingham, lived at Snaefell, 7, Roy Road, enlisted at Woldingham on 30 June 1915 when he was twenty-nine years old, as 2496, Private, 16th Middlesex Regiment. He served with the BEF in France from 17 November 1915 and was wounded by gunshot in the right leg on 1 July 1916, on the first day of the Battle of the Somme, at White City, near Beaumont Hamel, which resulted in a compound fracture of the tibia. He was operated on in France in the 16th general hospital at Rouen and was admitted to Northamptonshire War Hospital on 16 July 1916. His leg became shorter by ½ inch and it was recommended that he be discharged. He was discharged at Hounslow as being physically unfit on 19 June 1917 and died of pneumonia following influenza in October 1918, aged thirty-two. Son of Mr and Mrs William Edward Marrian of Chudleigh, Sandy Lodge Road, Northwood. He had been a scenic artist. He is not commemorated locally and it is not known where he is buried.

Marshall, William Edward Isley

Lieut., RAF. Accidentally killed while flying at Northolt on 26 June 1918. Whilst flying at 1,500ft his plane nosedived. He was a Liverpool man and had just returned from the Italian front. Son of Charles and Harriet Marshall of 19, Rockfield Road, Liverpool. Buried: Liverpool (Anfield) Cemetery.

Marston, George

Born at Watford in about 1878, enlisted at Northwood in July 1915, of 2 Cromer Terrace, Hallowell Road, Northwood. 83107, Private, 1st Sub-section, 139th (129th) Coy, Northamptonshire Regiment, Labour Corps. Formerly 32864 Middlesex Regiment. Killed instantly in action on 28 February 1918. For ten years before the war he was employed by Mr Henry Ainslie Redford of Linkside, Northwood. He is commemorated on the Emmanuel church, Northwood, and Northwood war memorials. Buried: Duhallows Advanced Dressing Station Cemetery, Ypres, Belgium.

Martin, Douglas Francis De Renzy

Captain, 1st Northumberland Fusiliers. In February 1917 the 3rd Division had moved up from the Somme to Arras. Earlier the enemy had withdrawn voluntarily to the newly prepared Hindenburg Line, stretching from the high ground immediately east of Arras, to Vailly on the Aisne. The Allied plan was for the British opposite Arras to break the northern hinge and the French 69th Division (151st 162nd and 267th regiments of infantry), 42nd Division (94th and 332nd infantry regiments and 8th and 16th battalions of chasseurs) and the French 165th Division comprising the 154th, 155th and 287th regiments of infantry northwards across the Aisne in the region of Berry-au-Bac to Juvincourt to outflank the German line. Douglas was killed in action near Gueumappe at the First Battle of the Scarpe on 13 April 1917, aged nineteen. The battle had begun on 9th April and the 9th Brigade had taken all their objectives and was due to be relieved on the night 13–14 April. However, before this could take place the 3rd Division became involved in fighting at Guemappe, where they were exposed to devastating flanking fire from Wancourt Tower, the hamlet itself and from the high ground to the south. The enemy was seen to be firing in the open across the valley. The 1st Northumberland Fusiliers suffered severely. He was the son of Sir A.R. Martin and Lady Martin of Alton, Hampshire. He is commemorated in Holy Trinity church, Northwood. Commemorated: Arras memorial, Pas de Calais, France.

May, Wilfred John, MC

Born at South Hackney. He had enlisted as Private, 1427 in the 15th London Regiment (Civil Service Rifles) and received a commission on 26 February 1917 as Second-Lieutenant, 2nd West Yorkshire Regiment (Prince of Wales's Own). He died of wounds on 1 August 1917, aged twenty-two. He had been wounded at the battle of Pilckem on the previous day. Most of July 1917 the 23rd Brigade had spent out of the line training, and on 23rd of that month moved up to Ypres. In the last week of July the West Yorkshires carried out a successful raid and afterwards retaliatory barrages cost the troops dear. He had been awarded the Military Cross for patrol work around Hendecourt during operations in the Arras sector in April 1917. Son of John Alchin May and Clara Elizabeth May, of 14 Roy Road, Northwood. He does not appear to be commemorated locally. Buried: Lijssenthoek Military Cemetery, Belgium.

Mclachlan, Berry, MC

Lieutenant RFA attd. 'C' Battery, 4th Brigade Royal Horse Artillery. He died of wounds probably received in the fighting around Le Cateau on 11 October 1918, aged twenty-eight. Awarded the Military Cross (supplement to *The London Gazette*, 6 April 1918) for conspicuous gallantry and devotion to duty in extracting two men from a dug-out which had been struck by a gas shell; he did not even pause to adjust his gas mask. He then went to do duty as forwarding observation officer and later that day had to go to hospital suffering from the effects of gas. The only son of Mrs Mary McLachlan of Arreton, Sandy Lodge Way, Northwood. He is not commemorated locally. Buried: Honnechy British Cemetery, Nord, France, C.17.

Mclarty, John

Northolt Aerodrome. Possibly Flight Sub-Lieut., John McLarty, RNAS. Accidentally killed on 24 August 1915 in a flying accident when the plane dived into the sea from 2,000ft and was completely wrecked in Southampton Water; he was twenty-three. Buried: Greenock Cemetery, Renfrewshire.

Messenger, Henry Herbert

G/10492, Lance Corporal, 4th Middlesex Regiment. Born at Teddington on 5 October 1882 and baptised at St Mary, Teddington, on 26 November 1882, son of James Arthur, a boatbuilder, and Eliza Jane Messenger of South Teddington. He enlisted at Northwood, and lived at The Lodge, The Close, Rickmansworth Road, Northwood. He died of wounds, probably in the 44th casualty clearing station at Nine Elms, on 29 March 1918, at the age of thirty-six. He may have been wounded on 8 March when the enemy heavily bombarded the 4th Middlesex trenches. On 21 March the Battalion held trenches north of Ypres. Husband of Kate Messenger of 221 High Street, Hampton Hill, Middlesex. He is commemorated on the Northwood war memorial. He buried at Nine Elms British Cemetery, Poperinghe, Belgium.

Michon, Albert Edward Roy

Born at Walthamstow, enlisted in London, lived at Leytonstone, Essex. Sergeant, 99172. 2nd/6th Durham Light Infantry. Formerly 11485, West Yorkshire Regiment. The 2/6th Durham Light Infantry had been a Garrison Battalion stationed at Frinton. On 10 May 1918, after embarking for Calais four days earlier, they were placed in the 177th Brigade (59th Division) at Hestrus. They were at first employed on the construction of rear defences, taking part in its first attack on 30 September 1918. Albert was later killed in action in the Advance to Victory, the last great concerted movement of the war, on 4 November 1918, aged twenty-four. He was the son of George Frederick and Annie Michon of Carbis, Glenalla Road, Ruislip, but he is not commemorated locally. Buried: Obigies Communal Cemetery, Belgium.

Milton, George Arthur

Born Harefield, on 9 August 1886 and baptised at St Mary's church, Harefield, twenty days later enlisted at Melbourne on 30 September 1914. 4445 (originally 1165, 1169 given in error), Private, 'D' Coy, 8th Battalion Australian Infantry, AIF. He was a machine gunner. He embarked at Melbourne on the *Themistocles* on 22 December 1914 but had to return to Australia to reattest as his papers had gone missing. He reembarked at Melbourne on RMS *Malwa* on 23 April 1916. He may have joined the 8th Battalion from another regiment when in Egypt. Died of wounds on 26 (or 28) October 1917 at the 2nd Australian field ambulance, aged thirty-one (or thirty-two). As the regiment was advancing, he was badly crushed when a shell knocked some boards on him in a machine-gun dug-out at about 7 a.m. near the lines at Passchendaele. He was conscious, complaining about pain in his arm and back. He was taken to the 2nd Australian field ambulance and died about two days later. He had probably been wounded on 26 October – as the rain poured down as heavily as ever – in a renewed advance and died on the latter date. He was the third son of Joshua and the late Sarah Ann Milton (who had passed away on 27 March 1909) of Laurel Cottage, 93 Church Road, Northwood, but was formerly of Harefield, where he was educated. One of his older brothers, Robert Frederick Milton, died from a fall from a ladder on 18 August 1900, aged twenty. George was a bricklayer, as was his father, and had served his apprenticeship with Messrs Gardener and Winch. In 1909, aged twenty-four, he went to Australia to do similar work. He joined up soon after the outbreak of war and while training in Egypt he was taken seriously ill and sent back to Australia. On recovery he went back to France. He is commemorated on the Emmanuel church, Northwood, Northwood, and Harefield war memorials. Buried: Bedford House Cemetery Enclosure No. 2, Ypres, West-Vlaanderen, Belgium.

Molyneux, G.

Northolt Aerodrome. Possibly 2nd Lieutenant RAF who died on 11 May 1918 and who is buried at Belfast.

It was reported in the local paper that a MOLYNEUX was flying over Ickenham Marsh in late July 1916 or early August 1916 'when his machine turned over in the evening and "he fell to the ground". When local people unstrapped him from the machine he was found to be dead. It is believed he is buried at Northampton.'

Molyneux, S.
Northolt Aerodrome. No more details are known.

Murch, James Charles
Born at Eastcote and baptised at St Martin's on 2 January 1859, son of Mary Bishop Murch, a single woman. He had been a groom when he enlisted as a Private in the 18th Hussars (2049), in London, on 5 November 1877. He was nineteen when he enlisted, and he lived in Hampstead. He was appointed Lance Corporal on 18 November 1878, promoted to Corporal on 13 October 1879 and to Sergeant on 8 January 1881. He was demoted to Private for making a false statement on 13 April 1881, reappointed to Lance Corporal on 10 December 1884, promoted to Corporal on 22 October 1885 and appointed Lance Sergeant on 2 January 1888. 28188, Sergeant, 11th Reserve Regiment of Cavalry. He was discharged as medically unfit, suffering from arterio sclerosis, in late January 1917, and died on 8 February 1917, aged fifty-eight. He does not appear to be commemorated locally. Husband of the late Jane Maria Murch, whom he had married at St Michael's, Islington, on 24 February 1889, and father of Ivy Isobel (who had been born in February 1904). Buried: St Pancras Cemetery, Middlesex.

Murphy, Vincent Patrick
Born on 3 March 1894. Captain, 25th Battalion, Canadian Infantry (Nova Scotia Regt) and RFC, Northolt Aerodrome. While carrying out a solo flight at Ruislip, the plane he was flying crashed into a field, killing him, on 12 March 1918. He was twenty-four. Vincent was the son of John S. and Charlotte Mary Murphy of New Ross, Nova Scotia. He had been a theatre manager and had also been in the Canadian Navy for two years. Buried: Brookwood Military Cemetery, Surrey.

Newland, Henry John
Second Lieutenant, 8th East Surrey Regiment. At the end of January 1917 and for the first ten days of February, the regiment was employed in tramway and light railway construction in the Thiepval area and the Ancre Valley line. On the evening of 11 February they moved back to their old position in Fabeck Trench, 1 mile east of Thiepval. On 16 February 1917, the first day of a thaw which turned the ground at first into one big slide and then into mud, the battalion moved to Warwick Huts in reserve. On the 18th they moved to Grandcourt Trench in Boom Ravine. It was decided to carry out the relief in daylight as the weather was misty. On the morning of 17 February, the troops were ordered to be in position at 4.45 a.m. – one hour earlier than the start of the battle. The relieving Surreys had been instructed to take over 200 yards more ground on the left of the Suffolks, but nobody knew where the Suffolk HQs were, although they had last been reported to be in Grandcourt Trench. While passing up the Ravine Valley, Henry was killed in action on 18 February 1917, at the age of twenty (though some reports say twenty-nine). The son of Henry and Emily Ann Newland of The Larches, Pinner Road, Northwood, he is commemorated on the Northwood war memorial and on Holy Trinity church memorial, Northwood. Buried: Regina Trench Cemetery, Somme, France.

Nichol, William Alexander

Born on 18 November 1888 and baptised at St Luke's, Chelsea, on 3 March 1889. He was a school teacher, the son of Emily and William Nichol of Ruislip. William was killed in Belgium on 23 June 1917. He was twenty-eight. He does not appear to be commemorated locally.

Probably William Alexander Nichol, Private 2645, 35th Btn, Australian Infantry, AIF, who enlisted on 3 October 1916 and died on 23 June 1917, after being wounded on a fatigue party while salvaging. At about 10.30 a.m. he had just passed a dressing station when he was hit by a shrapnel bullet which went through his mouth, choking him, and came out at the back of his neck. He was at Messines Ridge. Aged twenty-eight at the time of his death, he was a school teacher, the son of the late William and Emily; his wife was Maude Grace Nichol of Graman, New South Wales. He was a 'native of England'. He was buried near the 3rd divisional advanced dressing station, about 1 mile from Ploegsteert Village, and later re-interred in Kandahar Farm Cemetery, Heuvelland, West-Vlaanderen, Belgium.

Nightingale, Frederick

Born at Field End, Eastcote, enlisted in Harrow in September 1914, of Pinner. 3788, Private, 8th Royal Fusiliers. Frederick's father died in mid-1921 after one day's illness, aged seventy-nine. He had been born at Mount Pleasant in a house which stood on the garden of the house in which he passed away. Here he carried on the business as a hay dealer. He had travelled the district a good deal – but had never seen the sea. On 5 July 1916, the 8th RF took over a sector of the line in the village of La Boiselle, which had been captured the previous day. At 8.30 a.m. of 7 July, they participated in – and were aided by the 20th and 35th French Army Corps and one of the 'colonial' regiments – in an attack on Ovillers, then held by the 180th Regiment of Wurtembergers. They attacked from the west, also assaulting the trenches to the right across the Pozieres Road, where he was reported as missing, believed killed in action at Ovillers on that date. He was aged thirty-two. His regiment had hitherto been in reserve. While forming up in the assembly areas, a heavy barrage had caused great losses. Immediately 'D' Coy, forming the front line of the 8th Royal Fusiliers, left our trenches, it came under heavy machine-gun fire from Mash Valley. They were momentarily overwhelmed but the advance from the second and third lines carried on. The advance was frightful. Heavy weather had held down the fumes of poison shells and the craters in which the men took refuge were often found to be traps from which some never emerged again. Still the thin lines went forward. Machine guns were active on either flank of them and on their immediate front lay the rubbish heap, once a village. Amongst the ruins lay the Fusiliers of the Prussian Guard – reputed to be among the best soldiers in Europe. Bombing attacks and hand-to-hand fighting had taken place all day long. Son of James and Jane Nightingale of Field End Cottages, Eastcote. He also served in Gallipoli with the 7th Battalion and had been wounded twice times. In all he had been wounded four times. He is commemorated on the Eastcote, St Lawrence's church, Eastcote, St Martin's church, Ruislip, and Ruislip war memorials. Commemorated: Thiepval memorial, Somme, France.

Novikov, Andre Matveer

A Russian subject attached to the 35 Squadron, RFC, and a cadet stationed at Northolt Aerodrome. On 22 September 1917, while approaching Northolt Aerodrome in the day, his plane nosedived and crashed. Twenty-four-year-old Novikov was a capable pilot but he was unable to escape and burned to death. He was given the rites of the Orthodox Church. The cortege had come from Northolt Aerodrome and he was buried in Southall-Norwood Cemetery.

O'Halloran, Sylvester North East

Born in Ceylon on 6 or 7 December 1868, of Lansdowne House, Dene Road, Northwood. Captain 2nd Essex Regiment (56th Foot). He had served in the South African War, after which he became a bank clerk and volunteered for service on the outbreak of war in 1914. He obtained a commission as Lieutenant in the 9th Essex Regiment on 23 December 1914 and served with the Expeditionary Force from July 1915; acted as Adjutant to the 4th Infantry Base Depot at Rouen and went to the front line in September 1915. He was killed in action on 9 August 1917 by a bomb while leading his men at Monchy-le-Preux, near Arras, while serving as acting Captain. He was the son of Christopher O'Halloran. He had married Annie Eliza Pattinson at St Peter's church, Belsize Park, on 6 February 1904 and had two children. He is commemorated on the Northwood war memorial. Commemorated: Arras memorial, Pas de Calais, France.

Palmer, Arthur Bailey Bentinck ('Jimmie')

Born at Ealing and lived at 62 Twyford Avenue, Ealing. Lieutenant, R.A.F., 35th Training Depot Squadron and Middlesex Regiment, formerly Artists Rifles. Killed in an 'aeroplane accident' at Thetford on 23 August 1918, aged almost twenty-eight. Buried: Hanwell Cemetery.

Palmer, George

Born at Newbury, Berks., enlisted at Northwood, of Northwood. 225055, Private, 1st London Regiment (Royal Fusiliers), posted 12th Battalion. Formerly 2774 West Kent Yeomanry. Killed in action on 22 June 1917, aged thirty-three, and buried near where he fell. His body was later moved to its final resting place after the war. The husband of Elizabeth Ethel Palmer of 275 New Road, Croxley Green, Watford, he is commemorated on the Northwood war memorial. Buried: Poelcapelle British Cemetery, Langemark-Poelkapelle, Belgium.

Parker, Arthur

He is commemorated on Northwood war memorial and on Holy Trinity church memorial, Northwood. It is known he was a Private when he died. There is also an Arthur Parker commemorated on the Cowley war memorial as 'connected with the parish', who enlisted in the army before the end of 1915.

Two A. Parkers and one A.G. Parker from Ruislip/Northwood had enlisted in the early days of the war. Possibly Arthur Parker, who was born and lived at Rickmansworth and who enlisted in Harrow. He was a Private, 8072, in the 14th London Regiment (London Scottish), formerly 1176, 9th Middlesex Regiment. He died of wounds on 25 August 1916 and is buried in Aubigny Communal Cemetery, Pas de Calais, France.

Parker, Henry Tommy

Born at Harrow, enlisted in London. 194, Corporal, 10th Royal Fusiliers. Killed in action near Gavrelle on the first day of the Second Battle of the Scarpe, 23 April 1917, aged twenty-seven. The advance began at 4.45 a.m., at first light. The 111th Brigade at first advanced with a slight loss of men, but when they reached Cuba Trench, about 1,000 yards from the start, they came under a heavy enfilade of machine-gun fire and could make no further progress. He was the son of Mr and Mrs Parker of East Finchley; husband of Dora Parker of 'Sandy Hook', Northwood. He does not appear to be commemorated locally. Buried: Hervin Farm British Cemetery, St Laurent-Blagny, Pas de Calais, France, B.15.

Parker, T.W.

He had been a postman at Northwood.

Parkinson, James Frederick

Air Mechanic 1st Class, F/27459. HMS *President*, Royal Naval Air Service. He died at Hendon from pneumonia following influenza on Sunday, 24 November 1918, aged thirty-four. The husband of E. Mildred Parkinson of 42 Chester Road, Northwood, he does not appear to be commemorated locally. Buried/commemorated: Golders Green Crematorium.

Partington, Leigh B.

Born at Marylebone on 27 February 1895 and baptised at St John the Baptist, Walworth, on 1 March of the same year, son of Henry Leigh and Mary Partington, lived at Northwood. He was educated at University College School where he was in the OTC, and had served a two-year apprenticeship in the traffic department of the Great Northern Railway, after which he became a clerk with them. On 5 August 1915, he enlisted as Private 1527, 1/28th London Regiment (Artists Rifles), later becoming Lance Corporal and later Captain, 1st Northumberland Fusiliers on 12 June 1915. In the autumn of 1917 the 3rd Division had taken part in the Third Battle of Ypres (also known as Passchendaele). By March 1918 they had returned to the Arras sector and were holding the sector from Guemappe to Croisilles. He died on 28 March 1918. He may have been wounded in the fighting in the days previous in the German Offensive of 1918. He had been awarded the Croix de Guerre in Belgium and was also mentioned in Haig's dispatches. He is commemorated in Holy Trinity church, Northwood. Son of Henry Leigh Partington of Heron Deene, Hallowell Road, Northwood. Commemorated: Arras memorial, Pas de Calais, France.

Pengelly, Harold

Harold was born at Uxbridge or Harefield police station, although the latter is probably more correct, in 1892, and enlisted at Kingston on 25 April 1908 while still underage (although with the consent of his father). He had been a butcher's errand boy. He had lived at 2 York Road, Uxbridge, and latterly 37 Northcote Avenue, Southall. Private 9707, 1st East Surrey Regiment. On 9 September he was wounded, and on 12 September 1914 he was admitted to No. 3 stationary hospital, slightly wounded by shrapnel in the chest and head and with a broken leg and smashed knee-cap. He was transferred to a convalescent depot on 17

September. The case became complicated and he 'got rapidly worse' and was transferred to No. 13 stationary hospital at Boulogne – where, on 6 November 1914, he died at 9.45 a.m., aged twenty-two or twenty-three. Only son of Samuel M. Pengelly, formerly Warrant Officer at Uxbridge Police Court and Mary Ann Pengelley of Northolt, Ruislip, formerly of 2 York Road, Uxbridge. He had served with the Expeditionary Force in France. He does not appear to be commemorated locally. Buried: Boulogne Eastern Cemetery, Pas de Calais.

Penn-Gaskell, Leslie Da Costa

Major and Squadron-Commander RFC and Norfolk Regiment. On 31 January 1916 warning came through for aeroplanes to go up during a raid, weather permitting. Major Penn-Gaskell, the Squadron Commander, was in charge of the training squadron at Northolt, and set off in a BE2c, a two-seater tractor biplane, to investigate conditions before allowing others to take off on such a foggy night to intercept the Zeppelins attacking the Midlands. In a very heavy ground mist he took of at a quarter to seven but he hit an elm tree on the west side of Northolt airfield. He was seriously injured and died on 4 February 1916 at the Royal Flying Corps Hospital, 37 Dorset Square, London, aged thirty-four. He was the son of Miriam and Alexander Barclay Penn-Gaskell. Mentioned in dispatches. Buried: St Martin's churchyard, Ruislip.

Perry, Evelyn Walter Copland

Of Northwood. Lieutenant, Royal Flying Corps (Special Reserve). Killed instantly, with his pilot, on 16 August 1914 when his machine stalled and caught fire on leaving Amiens. He was educated at St David's (Mr Joyce's), Reigate, Repton and Trinity College, Cambridge and on leaving worked from February 1911 to August 1912 at the Royal Aircraft Factory. In August 1911 he had obtained his flying certificate. He joined the military wing of the Royal Flying Corps in about mid-1913, gazetted 2nd Lieutenant. Only child of his widowed mother, the second wife of Walter Copland Perry, who was the sister of Colonel Horace Robert Stopford of the Coldstream Guards; Stopford had been appointed a Lieutenant in 1874, Captain in 1885 and Major in 1893, but was hit in the neck and fell, gloriously, at the head of his men at Modder River on 28 November 1899 during the Boer War, having never previously been on war service. His father was the late Mr Walter Copland Perry of 25, Manchester Square, London, and father of Colonel Ottley Perry of Northwood. Lieutenant Perry is not commemorated locally. Buried: St Acheul French National Cemetery, Amiens, France.

Philbey, Ernest

Born at New Beckton, North Woolwich, enlisted at Stratford, of Fairholme, Church Road, Northwood. 3/929, Acting-Corporal, 2nd Essex Regiment. He was killed in action on Monday, 24 May 1915 at the battle of Bellewaarde Ridge in the Ypres Salient. The attack on that day had begun before dawn and at 2.45 a.m. a violent bombardment of gas shells was opened against our lines which ran from Wieltje, north-east of Ypres, to Hooge, on the Menin road, followed by a terrific barrage of artillery fire, shrapnel and high explosives, the largest yet experienced. He is not commemorated locally. Buried: New Irish Farm Cemetery, Ypres, Belgium.

Pickersgill-Cunliffe, John Reynolds

Born on 16 May 1895. Of Northwood. 2nd Lieutenant, Grenadier Guards. On Monday, 14 September 1914, the 2nd Grenadier Guards formed the advance-guard of the 8th Brigade, followed by the 3rd Coldstream Guards, Irish Guards and 2nd Coldstream Guards. After they had cleared Soupir village, the force was heavily shelled as they pushed on. Near La Cour-de-Soupir he was wounded in very heavy shelling and machine-gun fire as they ran into numerous enemy forces. While he lay wounded, he was shot dead by a German officer. He was nineteen years old. John had been educated at Evelyns and Eton and had been gazetted 2nd Lieutenant, Grenadier Guards, on 17 September 1913. He was an only son. He is not commemorated locally. Buried: Soupir Communal Cemetery, France.

Polhill, Robert, Mm

Born at Hastings, enlisted at Marylebone before the end of June 1915, of Northwood (or Littlestone-on-Sea). 20151, Lance-Corporal, 6th Dorsetshire Regiment, formerly M/2894, 7th DSC, Royal Army Service Corps. On 20 August 1918, General Mangin had pushed forward the 10th French Army, attacking along a 16-mile front from the Oise to the Aisne, thus connecting up the original operations with those initiated by Marshall Haig. Into the fray came various British regiments, with the 17th Division in support. Several days later, the 6th Dorsets, in spite of gas clouds and machine guns, crossed the Ancre in its narrowest reach, where some sort of bridges had been prepared, cleared up some front trenches near Thiepval but were driven back by an attack from the Schwaben Redoubt. Pushing on, they captured what they thought was Courcelette but which turned out to be Pozieres. About two days later he was killed in action in capturing Flers in the successful attack on Thiepval, Courcelette and the Stuff Redoubt on 27 August 1918. Since about 20 August they had taken turns in the front line in the Hebuterne sector. He was awarded the Military Medal (supplement to the *London Gazette*, 21 October 1918). He does not appear to be commemorated locally. Buried: Bulls Road Cemetery, Somme, France.

Pollock, James Mcgillveray

Born in Gibraltar, enlisted at Stirling, Stirlingshire. S/15113, Private, 6th Cameron Highlanders. In early February 1918, the 15th (Scottish) Division moved back to the Arras front. On 8th the northern boundary of the sector was extended as far as the Lagoon, immediately south of the Scarpe. The front line was then reorganised, the move being complete by 9 March 1918, the 45th Brigade in the Centre (Monchy) Section, where he was killed in action on 9 March 1918, aged twenty. On the day he was killed there had been a terrific and successful attack on the Armentieres front. James was the son of Mary Pollock of Eversholt, Eastcote, and the late Sergeant James Pollock (1st Battalion Cameron Highlanders). He is not commemorated locally. Buried: Monchy British Cemetery, Pas de Calais, C.18, France.

Pond, W.G.

He had been a postman at Northwood.

Ponton, Thomas

Born in Dundee, enlisted at Hendon. 41356, Private, 'B' Battery, VIII Platoon, 2nd Northamptonshire Regiment. Formerly Private, 4478 (T. L.) Essex Regiment. On 21 March 1918 the Germans had made a colossal thrust on the Somme and on 9 April had made another at the Lys and were planning a third desperate attempt at this very point, which was not strongly held. During the first fortnight of May 1918, the 2nd Northants were put into the line near Rheims where they held a front of about 15 miles. They were there on 27 May when the Germans launched a large attack on the thinly held Aisne front and he was reported as missing in action on that date, aged thirty-seven, on the first day of the Battle of the Aisne 1918 (also known as the Third Battle of the Aisne). Five British divisions had been sent to the supposedly quiet Chemin des Dames sector for a rest after terrific fighting on the Somme, but at 1 a.m. on that morning the Germans commenced a heavy bombardment of gas shells, high explosives and trench mortars. For four hours this continued. Both the front and support lines from Craonne to Berry-au-Bac were deluged with shells from upwards of 1,000 guns and at 4 a.m. German infantry also began to attack from Crecy-au-Mont to Berry-au-Bac and at 5 a.m., south of the Aisne. Thomas was the son of Mrs Ponton of 12 King Street, Dundee; husband of N.M. Cordell (formerly Ponton) of Cemetery Lodge, Northwood. He had married Nellie Green of Northwood at Holy Trinity church on 20 March 1915. His profession was listed as 'conductor' and his address given as Shepherd's Bush. He is not commemorated locally. Commemorated: Soissons memorial, Aisne, France.

Poole, Leslie Stanley Richard

Born at Walthamstow, he was the son of Richard Frank and Florence Poole of Killowen, Ducks Hill Road, Northwood. Lieutenant, 1st Balloon Wing, Royal Air Force. He had joined the Artists Rifles as 5868 and served with them for three and a half years and gazetted to the RFC 5 September 1916. He died of pneumonia on 22 November 1918 or 3 December 1918, aged thirty-two. He is not commemorated locally. It is thought that the address applied to another location the other side of London. Buried: Douai British Cemetery, Nord, France, C.30.

Popplewell, Harry Bury

Born in 1886. Captain, 3rd Royal Irish Rifles, and attached to the 3/3rd King's African Rifles, which at the beginning of the 1916 campaign in East Africa was the only native regiment. He was the younger son of the late Frank Popplewell, architect of Manchester, and of Mrs Lucy Popplewell of Haytor, Northwood. He was educated at Manchester Grammar School, Lurgan College, Ireland, and Lincoln College, Oxford, where he took a second-class in 'the Greats' in 1910. On leaving he was granted a commission in the Special Reserve Battalion of the Royal Irish Rifles but was seconded for civilian service in British East Africa and was appointed in 1910 as Assistant District Commissioner in that colony. He was retained in his administrative work in East Africa in the early years of the war but obtained leave to join up in 1917 and was attached to the King's African Rifles. He had twice been invalided back to Nairobi when finally he joined his battalion. On 20 July 1918 FITZCOL (3/3rd King's African Rifles and 4/4 KAR) reached the Namirrue stream at a ford about 25 miles west of the Portuguese boma (fort) at Namirrue. When the march was resumed on the following day, heavy fire was heard from the direction of Namirrue. The advance carried on all day along narrow tracks through dense bush. After a few hours' rest the column marched again before dawn on 22 and at 11 a.m. found themselves near a rocky ford near Namirrue. With the 3/3rd leading, FITZCOL crossed again to the left bank of the river and got astride the Alto Ligonha-Namirrue road. The 3/3rd African Rifles began to move forward across a succession of ridges running at right angles to a river, at about 4 p.m., with little darkness left. Within half an hour they had driven in the enemy's outposts and by 5 p.m., were heavily engaged. Good progress followed and when darkness fell, they were ordered to form a camp and dig in, but at 7 p.m. the Germans suddenly counter-attacked from the direction of the river. The 3/3rd had not yet completed the right face of the perimeter and within minutes the enemy was inside the camp. A desperate action followed. He was killed in action at Namirrue on 22 July 1918, aged thirty-one. He is not commemorated locally. Buried: Lumbo British Cemetery, Mozambique.

Powell, Thomas Henry Norman
Born at Warrnambool, Victoria. He embarked on HMAT *Wiltshire* at Melbourne on 19 October 1914 as Private, 2nd field ambulance. 2nd Lieut. RFC, Northolt Aerodrome. Formerly 255, S/Sgt, 1st Div., HQ, AIF. Died of accidental injuries on 24 April 1917 when his machine fell at Yeading and burst into flames, just before 8 o'clock in the evening. He was twenty-two years old. He was the son of Samuel James and Sarah Jane Powell of 23, Blair St, Coburg, Victoria, Australia. Buried: Brookwood Military Cemetery, Surrey.

Price, A.P.
Northolt Aerodrome. Possibly A.P. Price Sergeant, 2267 School of Aeronautics (Reading), RFC, who died on 25 January 1917, aged twenty-six. Son of George Price of 40 Mather Street, Failsworth, Lancashire. Buried: Failsworth Cemetery.

Price, J.W.
Of Northwood. It is known he was serving as a Private when he died.

Prince, Cecil Robert
Born at Northwood where he was baptised at Holy Trinity church on 11 July 1875, son of William and Elizabeth Prince, and lived at 5 Manor Cottages, Northwood with Annie Cox as his (common-law) wife, where he enlisted on 28 April 1915. He had been a scaffolder and had previously served with the Royal Scots. 22728, Sergeant, 'D' Coy, 2nd Royal Scots (Lothian Regiment). For a very short time he served with the 8th East Yorks, reverting back to the 2nd Royal Scots. Cecil was killed in action near Montauban at the battle of Bazentin Ridge on 16 July 1916, probably in the taking of Ovillers, which paved the way for an assault on Pozieres. He was aged forty-one. At 12.25 a.m. the assault battalions quietly filed up from Caterpillar Wood in No-Man's Land and at 2 a.m. they started to creep slowly forward. By 1 p.m. their objective was secure to a depth of 200 yards, but for 1½ hours prior to securing their objective a grim battle was fought below ground level. There had been a heavy bombardment on both sides all along the line. He was the son of the late William and Elizabeth Prince, and the husband of Mary Annie Prince of 5 Manor Cottages, Northwood. Her brother, Private Thomas Cox, 2nd Bucks Battalion, was killed in France; her cousin, Private Thomas Cox of the same battalion, was also killed. Cecil had

served in the South African campaign and is commemorated on the Holy Trinity church, Northwood, and Northwood war memorials. The family of a C. Prince received financial assistance from the Soldiers' and Sailors' Families Association. Commemorated: Thiepval memorial, Somme, France.

Prince, John W.

He is commemorated in Holy Trinity church, Northwood. A John Prince lived at Giffard Villas, Hallowell Road.

Prince, Percy Robert

Born at Northwood on 7 January 1897, where he was baptised at Holy Trinity church in March 1897, enlisted in London, lived at Northwood. 472916, Rifleman (Private), London Regiment 12th (City of London) Battalion, (The Rangers). Formerly 2991, 9th Middlesex Regiment. By 30 March, the British Army was north of Amiens. On 9 April they were assigned the capture of Neuville-Vitasse and the strong works which surrounded it. He was killed in action near Neuville-Vitasse on 9 April 1917 in the 'big push at Arras'. This was the first day of the Battle of Arras, Easter Monday 1917, fought on a front of 15 miles from Croisilles to the northern foot of the Vimy Ridge and included between 4 and 5 miles of the Hindenburg Line. At 7.45 a.m. the 56th Division moved to the assault. The 12th Londoners, after going through their first lines, met some uncut wire and a very heavy belt of fire which delayed them until around 10 a.m. and three further attempts were made, each impeded by the deep mud. Percy was the son of John and Rose Prince of Giffard Villas, Hallowell Road. He is commemorated on the Emmanuel church, Northwood, and Northwood war memorials. Buried: London Cemetery, Neuville-Vitasse, Pas de Calais, France.

Puddefoot, Ernest James

Born on 28 March 1894 and baptised at Holy Trinity church on 6 May 1894, the son of Henry and Annie Puddefoot. Able Seaman, 146875, Royal Navy, HM Submarine K4. Presumed drowned after the collision of his submarine in the North Sea on 31 January 1918, aged twenty-three. Son of Mr and Mrs Puddefoot of 50 Holywell Road, Watford; husband of Rose Puddefoot, née Bowden, of 2, St Mary's Villas, Church Road, Northwood, whom he had married at Emmanuel church on 10 April 1916. She also lost two of her brothers, William and John (*see* pp. 107–8). Ernest had been in the Navy since leaving school at Northwood and had been on HMS *Vanguard* for four and a half years when he volunteered for submarine service. The 'K4' was cut in half by her sister ship 'K6' and then run over by the 'K7' during exercises. All the crew was lost. He is commemorated on the Emmanuel church, Northwood, and Northwood war memorials. Commemorated: Chatham memorial, Kent.

Puddefoot, Reginald Henry, DCM

Born at Northwood in June 1896 and baptised at Holy Trinity church on 2 August that same year, son of Henry James and Anne Puddefoot, enlisted at Bedford. 51600, Sergeant, 'A' Battery, 11 Platoon, 1st Lincolnshire Regiment. Formerly 10055, Bedfordshire

Outside the War Office, London, crowds turned out to see the first captured enemy gun, a Krupp. It was captured by the Regiment of Reginald Henry Puddefoot, DCM, the 1st Battalion Lincolnshire Regiment.

Regiment. He was killed in action in Flanders on 6 April 1918 (or 16 April 1918). The Red Cross Enquiry List of Wounded and Missing records him as missing on 16 April 1918 after an engagement at Wytschaete where, as defenders in the front line, faced by the greater part of two divisions (49th Reserve and 17th Reserve), they were eventually overwhelmed by superior numbers. In about August 1917 he was awarded DCM while serving as a Sergeant with the Bedfordshire Regiment in 'leading his platoon to its objective through a stiff fight in spite of the fact that he was shot through the thigh while topping the parapet. He continued to do excellent work until he was wounded for the second time'. Husband of Mrs L. Puddefoot. He is commemorated in Holy Trinity church, Northwood. Commemorated: Tyne Cot memorial, Zonnebeke, West Vlaanderen, Belgium.

Puddifoot, Walter, MM
Born at Northwood where he was baptised at Holy Trinity church on 11 May 1884, and enlisted at Northwood, of Northwood. 3835, Corporal, 52nd Machine Gun Corps (Infantry). Formerly 10859 Middlesex Regiment. He was killed in action on 10 November 1917, in the resumed Battle of Passchendaele Ridge, during a short narrow thrust along the crest of Passchendaele hills towards Westroosebeek, aged thirty-three. The battle for Passchendaele and the Third Battle of Ypres was over. He was awarded the Military Medal. The son of Henry and Sarah of Carew Terrace, Church Road, Northwood; husband of Annie Ada Greenaway (formerly Puddifoot) of 86 Church Road, Northwood. He is commemorated on the Emmanuel church, Northwood, and Northwood war memorials. Buried: Solferino Farm Cemetery, Ypres, West Vlaanderen, Belgium.

Rackstraw, Joseph
Born at High Wycombe, enlisted at Richmond, Yorkshire. 3/8402, Corporal, 6th Yorkshire Regiment. They had sailed from Liverpool on 3 July 1915, going via Mudros to Suvla

Bay, disembarking on 6 August 1915. The plan of the attack at Suvla Bay provided that the first landing should be made by three brigades of the 11th (Northern) Division; they then concentrated at the island of Lemnos. They left in destroyers and motor lighters after dark on 6 August 1915 and disembarked at 10.30 p.m., one hour after the Anzacs had been timed to rush 'Old No. 3 Post'. The 32nd Brigade landed at Beach B, about 1.5 miles away from Lala Baba and just over 2 miles from Old No. 3 Post. Although farthest away, they were the first in action. Marching through the darkness along the coast from Beach B they found their way unswervingly to Lala Baba and dashed up the height with fixed bayonets, carrying it swiftly before pushing on along the sandy causeway to support the 34th Brigade which was in difficulties before Hill 10. It was here in Gallipoli, on 22 August 1915, that he was killed in action, aged forty-five. Son of the late Frederick and Joyce Rackstraw of High Wycombe; husband of Annie Elizabeth Rackstraw of 15, High Street, Northwood. The brother of Mrs Rackstraw, Alfred George Harris, was also killed in action. Joseph is commemorated in Emmanuel church, Northwood. Commemorated: Helles memorial, Turkey.

Rayson, John Langdon

Born Godalming, enlisted at Camden Town as a Private on 15 September 1914, of 87, Mayford Road, Balham. He had been appointed Lance Corporal on 25 September 1915, Lance Sergeant on 14 April 1916 and Sergeant on 11 May 1916. 3116, Sergeant, 1st/19th London Regiment. He was killed in action in capturing High Wood at the Battle of Flers-Courcelette in the fight for High Wood, when faced with the desperate resistance of the 2nd Bavarian Corps, on 15 September 1916, aged thirty-one. They had been held

Non-Commissioned officers of the 9th London Regiment (Queen Victoria's Rifles).

up by very heavy rifle and machine-gun fire and immediately afterwards were taken out of the line. This was the first day of the Battle of Ancre and also the first day of the third and final stage of operations on the Somme. The advance, which began at 6.20 a.m., was greatly helped by the tanks which had been brought into action for the very first time. Son of Annie Rayson of 80 Dene Road, Northwood, and the late John Woodgate Rayson, who had died on 9 April 1915, aged sixty-nine. Sergeant Rayson is commemorated on the Northwood war memorial and on Holy Trinity church memorial, Northwood. Commemorated: Thiepval memorial, Somme, France.

Richards, Frederick William

Born at Northwood where he was baptised at Holy Trinity church on 1 March 1896, enlisted at Shepherd's Bush, lived at Greenford. 498, Private, 22nd Royal Fusiliers. The 2nd Division had been brought down to the Somme battlefield where, on 16 July 1916, they took over from the 3rd Division in the area of Delville Wood. At 7 a.m. on the following morning Kellett's 99th Brigade (which included the 22nd Royal Fusiliers and was attached to the 2nd Division) was ordered to improve our position in the wood and make a determined advance, with the 22nd Royal Fusiliers in support. Frederick was killed in action somewhere in the 196 acre Delville Wood on 27 July 1916, aged twenty. Enemy rifle fire on that date was considerable but inaccurate, and from the vicinity of Longueval village the enemy was firing with machine guns for a time once the wood had been captured and Germans infantry began counter-attacks. Son of Mr F. William and Mrs Alice Louisa Richards of 2, London Road, Greenford. He is commemorated on Greenford war memorial but not on the Ruislip memorial. His brother, Martin, was killed in action while in reserve during Guillemont operations on 15 August 1916, aged nineteen. There is an F. W. Richards who is commemorated on the GWR memorial: he had worked at Old Oak Common. Buried: Delville Wood Cemetery, Longueval, Somme, France.

Richardson, M.

He is commemorated on Emmanuel church, Northwood, and Northwood war memorials. He was a Private serving with the Middlesex Regiment.

Rodgman, Arthur George Banfield

Sergeant, 9940 Pilot, RFC, Northolt Aerodrome. He was killed while flying at Wolvercote, near Oxford, on 20 August 1917, aged twenty-two. He was at a height of about 100ft when smoke was seen issuing from the aeroplane. The machine fell to the ground, blazing furiously. He had flown from Northolt and was on his return journey when the accident happened. He was the son of George and Elizabeth Rodgman of 33 Baker Street, Heavitree, Exeter. Buried: Exeter Higher Cemetery, Devon.

Rolfe, William Caleb

Born on 16 January 1897 and baptised at Ruislip on 3 April 1898, the son of Caleb and Elizabeth Rolfe. CH/18843, Private, 'C' Coy, XII Platoon, 2nd RM Battalion, Royal Marine Light Infantry. He had enlisted on 26 August 1914 and embarked with the Royal Marine Brigade on 20 November 1914. He was serving with the Deal Battalion

Mediterranean Expeditionary Force when, on 3rd July 1915, he was wounded in the face by shrapnel in an engagement in the Dardanelles. He rejoined his battalion on 3 August 1915 until 9 November 1916, when he went to the Lewis Gun School at Étaples. Ten days later he rejoined the 1st Royal Marine Battalion. Reported missing, presumed killed, at the battle of Arleux at Gavrelle, during the Arras offensive – one of the deadliest of all battles for infantryman – on 28 April 1917, aged nineteen. He was the son of the late Caleb and Elizabeth Smith (formerly Rolfe) and stepson of W. Smith of 96 Hallowell Road, Northwood. He had been a fishmonger's assistant. The family of a W.C. Rolf received financial assistance from the Soldiers' and Sailors' Families Associations (Uxbridge Division) in the first year or so of the war – and maybe later. He is commemorated on the Emmanuel church, Northwood, and Northwood war memorials. Commemorated: Arras memorial, Pas de Calais, France.

Rose, Alfred Daniel

Born at Ruislip, enlisted at Uxbridge in early September 1914, and lived at Brentford. 8208, Private, 9th Royal Fusiliers. The 12th Division, which had seen much hard fighting at Loos in September 1915, had, by 5 July 1916, taken over part of the trenches of the 8th Division. They found themselves facing Ovillers, defended by the 180th Wurtembergers of the 26th Reserve Division. On the afternoon of 6 July 1916, the 36th Brigade had taken over the trenches near the Sunken Road. The following morning an attack took place on Ovillers, during the Battle of the Somme. Despite terrible casualties on the preceding days, the 9th Royal Fusiliers were very keen to get on with the task and gave up all but twelve hours of their rest. At 3 a.m. on 7 July, the 35th and 37th Brigades carried out an attack on Ovillers and the trenches to the right across the Pozieres Road. The 36th Brigade (which included the 9th Fusiliers) was in reserve. To the north of La Boiselle there was a group of enemy machine guns which were so deadly that the assaulting battalions, after a hard struggle, fell back on the British line. The assault was later renewed, the fresh troops attacking at 8 a.m. in the morning of 7 July, approaching Ovillers to attack from the south and overrun the machine guns. Meanwhile, at 8.30, the 36th Brigade planned to advance on Ovillers from the west. It was hoped that with half an hour's difference in starting off times, the fresh troops would destroy the machine guns before the 36th Brigade got there. The machine guns, however, were still active, and immediately in front of the 36th Brigade lay a mass of ruins, once a village. Before the 36th Brigade had even sprung to the parapet they were beaten to pieces by a terrible enemy barrage of shells and lost 225 men. The left of the 36th Brigade had been kept on the south side of the Leiptiz spur to avoid, as much as possible, the machine-gun fire from the Leipzig salient. As they crossed No Man's Land, bullets beat upon them from every side. Men took shelter in shell-holes filled with the fumes of poison gas shells, and perished there. A blast of fire greeted them as they went into the second trench. Only 500 men were left, but these 500 still went forward and gained their first and second objectives. Sometime on this day, Private Rose was killed in action. He is commemorated on Northwood war memorial. Commemorated: Thiepval memorial, Somme, France.

Rostern, Joseph Norman

Born at Prestwich, near Manchester. Lieutenant, 2nd/7th Manchester Regiment. On 21 March 1918 the 66th Lancashire Territorial Division (with the 24th Division) covered a front from south of Ronssoy to south of Maisemy. The Lancashire Division, which had behaved so splendidly in the mud battle of Broodseinde, had all three brigades in the front, covering 4,000 yards and was exposed all day to a most terrific assault. By the end of the day the whole forward zone was in the hands of the enemy. This action was the Battle of St Quentin which lasted until 23 March. From that date until about dusk on 25 March, the 66th Division suffered very heavily in guarding the crossings along the Peronne sector with only about 1,500 rifles. They had fought continuously from dawn on 21 March until the night of 30-31 March and its casualties were perhaps the heaviest of any. They were so short of officers that its depleted companies were improvised small teams. Nevertheless they carried on stoically, and somehow contrived to make counter-strokes on the afternoon of 30 March. Joseph was reported missing at Peronne, but officially reported as killed in action or died of wounds on (or just after) 28 March 1918, aged twenty-three. Between 21 March and 5 April 1918, the 66th Division had lost thirty-two officers killed, 130 wounded and 178 missing. Of the other ranks, 341 had been killed, 1,254 were wounded and 5,088 were missing – a total of 7,023 men.

Joseph was the younger son of Joseph Rostern, CBE, chief goods manager with the Great Central Railway, and Clara Rostern of Prestwych, Dene Road, Northwood. He had been educated at Aldenham School, Elstree, Hertfordshire. He had enlisted in September 1915 in the King's Own Loyal Lancashire Regiment. In January 1916 he was given a commission in the Manchester Regiment and went to France in March 1917. He is commemorated on the Northwood war memorial and on Holy Trinity church memorial, Northwood, where there is a memorial window in his memory. Buried: Peronne Communal Cemetery Extension, Ste Radegonde, Somme, France, P.27.

Rufey, William

Born at Donnington, Berks., enlisted at Mill Hill in June 1916 in the 5th Middlesex Regiment, of 5, Kathleen Villas, Hallowell Road, Northwood. He had been transferred a number of times into other Middlesex regiments, but at the time of his death was serving as G/22776, Private, 13th Middlesex Regiment. He was killed in action near Messines while acting as a stretcher-bearer on 10 June 1917, aged thirty-five. Both sides had been shelling each other heavily at intervals all day. William was the son of E. and E. Rufey of Donnington, Newbury, Berks., and husband of Edith Rufey, of 132 Hallowell Road, Northwood. He was sent home in January 1917 suffering with trench foot and spent some time in Cork Hospital. He had been employed as a gardener by Mr C. Cooper of Maxwell Road; before that he was gardener at Denham Court. He left a widow and two young children. He is commemorated on the Emmanuel church, Northwood, and Northwood war memorials. Commemorated: Ypres (Menin Gate) memorial, Ypres, West Vlaanderen, Belgium.

Maxwell Road, Northwood. (Courtesy of Hillingdon Local Studies, Archives and Museum Service)

Sampson, Archibald Frank

Born at Ruislip, enlisted at Chelmsford, and lived at Braintree. 12159, Lance-Corporal, 'A' Coy, 11th Battalion attd. Prisoner of War Coy, Essex Regiment. He died of wounds in hospital on 14 April 1918, aged twenty-seven. He had at first been wounded and unofficially reported as missing on 21 March 1918, where the prisoners and guns captured by the Germans in this (and in the attack on 27 May) exceeded the highest record of the Allies in any of their great offensives. We had been overpowered by an enemy who outnumbered the defenders by three to one. He was probably a POW. Archibald was the son of Thomas and Elizabeth Lavinia Sampson of Thelma House, Rayne Road, Braintree, Essex. He does not appear to be commemorated locally. Buried: Soignies (Zinnik) Communal Cemetery, Soignies, Hainaut, Belgium.

Sankey, Cecil Martin, MC

Lieut., The Buffs., attd RAF, Northolt Aerodrome. He was accidentally killed near Northolt on 15 May 1918 while flying. Cecil was the only son of Mr and Mrs Sankey of 7, Tring Avenue, Ealing. He obtained a commission in September 1914 in the 2nd County of London Regiment (Queen Victoria's Rifles) and promoted to Lieutenant on 10 July 1915. He had been awarded the Military Cross for conspicuous gallantry and devotion to duty – leading his men in a most successful attack on the enemy at Loos. He was transferred to the RAF in December 1917 and had only qualified as a pilot two weeks before his death. Buried: Westminster Cemetery, Hanwell.

Sayer, G.

All that is positively known is that he was of Northwood and was a 'Gunner' in the 'RFA' who was dead before June 1915. He is not commemorated locally.

Possibly George Alfred Sayers, 49120, Gunner, RFA, The Chestnut Troop 'A' Battery RHA). He was born at Brighton and died on 15 February 1915, aged twenty-five. He was the son of Henry and Emma Sayers of Brighton. Buried: Royal Irish Rifles Graveyard, Laventie, Pas de Calais, France

Schilling, Ernest Harold

Born in London, son of Ernest Francis and Rose Schilling who lived at The Ferns, Roy Road, Northwood. He is commemorated on the Emmanuel church, Northwood, and Northwood war memorials. He was a banker's clerk and enlisted at Bury St Edmunds on 6 June 1916 in the Suffolk Yeomanry. He qualified as a 1st Class Instructor in Musketry at Bisley on 21 December 1917 and was posted to the 1/10th Royal Scots as Sergeant Instructor, 62497. After the war ended he was retained for service in the Armies of Occupation and sent to Curragh for further training. He died at Ballinrobe Hospital of pneumonia following from influenza on 20 February 1919, aged twenty-one. Buried: Ballinrobe (St Mary) church of Ireland churchyard, County Mayo, Republic of Ireland.

Selby, A.

He had been a postman at Northwood.

Shambrook, Charles William

Born at Uxbridge, enlisted at Croydon, and lived at Ivor Villa, Merstham, Surrey. SE/88, Private, Royal Army Veterinary Corps. He was a farrier. Charles died of pneumonia at the Red Cross Hospital, Great Western Road, Gloucester, on 14 January 1917, at the age of thirty-two or thirty-five. Son of the late James Harding Shambrook; husband of Marion Marshall Shambrook of 18 Grange Road, Alresford, Hants, whom he had married at St Martin's, Ruislip, on 11 December 1905. Both were 'of this parish'. He is not commemorated locally. Buried: St Martin's churchyard, Ruislip.

Simons, Archibald ('Archie')

Born at Naunton (maybe a mistake for Launton), enlisted Northwood, of Northwood. G/6012, Private, 2nd Middlesex Regiment. The 8th Division had fought with the 70th Brigade of the 23rd Division with distinction on 1 July 1916; although the attack failed, it was repeated at dawn on 29 September with success. For a time the fighting died down and on 22 October 1916 the regiment moved up into trenches south-east of Flers. On 23 October 1916 an attack was launched at 2.30 p.m. against the salient, west of Le Transloy, formed by the Zenith and Eclipse Trenches. For the 23rd Brigade, with Zenith as its objective, the attack went well, and the advanced troops even reached Orion Trench. Other brigades did not far so well so the 23rd Brigade with no support on the flank was compelled to fall back on Orion and Zenith Trenches. On 24 October, the 2nd Middlesex held Zenith in part, but Archie was killed in action on this day, aged twenty. He was the son

Elm Avenue, Ruislip, looking towards Eastcote. (Courtesy of Hillingdon Local Studies, Archives and Museum Service)

of Mr and Mrs Charles Simons of Station Road, Launton, Bicester. He is commemorated on the Northwood war memorial. Buried: AIF Burial Ground, Flers, Somme, France.

Simpson, N.J.

Born at Newport, Fife. 25979, Private, 11th Cameronians (Scottish Rifles). In November 1915 two British divisions left France for service in Salonika, where malaria, heat-stroke and dysentery took a heavy toll. During the first summer, over 3,000 malaria-stricken troops were admitted to the casualty clearing stations in one day from two divisions on the Struma front. They were later joined by other troops of the 26th Division. He died on 19 September 1918, aged thirty-eight. The 29th general hospital at Doiran was there by November 1916, although more hospitals may have been put up later. He was the youngest son of William Simpson of The Homestead, Elm Avenue, Eastcote, and the late Isabella Simpson, late of Duneaves, Wormit, Fife. He does not appear to be commemorated on any local memorial. Buried: Doiran Military Cemetery, Greece, B.32.

Skey, Henry

Born at Aylesbury, enlisted in London, of Ruislip. 98489, Bombardier 'A' Bty, 54th Brigade RFA. He was the youngest son of Mr Arthur Skey, of Fernleigh, West End Road, Ruislip, stationmaster at Ruislip Metropolitan station. Henry drowned at Alexandria on

23 September 1915, aged twenty-one. Before joining the Army he was secretary of the local branch of the CEMS (Church of England Men's Society). He is commemorated on the St Martin's church, Ruislip, and Ruislip war memorials. Commemorated: Jerusalem memorial, Israel.

Small, Frederick John (John Fredrick?)

Born at Ruislip or Reading (which is more likely to be correct), enlisted at Harrow in June 1916, and of Ruislip. He rented one furnished room on the first floor of his parent's home at Little Manor Farm for the sum of 10s per week. G/23326, Private, 'D' Coy, 11th Middlesex Regiment. At the beginning of January 1917, information reached the divisions that a British offensive would be carried out in the spring of that year. On 14 January the 12th Division, which included the 11th Middlesex, took over a sector of 2,000 yards, extending from 700 yards south of Faubourg St Sauveur to the River Scarpe. Although preparations had been taken in hand for the forthcoming offensive, there was much to do. As command of No Man's Land was very important, frequent raids were carried out. It may have been in one of these raids that Private Small was killed in action on 3 March 1917, aged thirty-two. He was the only son of Francis James Small and Elizabeth Small of Little Manor Farm Dairy, Ruislip, later of Orchard House, Galmington, Taunton, Somerset. Before joining up, Private Small was manager of the farm and did the milk round until called up for service. He is commemorated on the Ruislip Common, Ruislip and St Martin's church, Ruislip war memorials. Buried: Faubourg D'Amiens Cemetery, Arras, Pas de Calais, France.

Smalley, Horace Edward

Enlisted at Woolwich, Kent, of Northwood. G/17865, Lance-Corporal, 1st Middlesex Regiment. Died of wounds in France on 1 May 1917, probably in one of the CCSs at Warlincourt (20th or 43rd), aged twenty-eight. He may have been wounded in the battle at Arras at the Second Battle of the Scarpe, which opened on 23 April 1917, when the 1st Middlesex attacked the enemy east of Monchy, capturing Guemappe and Gavrelle. It was a day of heavy fighting with comparatively very limited gains. Near the Sensee River the 33rd Division's forward position had exposed the whole left flank and its advanced units cut off. With the first light of morning two battalions from the 19th Brigade pushed forward to clear up the situation and found some 1st Middlesex men who had spent some fifteen hours in the heart of the German's advance – in their shell holes were found a group of some twenty or more prisoners. Altogether on 23rd/24th April the 33rd Division took 750 prisoners from the German 61st Division. On 24th they were relieved. Horace was the son of Henry and Annie Smalley; husband of Eva Constance Smalley of 91 Church Road, Northwood. He is commemorated on the Emmanuel church, Northwood, and Northwood war memorials. Buried: Warlincourt Halte British Cemetery, Saulty, Pas de Calais, France, G.2.

Smirnov, George Vladimivoctah

A Russian Cadet who was a pupil at Northolt. Died of syncope in Southall Auxiliary Military Hospital on 4 May 1917. He was under instruction in Captain Waines' machine

Batchworth Heath. (Courtesy of Hillingdon Local Studies, Archives and Museum Service)

which crashed from about 200ft early in the morning of 4 May. Captain Waine died instantly, but it was only later that it was discovered that Cadet Smirnov was still in the machine. He arrived at the hospital at about 9 a.m., unconscious, suffering from fractured thighs. He was buried at Southall.

Smith, Charles

Born at Cloberly, Gloucs., resided at Northwood. 41674, Private, 8th Lincolnshire Regiment. Formerly 184881, Royal Army Service Corps. Died of wounds on 10 August 1917, aged thirty-two. He had been a POW in German-occupied Ghent. He may have been wounded and/or taken prisoner in the action on 31 July 1917 at Ypres. Charles was the husband of Mrs M.E. Smith of 1 Batchworth Heath, Rickmansworth. He is commemorated in Holy Trinity church, Northwood. Buried: Ghent City Cemetery, Ghent, Oost-Vlaanderen, Belgium.

Smith, Duncan Vaughan, DSO

Of Kewferry Lodge, Kewferry Road, Northwood. Lieutenant Colonel, Duncan Vaughan Smith, DSO, 1st Royal Fusiliers. Vast preparations were in hand for an attack at Arras, including the construction of a huge dressing-station with 700 beds, for an assault extending from the neighbourhood of Lens in the north to Arras in the south, a front of more than 12 miles. Roughly 120,000 men were in the storming line with 40,000 advancing behind them. The Germans had six divisions, the 11th Prussian, 14th Bavarian, 1st Bavarian Reserve, and the 17th, 18th and 79th reserve in line. By 9 April all was in order for the assault, and at 5.30 a.m. the word was given. Duncan was wounded on 9 April and died in hospital at Rouen on 13 April 1917 of wounds 'received at the Battle of Arras' on 9 April, aged thirty-eight. The point of the Vimy Ridge, near Givenchy-en-Gohelle marked the northernmost limit of the First Army's attack on 9 April 2 miles to the south and on the far side of the Carency River; Angres, Lievan and Cite St Pierre were all successfully taken. He was the son of Mr and Mrs Frederick Smith of 2 Clarence Terrace, Regent's Park, London, and husband of Nora E.B. Smith of Kewferry Lodge, Northwood. He is commemorated on Northwood war memorial and on Holy Trinity church memorial, Northwood. Buried: St Sever Cemetery, Rouen, Seine-Maritime, France.

Stanescu, Peter John

2nd Air Mechanic, 58732, RFC, Northolt Aerodrome. He had accompanied Captain Harold Hamber on his last tragic flight. Stanescu was killed outright when the plane crashed at Cherry Lane, Harlington on 22 June 1917. His neck was broken. Buried: Hayes and Harlington (Harlington) Burial Ground.

Stanley, Horace

Born at Bethnal Green, enlisted at Mill Hill, of Northwood. G/11476, Private, 'C' Coy, 21st Middlesex Regiment. Died of pneumonia on 19 October 1918, aged twenty-three, probably as a prisoner of war. He was the son of Mrs E. Stanley of 2 Ivy Cottages, Church Road, Northwood. He is commemorated on the Emmanuel church, Northwood, and Northwood war memorials. Buried: Berlin South-Western Cemetery, Germany.

Stent, Arthur

Born and lived at Ruislip, enlisted at Northwood. 265269, Private, 2/5th Lincolnshire Regiment. At noon on 21 March 1918, the 2/5th Sherwood Foresters, greatly reduced in strength, were still clinging on near the south-west corner of Noreuil. The 2/5th Lincolnshires were sent up from divisional reserve in support, having a march of about 4 miles to reach its objective. At about 12.30 p.m. runners reported that they had seen the leading parties of the 2/5th Lincs in a trench 500 yards behind Noreuil. German aeroplanes soon afterwards began bombing around Mory and along the Bapaume-Vaulx road, causing a delay and much confusion. The 2/5th Lincs moved by successive platoons along the ridge north of the Hirondelle Valley. After passing through the rear defences of the battle zone they came under fire from machine guns and rifles. Heavy casualties brought the rapid advance to a sudden stop and after further efforts to hold their ground, they were driven back, eventually taking cover in a switch trench running southwards from Noreuil. The remnants were soon surrounded and overpowered. Sometime on this day, 21 March 1918, Arthur was killed in action. The prisoners and guns captured by the Germans in this (and in the attack on 27 May) exceeded the highest record of the Allies in any of their great offensives. We had been overpowered by an enemy who outnumbered the defenders by three to one. He was the husband of Mrs Elsie Maud Stent of Reservoir Road, Ruislip Common, daughter of Mr and Mrs J. Lavender of Ruislip Common. They had married at St Martin's church on 19 October 1912. In June 1930 or 1931, Elsie married Ralph Bysh at Northwood Primitive Methodist church. Arthur had worked for Mr Beer, of Northwood, being the chief plumber (as well as house carpenter and decorator of Hallowell Road) in the district and when war broke out was 'connected' to the special constabulary. He is commemorated on the Ruislip Common, St Martin's church, Ruislip, and Ruislip war memorials. Commemorated: Arras memorial, Pas de Calais, France.

Stevens, Robert Gray

Born at Cove, Dumbartonshire on 28 March 1896, he lived at Eildon, Hallowell Road, Northwood. He had been in the employ of the London & North Western Railway Company as a clerk at Euston station and joined the RNVR in February 1914. He was called up at the beginning of the war and went with the Royal Naval Division to Antwerp and afterwards to Egypt. He served with the Drake Battalion RNVR from 22 August 1914 and had taken part in the landing at Gallipoli on 25 April 1915. He was wounded by gunshot in his right upper arm in the following 6 June, when still a Private, and invalided to Malta and Alexandria. On recovery he rejoined his regiment but in October 1915 was invalided home to England suffering from dysentery and admitted to the London Homeopathic Hospital. He was drafted for the BEF as a Stokes Gunner, and served with the Expeditionary Force in France and Flanders from July 1916 and took part in operations on the Somme and Ancre. On 10 July 1916 he joined the Howe Battalion, at some time becoming London 8/3137, Leading Seaman, Howe Btn, Royal Navy Volunteer Reserve. He was injured in the abdomen and thigh by a trench mortar and died at the 149th (RN) field ambulance on 13 September 1917, and buried in the British Military Cemetery at Gavrelle. His body was later moved. He is commemorated on the Emmanuel church, Northwood, and Northwood war memorials. He had played for Northwood Cricket Club and was also a member of the Ruislip Rifle Club. He was the son of Elizabeth M. Stevens and the late Robert Stevens of Glasgow. Buried: Point-du-Jour Military Cemetery, Athies, Pas de Calais, France.

Strong, Thomas William

Born in Scotland. Second Lieutenant, 4th South Staffordshire Regiment. Accidentally killed on 26 (or 28) May 1918, during the Battle of the Chemin-des-Dames, aged twenty-five. On 9 May 1918, the 25th Division, which had recently been in the fighting both in Flanders and on the Somme since the start of the great German offensive, entrained at Rexpoede and other small sidings near Poperinghe for their long 30-hour journey to the district near Fismes. Around the middle of the month, reports came in from escaped French prisoners that immense dumps of ammunition had formed behind the German front, telephone cable and field guns dug in – the Germans were preparing for an attack. Meanwhile a (25th) Divisional School had been opened at Coulognes where classes of instruction in musketry, Lewis Guns, and trench mortars took place. It may well have been here that he met with his accident. On the afternoon of 26 May definite information was received that the enemy intended to deliver an attack the following morning and in the evening Germans were seen pouring down to their front lines. On 19 May the enemy had moved fourteen divisions from Amiens to the neighbourhood; by 26 May these enemy troops have received reinforcements – a total of forty-two divisions on a front of 75 kilometers, in particular thirty divisions on a front of 45 kilometers corresponding to the Chemin-des-Dames. At 9.15 p.m. the same evening all brigades moved up in close support and by daybreak, the 7th, 74th and 75th Brigades had reached Guyencourt, Muscourt and Venteley respectively, between 2 and 3 miles south of the Aisne. At 1 a.m. on 27 May, the first day of the Battle of the Aisne, the Germans commenced a heavy bombardment of gas shells of every description and of high explosives. The 25th Division, which was in Corps reserve near Fismes, was instructed to hold the second line of defense south of the Aisne along the heights of the Maizy-Cormicy Road, thence bending back south-east to Trigny – a line of about 12 miles. By 10 a.m., the 4th South Staffs were holding a line from Cormicy to Bouffignereux. By mid-afternoon, they had become almost surrounded and forced to retire. On the morning of 28th, the 4th South Staffs (part of the 7th Brigade) were found all along the high ground east of Prouilly. It has been difficult to establish how Tom met his end: although the 4th South Staffs were part of the 25th Division at that time, there is no record of his death amongst those mentioned as killed in the Divisional diary. He was the (twin) son and only surviving child of Frederick and Jemima Strong of High Grove Lodge, Eastcote. A younger brother, Fred, died on 25 October 1911, at the age of fourteen.

Tom enlisted in the Coldstream Guards at Uxbridge in September 1914 as a Private and had been twice wounded, once in early October 1915 at Loos (when he was wounded in the left hand by a German bomb) and again in September 1916 when he was hospitalised at Bristol. He was later recommended for a commission, maybe joining the 4th South Staffs when it was raised sometime in 1917, joining the 25th Division from England in October 1917. Prior to enlisting he had worked for the *Advertiser* where he had been employed since leaving school; he had been a frequent writer to the paper. Commemorated on the Eastcote, St Lawrence's church, Eastcote, St Martin's church, Ruislip, and Ruislip war memorials. Buried: Marfaux British Cemetery, Marne, A.2, France.

Suthers, Robert Eric

Enlisted at Mill Hill. 79019, Private, 'A' Coy, IV Platoon, 1st/4th Northumberland Fusiliers. Died on 2 August 1918, aged nineteen. He was buried in a small cemetery and reburied after the Armistice where he now sleeps in eternal rest. He had previously been unofficially reported as missing near Berry-au-Bac at the Battle of the Chemin-des-Dames on 27 May 1918 – the renewal of the German offensive on the Aisne. Between 21 March 1918 and 20 April that same year, fresh British drafts totalling almost 20,000 men had been sent to France, including, as a result of the emergency, youths under the age of nineteen years. Robert was the son of Robert Bentley Suthers and Alice Elizabeth Suthers of 60 Manor Way, Ruislip. He is not commemorated locally. Buried/commemorated: Chauny Communal Cemetery, Aisne, France, special memorial 'E'. No. 22.

Taylor, James

Born Crosshill, Glasgow on 31 May 1890. Second Lieutenant, 9th (Service) Battalion, Black Watch. Killed in action in attacks on Passchendaele and Broodseinde at the Battle of the Ridges at Frezenberg on 31 July 1917, aged twenty-seven. On this day, the great Ypres offensive known as 'the Third Battle of Ypres' was opened on a front of 15 miles from La Basse Ville, on the River Lys to Steenstraate on the Yser Canal, the main object being an arc of small hills in front of the British valley positions around Ypres. Twelve divisions advanced on an 11-mile front in pouring rain. The 44th Brigade of the 15th (Scottish) Division was one of the two brigades which led the advance. Verlorenhoek had fallen to the Scottish troops of the 15th Division (which included the 9th Black Watch) who later that day were engaged in stiff fighting round Frezenberg before it (and its defences) fell to the British. They had that day succeeded in exploiting their initial successes and had managed to advance to their Green Line objectives approaching the low London Ridge. He had joined the 7th Battalion the Scottish Rifles in January 1911 and was mobilised on 4 August 1914. He went with his regiment to Egypt in February 1915 and then to Gallipoli in that June. He was invalided home with frostbitten feet and discharged from the Army as physically unfit in February 1916. The following June he reenlisted in the Argyle and Sutherland Highlanders and in October 1916 was gazetted 2nd Lieutenant 3rd (Reserve) Battalion, Black Watch. He returned to France in April 1917 and was transferred to the 9th Battalion of the same regiment.

He was the son of John Taylor of Glasgow, formerly of Widcombe, Northwood; husband of Effie Proctor Wright (formerly Taylor, née Nance), of Kelvin, Gate End, Northwood. He does not appear to be commemorated locally. Commemorated: Ypres (Menin Gate) memorial, Ypres, West Vlaanderen, Belgium.

Taylor, James Wood Colin

Born at Rickmansworth. Lieutenant, attd. 2nd Battalion Sherwood Foresters (Notts and Derby Regiment). He joined the 2nd Battalion HAC, as Private 1863, in September 1914 and in December obtained a commission in the 3rd Sherwood Foresters. In July 1915 he was sent abroad, attached to the 2nd Battalion serving at the front. The 6th Division had been in trenches near Wieltje and Pitijze and was brought out to relieve the luckless 14th Division on 6 August 1915. He was killed in action in an attack on the trenches at Hooge on 9 August 1915, aged twenty-eight. From 9.30 a.m. until 8.30 p.m., when they were withdrawn, enemy minenwerfers and artillery fire was incessant. He was the only son of Colin Taylor of Widcombe, Northwood, Middlesex, and the late Annie Elizabeth Taylor. He is commemorated in Holy Trinity church, Northwood. Commemorated: Ypres (Menin Gate) memorial, Ypres, West Vlaanderen, Belgium.

Thackham, George

Born at Croxley Green, son of David and Ellen, enlisted at Watford, lived at Northwood. 4/6640, Private, 2nd Bedfordshire Regiment. Early in May 1915 the British offensive was switched south of Neuve Chapelle to Festubert, north of Givenchy. On 10 May 1915, the 7th Division moved towards Bethune and by the evening the 21st Brigade was established around Le Touret. To delude the enemy as to the exact hour of a planned assault on Aubers Ridge and Festubert, deliberate bombardments were spread over a number of the following days. On 10/11 May they reached their destination in reserve, west of Bethune. On the night of 11 May, the 21st Brigade began relieving the 47th Division on the frontage from which the 7th Division was to attack, running from Prince's Road to the road running north-east from Festubert through La Quinque Rue. The Bedfords, busy trying to prevent the enemy repairing their damaged trenches or mending the gaps in their wire by keeping them under constant rifle and machine-gun fire, were met by a vigorous retaliation. He was killed in action on 11 May 1915 at the battle of Aubers Ridge. He does not appear to be commemorated locally. Buried: Guards Cemetery, Windy Corner, Cuinchy, Pas de Calais, France.

Thompson, Albert

Born at Eastcote and baptised at St Martin's, Ruislip, on 1 November 1896, enlisted at Harrow. L/16028, Lance-Corporal, 11th Middlesex Regiment. On 7 October 1916 an offensive, an infantry attack, planned for the 5th but postponed because of the inclement weather for 48 hours, began. The objectives of the 12th Division, which included the 11th Middx, were Bayonet Trench and then a further advance of 500 yards. This infantry attack on the trench system was carried out by the 41st, 12th, 20th and 50th Divisions, together with the French 150th, 161st, 154th and 155th Infantry Regiments. The attack was at 1.45 p.m., on a front of 25 kilometres, and the troops advanced under a heavy barrage along the whole sodden and slippery front. He was killed in action at the Battle of the Transloy Ridges during heavy shelling on 8 October 1916, aged twenty-one. He was the youngest son of Obed and Frances E. Thompson of Park Cottage, Eastcote; husband of Catherine Oliver Lockey (formerly Thompson, née Pollock) of 'Eversholt', Cuckoo Hill, Eastcote. Brother of Charles, below. An older brother, thirty-two-year-old Edward Charles Thompson, had been accidentally killed at Yiewsley on 16 November 1912 on his very first day of his employment with Messrs Squires' factory. As he was leading a horse out of a shed, the shaft of the cart caught him in the chest as he turned, pinning him against the wall. He died shortly afterwards, at 3 p.m., and is buried at Ruislip. Lance Corporal Thompson's married son, James Edward Thompson, of 7, Wiltshire Lane, Eastcote, who had been educated at Bishopshalt, was serving in the Second World War as a Pilot Officer in the RAFVR, having joined the London Scottish on the outbreak of war, later transferring to the Gordon Highlanders. He then had volunteered for flying duties with the RAF and was killed when his plane crashed at Ragdale Bombing Range, Leicestershire, on 17 July 1944, aged twenty-seven. Lance Cpl Thompson is commemorated on the Eastcote, St Lawrence's church, Eastcote, St Martin's church, Ruislip, and Ruislip war memorials. Buried: Bancourt British Cemetery, Pas de Calais, France.

Thompson, Charles Arthur, DCM

Born at Hillingdon on 29 August 1888 and baptised at St John the Baptist church, Hillingdon, on 30 September 1888, son of Obed, a jobbing gardener, and Francis Emma Thompson. He enlisted in London, of Uxbridge. 252, Sergeant, 1st Battery Machine Gun Corps (Motors). Formerly 2343, Royal Sussex Regiment. Killed instantly in action on 12 April 1918, aged twenty-nine. Awarded

The Distinguished Conduct Medal, awarded to non-commissioned soldiers for acts of personal distinction on the field of battle.

the DCM, probably while serving with the MGC. Son of Mr and Mrs Thompson of Park Cottages, Southill Road, Eastcote; husband of Florrie (or Flora) Emilie Thompson of 25 Austin Waye, Uxbridge, whom he had married at St John the Evangelist church, Uxbridge Moor, on 27 March 1916, and brother of Albert (above). He had worked for Messrs Gurney and Ewer, engineers of Bury Street. Charles is commemorated on St John's, Uxbridge Moor's Roll of Honour and on Ruislip (Manor Farm) war memorial. Commemorated: Pozieres memorial, Somme, France.

Thornhill, Geoffrey Holland

Born at Primrose Hill on 26 October 1888, of Northwood. He was an engineer and had obtained a commission in the 3rd Royal Warwickshire Regiment on 7 August 1914. He served with the Expeditionary Force in France and Flanders and was for a long time in the trenches, where he contracted rheumatism. He had been twice wounded and had suffered concussion after an injury in France in October 1914, resulting in traumatic neuralgia of the head and spine, depression and sleeplessness; he was invalided home in January 1915 with a nervous breakdown. On recovery he took light duties and was transferred to the 2nd (or 12th) (Labour) Battalion, Devonshire Regiment and worked at the Rugby Recruiting Office for some time. He was taken ill and admitted to 3rd southern general hospital, St Peter-in-the-East, Oxford on 7 May 1917; he died at 3.55 a.m. on 10 May 1917 at the Sommerville Section, aged twenty-eight. The cause was pneumonia. At the time of his death, two brothers were still on active service, another had been invalided from France and another was working for the Ministry of Munitions. Sixth son of Mary Elizabeth Thornhill (who died in 1945) of Chase Side, Rickmansworth, formerly of Cranford, Dene Road, Northwood, and the late Edward Baylies Thornhill (who had died prior to 1913). Geoffrey is commemorated on Northwood war memorial. Buried: Rickmansworth Cemetery, Herts.

Tierney, Alfred George

Born at Twickenham on 6 November 1894 and baptised at Holy Trinity church, Twickenham, on 18 September 1895, enlisted at Hounslow, of Northwood. L/9996, Private, 1st Royal West Kent Regiment. On the afternoon of 22 April 1915, the 1st West Kents had moved off to relieve the 15th Brigade near Hill 60. As they approached Vlamertinghe, confusion reigned: every description of vehicle, along with crowds of fugitives, blocked the road. Poison gas was also hanging in the air. The relief was cancelled and they were diverted to a position of readiness in fields just west of Ypres, where they remained all night. Early next morning fresh orders were received and they moved off north-east to a position near Brielen. After a short stay they pushed on, crossing the Ypres-Yser canal north of Ypres. At 2 p.m. the battalion received orders to move off to St Jean. The march was carried out under shell fire but they reached their position in time, at 3 p.m. Private Tierney was killed in action here north of Ypres after going back to rescue a wounded officer on Friday, 23 April 1915 at the Second Battle of Ypres. The Germans had swept the British brigade, front and flank, with machine-gun fire and sprayed it with shrapnel. Wave after wave fell. Third son of Mr Patrick (but known as James) Tierney of 7 Clifton Villas, Church Road, Northwood, later of Ealing and Louisa, his estranged wife (he had left his wife some six years previously). Alfred is commemorated on the Northwood war memorial. Commemorated: Ypres (Menin Gate) memorial, Ypres, West Vlaanderen, Belgium.

Tilley, Alan Herbert

Born on 24 October 1896 and baptised at Holy Trinity church on 16 December 1896. Second Lieutenant 2nd/4th Battalion Oxford and Bucks Light Infantry. On the last day of March 1917 until 10 April a prolonged attack was made by the 184th Brigade at Soyecourt. The Battalion's objective was a line of trenches recently dug by the enemy and running between Le Vergier and the river. In its advance on 7 April, 'A' Company lost men from our own shells, of which nearly all were seen to be falling very short. The German wire was found uncut and men were trying to find a gap. Enemy machine guns were manned, which swept the ground with a fierce enfilade fire. On this day, Alan was wounded in this action near St Quentin and died at Nesle, probably in the 21st casualty clearing station at Nesle, on 10 April 1917, aged twenty. He had at first been reported as missing on 7 April 1917. He was the son of John Wesley Tilley (who died on 18 January 1932) and Louise Annie Tilley (who died on 6 March 1951, aged ninety), of The Knoll, Northwood. His nephew, Roland Kenneth Tilley, who was serving as a Corporal in the RAF, was killed in Singapore during the Second World War. Alan is commemorated on the Northwood war memorial and Holy Trinity church memorial, Northwood. Buried: Nesle Communal Cemetery, Somme, France, B.21.

Tillyard, William

Born and lived at Northwood, enlisted in London before the end of June 1915. 15617, Private (or Lance Corporal), 'D' Coy, XV Platoon, 13th Royal Fusiliers. On 23 April 1917, the 37th Division renewed its attack on a large scale north of the Scarpe. Indeed, on that date there was a renewal of an advance all along the British line, which took for its objectives, counting from the south, Bois du Vert, Bois de Sart, Pelves, Roeux, Gavrelle, Oppy, and Acheville, to name but a few. For several days they were subjected to frequent and heavy bombardments and several times counter-attacked. William was killed in action near Gavrelle on 29 April 1917. The son of Mrs C. H. Hughes of 104 Hallowell Road, Northwood. He is commemorated on the Emmanuel church, Northwood, and Northwood war memorials. Buried: Chili Trench Cemetery, Gavrelle, Pas de Calais, France, D.14.

Tobutt, Charlie

Born at Pinner where he was baptised on 30 July 1893, son of Edward and Charlotte of Canon's Lane, enlisted at Northwood on 20 January 1918, lived at Reginald Road, Northwood. He served in the 6th, 11th and finally as S/12077, Lance-Corporal in the 1st/7th Middlesex Regiment. Throughout March 1918, the 7th Middlesex had been in and out of the line. On 21 March they were holding the Gavrelle sector (as usual). They were relieved that night and moved back into reserve at Roclincourt. At 3 a.m. on 28 March 1918, an intensive bombardment which gradually got heavier and heavier began. At 7 a.m. the 7th Middlesex in Wakefield Camp in reserve received orders to move forward to their assembly positions and at 8.45 a.m. they moved forward to a position near Canticler Junction. By 11 a.m. they were developing their attack. The enemy attacked in great force along the valley of the Scarpe at Arras and a bombardment of great violence with gas and high-explosive shells had swept the British lines. However, the 7th Middlesex had only been heavily shelled once, during which six men were killed. One of them was Lance Corporal Tobutt, who was killed in action at the First Battle of Arras, a week after his twenty-fifth birthday. The same day he was killed, his brother, Private H. Tobutt, was admitted to a hospital wounded. Son of Edward Tobutt of Strathnairn, 50, Reginald Road, Northwood; husband of Daisy Maria Tobutt of 37 Collingwood Road, Clyde Road, Tottenham (whom he had married at Emmanuel church on 25 November 1917). He had attended Pinner Road School and was a postman. He is commemorated on the Emmanuel church, Northwood, and Northwood war memorials. Buried: Maroeuil British Cemetery, Pas de Calais, France, J.9.

Todman, Henry William

He is commemorated on Northwood war memorial.

Probably Henry William Todman, who was born at Graffham, Sussex. Private, L/7465 'A' Coy, 2nd Royal Sussex Regiment. During the night of 8-9 May 1915, the 2nd and 3rd Brigades moved into their assembly positions behind breastworks, previously prepared, in rear of the front line. At 5.30 a.m. the first battalions of both brigades mounted the ladder to go over the top into No Man's Land – which varied in width from 500 yards to 100, intersected by wide ditches full of water – to establish themselves about 80 yards from the German parapet. Unknown to our troops, the Germans had seen every movement. As soon as the leading waves left the shelter of the trenches, heavy machine-gun fire began. Many men fell dead on the ladders and on the parapet. Others managed to move forward into No Man's Land and a general line was formed not far short of the intended one. Ten minutes later, at 5.40 a.m., the leading waves rushed forward towards the German defences. The charge was met by a devastating fire of machine guns and rifles. This attack on the Aubers Ridge had been the more devastating than any German fire to that date. Henry was officially reported as wounded and missing at Richebourg on Sunday, 9 May 1915, in an attack at Rue des Bois with the 9th French Corps, north-west of La Bassee in the direction of Dor (which failed within a few hours). He is commemorated on Le Touret memorial, Pas de Calais, France.

Tripp, Percy William

Born at Northwood in about 1889, son of Lowing and Sarah Tripp, he enlisted in London, but resided at Brighton. B/203566, Rifleman, 1st Rifle Brigade. Formerly Private, R/16796 King's Royal Rifle Corps. Killed in action in the Bouchavesnes sector during a heavy bombardment on 18 February 1917. His father, a nonconformist, had been a blacksmith and lived with his family at Tubb's Farm. He was taken ill and had been ill for some time when he died, suddenly and unexpectedly, on 28 December 1899. Percy is not commemorated locally. Commemorated: Thiepval memorial, Somme, France.

Turner, Albert

Douglas Haig outside the fallen German Headquarters in Cambrai in 1918.

Born in Bucks, enlisted at Harrow, of Eastcote. 48456, Private, 22nd Royal Fusiliers. Killed in action during heavy fighting near Cambrai on 30 December 1917. His regiment had been in furious fighting on 30 November 1917 when suddenly on the crest, looking down on the British lines a few yards off, unlimbered German field guns appeared. It may have been in this fighting (rather than 30 December) that Albert was killed. He was aged thirty-three. He was the son of William and Maria Turner of Spriggs Hollies, Bucks; husband of Henrietta Turner of 32 Solihull Road, Sparkhill, Birmingham. He is commemorated on Eastcote, St Martin's church, Ruislip, and Ruislip war memorials. Buried: Louverval Military Cemetery, Doignes, Nord, France.

Vines, William Samuel Thomas

Born at Pinner and baptised on 1 November 1893 at St Mary's, Harrow. He was a grocer and enlisted at Mill Hill on 10 December 1915, of Eastcote. He was mobilised on 10 February 1916, having spent time in the Army Reserve, and was posted to the 27th Middlesex Regiment, then to the 23rd on 21 March 1916. F/3232, Private, 23rd Middlesex Regiment. He had been eighteen months in France, and had been in action on the Somme, when the 41st Division took Flers. He was wounded in the right leg by gunshot at Messines on 8 June 1917 near the Dammstrasse, beyond which was Ravine Wood with its lurking guns and criss-cross of wire, and died of blood poisoning at 12.10 p.m. 'on the evening of his birthday', 19 June 1917, aged twenty-six. He had been brought to the Military Hospital, Western Heights at Dover, where his leg had to be amputated as gangrene had set in. He succumbed during the operation. His body was brought back to Ruislip on 21 June and he was buried the following day. He was the son of Henry Thomas and Jane Vines of 19 Council Houses, Wiltshire Lane, Eastcote. He is commemorated on the Eastcote, St Lawrence's church, Eastcote, St Martin's church, Ruislip, and Ruislip war memorials. Buried: St Martin's churchyard, Ruislip.

Volk, James
Born in England and educated at Brighton. 763, Private, 2nd Australian Brigade HQ, formerly 5th Australian Infantry. He embarked at Melbourne on HMAT *Orvieto* on 21 October 1914. He was found dead on the railway line near Northwood in the early morning of 27 January 1916. Apparently there had been a struggle in a train when he had tried to prevent a young lady getting out. The inquest decided that he had broken his neck and death was due to misadventure. Buried: Chorleywood Road Cemetery, Rickmansworth.

Waine, Malcolm Lyle
Captain Canadian Army Service Corps/attd. RFC Killed instantly after a spin while flying at Northolt at 6.35 a.m. on 4 May 1917, aged twenty-four. The plane had been heard to crack as though some part of the machine had given way. Medical evidence showed that he had probably died from shock and a fractured skull. His passenger, George Smirnov, died later. He was the son of the late G.A. and F.E. Waine of Ottawa; husband of Anna Waine of 83, Cartier Street, Ottawa. Buried: St Martin's churchyard, Ruislip.

Walden, Daniel
Enlisted at Northwood, of Dianthus, Hilliard Road, Northwood. 5141 Private, 1/4th Northumberland Fusiliers (Territorials), formerly 5869 Norfolk Regiment. The battalion was in the front line (Snag Trench) on 11 November 1916. On 13 November they withdrew to Hexham Road and Flers where he was killed in action on 13 November 1916, on the first day of the Battle of the Ancre. He was about twenty-five. It was the last concerted operation of the year but was not a success. Daniel was the son of William Walden and husband of Emily, née Stanhope, whom he had married at Emmanuel church on 21 June 1913. He is commemorated on the Emmanuel church, Northwood, and Northwood war memorials. Commemorated: Thiepval memorial, Somme, France.

Walters, Joseph Henry
Born at Reading, lived and enlisted at Northwood. 47111, Private, 'D' Coy, 22nd Royal Fusiliers. Big successes at Thiepval, and at Beaumont Hamel earlier, had worryingly left the Germans in a salient projecting westward like a pyramid. On the afternoon of 16 February 1917 the battalion, less 'B' Coy, had moved up from their temporary home in Wolfe Huts and

Ovillers Huts and proceeded to battle positions between the East and West Miraumont roads, 'D' Coy to form a defensive flank across No Man's Land as the 23rd Royal Fusiliers advanced. Their aim was to capture Hill 130, attacking towards a line between Miraumont and Pys village in a northerly direction. An attack on the day following at Courcelette by two companies of the 22nd RF was thwarted by constant enemy shelling, mainly on communication trenches and tracks leading to the rear. The attack had begun at 5.45 a.m., although the enemy barrage had begun at 5 a.m., especially round the shell holes occupied by 'D' Coy, who found the wire uncut and protected by a machine gun. Joseph was killed in action here at the battle of Boom Ravine on 17 February 1917, the first day of the thaw, after five weeks of biting frost. He was thirty-six. The attack was not a success. Two men, probably of the same division, had treacherously revealed the hour of the offensive to the enemy. He was the son of John and Julia Walters of Church Road, Northwood; husband of Alice Louisa Walters, née Stacey, whom he had married at Emmanuel church on 19 August 1912, of 86 Hilliard Road, Northwood. He is commemorated on the Emmanuel church, Northwood, and Northwood war memorials. Buried: Serre Road Cemetery No. 1, Pas de Calais, France, E.19.

Warburton, Arthur John Egerton

Born at Northwood on 4 April 1895 and baptised at Holy Trinity church on 15 May 1895, son of Arthur and Evelyn, enlisted at Camberley, of East Molesey. 650435, Rifleman, 2nd London Regiment (First Surrey Rifles). On 30 November 1916, the battalion sailed on the Ivernia, reaching Salonica on 8 December, where he died of pneumonia, probably in the No. 1 stationary hospital at Salonika on 14 August 1917, aged twenty-two. He was the son of Mrs Evelyn Morgan (formerly Warburton), of Arley, East Molesey, Surrey, and the late Arthur Warburton (MD). He was on active service from August 1914 until his death in August 1917. The Nos. 37 general hospital at Veryekop and 38 general hospital at Samlis were both within a few miles of Salonika. They were there by the autumn of 1916, as was the No. 1 stationary hospital at Salonika, although some hospitals may have come later. He is not commemorated locally. Buried: Salonika (Lembet Road) Military Cemetery, Greece.

Ward, Harold Henshaw

Midshipman RN, who lost his life on HMS *Hogue*, a cruiser, which had been sunk by the German U.29 while on patrol off the Dutch coast early in the morning on 22 September 1914, aged fifteen. The *Hogue*, with her sister ships, the *Cressy* and *Aboukir*, was trying to prevent the German forces moving south to attack Channel troop convoys. Amongst those who died were boys from HMS *Ganges* and officer cadets from the Britannia Royal Naval College at Dartmouth. Harold may have been one of them. He was the younger son of Thomas James Ward of Petrograd, Russia, and nephew of Mr and Mrs Needham of Chester Road, Northwood, where he was well known. Brother of Norman. He was educated at Wadham House School, Hale, Cheshire. He is commemorated on Northwood war memorial and on Holy Trinity church memorial, Northwood. Commemorated: Chatham Naval memorial, Kent.

Ward, Norman Hartley North

2nd Lieut., 5th Middlesex Regiment attd., 1st Loyal North Lancashire Regiment. He was killed in action on 8 March 1917, aged nineteen. He was the only surviving son of Mr

Thomas James Ward of Petrograd and Northwood. He was educated at Wadham House School, Hale, Cheshire. He is commemorated on Northwood war memorial and on Holy Trinity church memorial, Northwood. Buried: Bray Military Cemetery, Somme, France.

Watson, Walter Ernest Mansell

Born at Ruislip, enlisted in London, lived at Rickmansworth. 7584, Private, 1/22nd (County of London) Battalion (The Queen's) London Regiment. Formerly 5626, 3/12th London Regiment. Killed in action on 17 September 1916 near the ghastly charnel-house of High Wood, itself taken and retaken so often but still mainly in enemy hands until that day. At 6.20 a.m. the assault went forward along the line. He is not commemorated locally. Commemorated: Thiepval memorial, Somme, France.

Way, Bernard Walter

Born at Crediton, Devon, enlisted at Cardiff, of Northwood (or Crediton). 11946, Private, 2nd Devonshire Regiment. Died of wounds, probably in the 34th or 2/2nd London casualty clearing stations, known to the troops as Grove Town, on 31 December 1916, aged nineteen. After being in action on the Givenchy front from July to the beginning of October 1916, on 14 October the 2nd Devons entrained at Chocques for another turn on the Somme. The first attack they took part in was upon German trenches south-west of Le Transloy. On 22 October they moved up into trenches north-east of Flers, from where they advanced at 2.30 p.m. in an attack on the following day on Zenith Trench. On the 24th the attack was abandoned and the battalion was relieved and went back to camp near Meaulte. On 29 October they relieved the 1st Sherwood Foresters in the front line at Misty Trench where, between 29 and 30 October, thirty casualties were reported. After a week out of line, the 2nd Devons took over front-line trenches near Le Transloy on 7 November; there, on 8th and 9th, they advanced almost to the crest line of the ridge, digging a new trench – Fall Trench. On the next night they withdrew to the Flers line in Brigade reserve. On 20 November they went to Vergies, near Oisemont, for a month's rest. On 27 December they moved to a new section of the line near Bouchavesnes where they held a series of shell holes converted into posts in front of St Pierre Vaast Wood. Bernard does not appear to be commemorated locally but he is commemorated on the Crediton war memorial. Buried: Grove Town Cemetery, Meulte, Somme, France.

Weatherley, Charles William

Born at Northwood in August 1897 and baptised at Holy Trinity church on 3 October 1897, enlisted at Willesden before June 1915, of Northwood. T.F. 3856, Private, 1/8th Middlesex Regiment. Died of wounds on 16 September 1916, probably in either the 34th or 2/2nd London CCS at Meaulte, known to the troops as Grovetown, which had been set up to deal with casualties from the Somme battlefield. He may have been wounded in an attack at Flers-Courcelette between 12-15 September. Day firing commenced at 6 a.m. and went on until 6.30 p.m. and during the night lethal shells were used. He was the son of Annie Western (formerly Weatherley) of 96 Victoria Road, Harlesden and the late

William Weatherley. Charles is commemorated on the Emmanuel church, Northwood, and Northwood war memorials. His family was amongst those who claimed financial relief from the Soldiers' and Sailors' Families (Uxbridge Division) sometime in 1914-15 or early 1916 and maybe later. Buried: Grove Town Cemetery, Meaulte, Somme, France.

Whatmoor, Donald Gurney

Born on 6 June 1892. He was educated at Berkhamsted Collegiate School and was in the OTC there from 1905 until he left in 1908, as a Private. He was employed by the National Provincial and Union Bank of England. On 31 August 1914 he enlisted in London in the 15th London Regiment, gazetted 2nd Lieutenant on 8 February 1915 and joined the 7th Bedfordshire Regiment on the Western Front, around Fricourt and Carnoy, on 1 August 1915. His period of service was carried out on that front at the southern end of the British line. He was killed in action during heavy shelling from opposing enemy trenches on 17 January 1916, aged twenty-three, and buried south of Albert. Son of Herbert Wade (or Ware) Whatmoor and E. Mary Whatmoor of Brairfield, The Drive, Northwood. He is not commemorated locally. Buried: Meaulte Military Cemetery, Somme, France, A.13.

White, Lionel John

Son of Alexander John White, who is buried at Ruislip. Killed in action on 18 July 1916, aged twenty-five. He does not appear to be commemorated locally.

Probably, CH/16412, Private, RMLI, 1st Bn. RN Division. He had embarked with the RM Brigade on 25 September 1915 and joined the battalion at Cape Helles on 22 October 1915. He was killed in action on 18 July 1916 and is buried in Tranchee De Mecknes Cemetery, Aix-Noulette.

Whittaker, Frederick Poulton

Born at Northampton. 2nd Lieut., No. 54 Training Squadron, R.A.F., Northolt, attached to the Fairlop Aerodrome. Formerly 8th Manchester Regiment. Accidentally killed while flying on 25 October 1918, aged twenty-one. When about 1,500ft from the ground something went wrong with the engine and the machine came down near Ruislip. He died instantly. The inquest verdict was that he died from a fractured skull and other injuries. Son of Orlando and Grace Whittaker of 24 Regent Road, Blackpool. Buried: Blackpool Cemetery.

Wiggington, Frank Cecil

Killed in action in 1916, aged twenty-three. Son of Maurice and Jane Wiggington of Ruislip. He does not appear to be commemorated locally.

Probably Frank Wigginton, born at Stoke Newington, enlisted in London. 19372, Lance-Sgt, 4th Grenadier Guards, who was killed in action on 25 September 1916 and is commemorated on the Thiepval memorial. On that date, the English had been allotted the task of taking Lesboeufs and Morval. The attack began at 12.35 p.m. In the attack they took Lesboeufs and surrounded Morval, which they later that day took, and Combles was encircled. On the night of 25-26 September 1916, the 74th French Infantry attacking from the south-west, the 110th French Infantry attacking by the north-east and the British attacking from the north, took Combles, the principal pillar of the German defense, and in the north, the British also took Thiepval.

Willey, Sidney George

Born at Henbury, Glos., enlisted at Northwood, lived at The Lodge, Horsens Ducks Hill, Northwood with his wife, Rachel, née Austin, whom he had married in 1909. He was a gardener. 85817, Private, 75th Divisional Machine Gun Corps (Infantry), formerly T4/172813, 229 Coy, Royal Army Service Corps. His regiment disembarked at Alexandria on about 1 June 1917. He was taken ill on 15th June 1917 and admitted to 17th general hospital. On 7 March 1918 he was posted to the Machine Gun Corps. On 20 October 1918 he was taken ill and admitted to the 27th general hospital, where he died in Palestine on 31 October 1918 from broncho-pneumonia. He is commemorated on the Northwood war memorial. Buried: Cairo War Memorial Cemetery, Egypt.

Williamson, William Robert

Baptised at Holy Trinity church on 1 March 1896. Able Seaman, London 8/3138, Drake Battalion, Royal Naval Reserve. On 28 February 1915 the Royal Naval Division embarked at Avonmouth in the *Franconia*, the *Braemar Castle*, the *Gloucester Castle*, the *Grantully Castle*, the *Minnetonka* and the *Astrian* for Gallipoli. There, on 28 April, they were in action at Cape Helles. William was killed in action in the Dardanelles on 25 May 1915 (or 9 June), aged nineteen. Only son of William and Agnes Williamson of Eildon, 83 Hallowell Road, Northwood, and grandson of Robert Gray (died 1912) and Janet Gray (died 1918). Had been a scholar at Holy Trinity church School and John Lyon School, and finished his education under Mr E.A. Cave of Harrow. He had worked for the London & North Western Railway as a clerk before joining the RND in April 1914 and was called up when war broke out. He had played for Northwood Cricket Club. He is commemorated on the Emmanuel church, Northwood, and Northwood war memorials. Commemorated: Helles memorial, Turkey.

Wills, Alfred Leslie

Born at Hendon. He was educated at Gresham School, where he was in the OTC, after which he was articled to a firm of solicitors. He enlisted on 10 September 1914 at St James's as a Private. On 15 September 1914 he was promoted to Corporal but reverted to Private at his own request, passed through Sandhurst and obtained his commission in the Worcester Regiment on 17 March 1915. On 16 September 1915 he embarked (as 4th attd. 5th Worcesters) at Southampton for Suvla in Gallipoli. On 8 October 1915 he was wounded in his right chest by gunshot, spending a week in hospital in Malta before being sent back on HMS *Italia* to England and the Royal Free Hospital. When he was getting better he spent some time on light duties at home, and on recovery he went to the front in March 1916 as Lieutenant, 4th Worcestershire Regiment. By 4 a.m. on St George's Day 1917, the battalion was in its jumping off positions south of Monchy-le-Preux in the sector between Monchy and La Bergere on the Arras-Cambrai road. Lieutenant Wills was killed in action leading his men before reaching the battalion's final objective, on 23 April 1917, aged twenty-three. On that date, our second general attack at Arras had taken place all along the line, but the German defences proved themselves and troops, especially those in the front line, were subjected to violent counter-attacks. The Worcester suffered very heavy casualties. He was the second son of Mr and Mrs Alfred Wills of Sandy Lodge, Northwood. He is not commemorated locally. Commemorated: Arras memorial, Pas de Calais, France.

Wilsher, Harold Ernest

Born at Hove, Sussex. Wireless Operator, SS *Tatarrax*. Mercantile Marine. Drowned as a result of fire on board the oil tanker on 10 August 1918, aged nineteen. It was en route from Port Said to France when it was torpedoed by the UC34. Son of Edwin John and Mary Amelia Wilsher (née Jacob), of The Lillies, 99 Hallowell Road, Northwood. He is commemorated on Northwood war memorial. Commemorated: Tower Hill memorial, London.

Wilson, Arthur James

Born at Enfield. He was a commercial clerk and enlisted at Willesden on 10th August 1914, and lived with his parents at Northwood. T.F.265424 (also 1546), Private, 'C' Coy, 1/9th Middlesex Regiment. In India he contracted a tropical disease transmitted by sand flies and was treated in Rawal Pindi Hospital. He was brought back to England on 8 March 1917 and taken to Stepping Hill Military Hospital, Hazelgrove (near Stockport) where he died of Kala Azar and internal haemorrhage on 2 April 1917, aged nineteen. He was the son of Arthur Edward Wilson and Rosina Caroline Wilson (née Cannon), of 'Rosslyn', 71 Hilliard Road, Northwood. He is commemorated on the Emmanuel church, Northwood, and Northwood war memorials. Buried: Northwood Cemetery.

Woodman, Alfred William

Born and lived at Ruislip, enlisted in London. 11795, Private, 2nd Coldstream Guards. At sometime around the end of the first week of September 1916 or at the beginning of the second, the Guards Division had taken over the Ginchy Section from the Irish Division, who had taken Ginchy on 3 September and then lost it again. At once they found themselves involved in some very heavy fighting, which left them weakened for the great advance due to take place on 15 September. They were faced by a strong system of trenches and especially the Quadrilateral, German front-line work, 1¼ miles north-east of Festubert. On 13 September 1916 the 2nd Coldstream Guards were at Carnoy, and during the night of 14-15 September moved forward to their assembly positions – their starting-off position was in a recently captured orchard. On the signal for the general advance, the Guards Division advanced to the front between Delville Wood and Ginchy. By dusk they were holding their second objective with its left on the Ginchy-Gueudecourt road. On the front of the 1st Guards Brigade, the night passed comparatively quietly. On the following day, 16 September 1916, Alfred was killed in action when the divisional front was very severely bombarded throughout the day by the enemy's artillery. He was twenty-seven or twenty-eight. For five nights they had had practically no sleep. Alfred was the son of Alfred and Matilda Woodman of Hope Cottages, Ruislip Common. Matilda Woodman died on 24 December 1919 after a long illness, aged sixty-three. She is buried at Ruislip He is commemorated on the Ruislip Common, St Martin's church, Ruislip, and Ruislip war memorials. Commemorated: Thiepval memorial, Somme, France.

Woodman, Percival Christopher

Born at Northwood on 3 July 1895 and baptised at Pinner on 29 September 1895, he lived at Northwood, and enlisted at Harrow in 1915 in the 6th Middlesex Regiment, later transferring to the 1st Middlesex Regiment. G/27318, Private, 1st Middlesex Regiment. He had volunteered for a bombing expedition with six others and was shot in the head. He was taken unconscious to a hospital where he died on 19 June 1918 at 5.30 a.m., about a week before his twenty-fourth birthday. All the others were also killed. In June 1918, the 1st Middlesex had moved back into the front line on the southern edge of the Ypres-Comines Canal, north of Voormezeele where, on the night of 19/20 June, the Battalion raided the enemy. He may have been injured in this action or before. In 1917 he had been badly gassed at the front and had contracted trench feet. He was educated at Pinner Road School and had previously been employed at the Harrow Observer Printing Works in the machine room for about nine years. He was the son of George Christopher and Rhoda Georgina Woodman of Inverness, 64 Hilliard Road, Northwood. He is commemorated on the Emmanuel church, Northwood, and Northwood war memorials. Buried: Esquelbecq Military Cemetery, Nord, France, B. 27.

SELECT BIBLIOGRAPHY

ADDISON, C. *Four and a half years* (2 volumes), Hutchinson, 1934

BEA Magazine, August 1954

BISHOP, W. A. *The courage of the early morning*, Bookprint Limited, 1966

BOURNE, J. *Britain and the First World War 1914-1918*, Edward Arnold, 1994

BOWLEY, A.L. *Prices and wages in the United Kingdom, 1914-1920*, Oxford (Clarendon Press), 1921

BOWLT, E.M. *The goodliest place in Middlesex: a history of the ancient parish of Ruislip from the Domesday Book to modern times*, LBH, 1989

————'Munitions in Ruislip during the First Word War: something of a puzzle' in *Ruislip, Northwood and Eastcote Local History Society Journal*, 1998

————'Munitions in Ruislip during World War One: a puzzle solved' in *Ruislip, Northwood and Eastcote Local History Society Journal*, 2001

British Red Cross & Order of St John Enquiry List of the Wounded and missing (various), Imperial War Museum

Citations of the Distinguished Conduct Medal in the First World War 1914-1920, N.& M. Press, 2007

CLUTTERBUCK, L.A. *The Bond of Sacrifice: a biographical record of British Officers who fell in the First World War*, N. & M. Press, 2002

COLE, C. *The air defence of Britain 1914-1918*, Putman, 1984

De RUVIGNY'S Roll of Honour, N and M Press, 2003

DOYLE, A.C. *The British Campaigns in Europe 1914-1918*, Geoffrey Bles, 1923

EDWARDS, R. *Eastcote – From village to suburb*, Hillingdon Borough Libraries, 1967

EVERETT, S. *World War I*, Bison Books, 1985

FAY, S. *The War Office at War*, EP Publishing Ltd, 1973

Francis Edwards Scrapbook: Northwood at War (a collection of ephemera), 2 vols

FRAZER, W.M. *A History of English Public Health 1834-1939*, Bailliere Tindall and Cox, 1950

GASKELL, M. *Harry Neal: a family of builders*, Granta Editions, 1989

GIBSON, J.A. *The history of Northwood College*, Northwood College, 1993

GILLMAN, P. *Collar the lot! How Britain interned and expelled its wartime refugees,* Quartet Books, 1980

HALLEY, J.J. *Squadrons of the Royal Air Force*, Air–Britain, 1980

HALPENNY, B. B. *Action Stations 8: Military airfields of Greater London*, Patrick Stephens, 1984

HAMILTON, J.A.B. *Britain's railways in World War I*, George Allen and Unwin, 1967

Harefield – 'At that time of day': life in a Middlesex village 1800 to the 1930s, Harefield Local History Society, 1978

HEAD, B. *The Northwood Book: a photographic essay*, Barry Head

HOUNSELL, F. *Greenford, Northolt and Perivale Past*, Historical Publications, 1999

HUGHES, J. *London since 1912*, HMSO, 1973

IVE, H. *The wind of change*, Typescript manuscript, no date

JACKSON, A.A. *London's local railways*, David and Charles, 1978

Kelly's *Directory of Harrow* 1915

KING, P. *Women rule the plot: the story of the 100 year fight to establish women's place in farm and garden*, Duckworth, 1999

LEWIS, P. *Squadron histories, RFC, RNAS and RAF,* 1912-59, Putnam, 1959

LIDDLE, P. *The airman's war,* Blandford Press, 1987

MACDERMOT, E.T. *History of the Great Western Railway,* volume II 1863-1921, GWR Co., 1931

McMILLAN, J. *The way it was 1914-1934,* William Kimber and Co. Ltd,, 1979

MASSEY, D. *Ruislip-Northwood: the development of the suburb with special reference to the period 1887-1914,* Ruislip, Northwood and Eastcote Local History Society, 1967

The Middlesex County Times (various dates)

Middlesex Register of Electors: Uxbridge Division 1914

MORGAN, D. *Lest we forget 1939-1945: Ruislip, Northwood, Eastcote*

MORRIS, J. *The German air raids on Great Britain 1914-1918,* H. Pordes, 1969

NORRIS, G. *The Royal Flying Corps: a history,* Frederick Muller, 1965

NORRIS, P. and HAYWARD, K., *A short history of RAF Northolt,* Chiltern Aviation Society, 1980

Northwood VAD Hospital Reports and Summary of Accounts 1915-1919

PARISH, H.J. *A history of immunization,* E. and S. Livingstone, 1965

PLUMRIDGE, J.H. *Hospital ships and ambulance trains,* Seeley, Service & Co., 1975

PRATT, E.A. *British railways and the First World War,* Selwyn and Blount, 1921

Prisoners of War Bureau, list of places of internment, no date

RAWLINSON, A. *The defence of London, 1915-1918,* Andrew Melrose, 1924

ROBINSON, D.H. *The Zeppelin in combat: a history of the German Naval Airship Division, 1912-1918,* G.T. Foulis, 1971

Royal Flying Corps Communiqués 1914-1918 (several authors and publishers)

Ruislip-Northwood: the development of an Urban District 1904-1965, Rawlinson (Printers) Ltd, 1965

Ruislip-Northwood UDC Medical Officer of Health Annual Reports 1914-1915

Silhouettes of aeroplanes, HMSO, 1917

Soldiers' and Sailors' Families Associations (Uxbridge Division of Middlesex) reports 1914- c1916,

SOUTHERTON, P. *The story of a prison,* Osprey, 1975

STURVIVANT, R. *Aircraft Serials and Units 1911-1919,* Air Britain, 1992

TAYLOR, A.J.P. *English history 1914-1945,* Oxford at the Clarendon Press, 1976

The Times History of the War, The Times, 1914-1919

The Times newspaper 1914-1919

TOTTMAN, D. 'Ruislip-Northwood: an early example of town planning and its consequences' in *Ruislip, Northwood and Eastcote Local History Society* Occasional paper No. 2 June 1982

TWINCH, C. *Women on the land: their story during two World Wars,* Lutterworth Press, 1990

WILLIAMS, J. *The home fronts: Britain, France and Germany 1914-1918,* Constable, 1972

WILSON, T. *The Myriad faces of war: Britain and the First World War 1914-1918,* Polity Press, 1988

WINTER, J.M. *The First World War and the British People,* Palgrave Macmillan, 2003

WINTER, JAY and ROBERT, JEAN-LOUIS, (eds) *Capital Cities at War: Paris, London, Berlin, 1914-1919,* Cambridge, 1999

PLUS various regimental and divisional histories, in particular:

ATKINSON, C.T. *The Seventh Division 1914-1918,* John Murray, 1927

HEADLAM, Cuthbert. *History of the Guards Division in the First World War 1915-1918, Volume 1,* John Murray, 1924

La Grande Guerre vecue-racontee-illustree par les combatants 1914-1918, Librarie Aristide Quillet, 1930

MOSER, Otto Von. *Die Wurttemberger im Weltkrieg,* Belagsbuchhandlung, 1927

NICHOLS, G.H.F. *The 18th Devision in the Great War,* Blackwood, 1922

SCOTT, A.B., *History of the 12th (Eastern) Division in the Great War 1914-1918,* Nisbet, 1923

SCOTT, MAJOR GENERAL SIR ARTHUR (ed) *History of the 12th (Eastern) Division in the First World War, 1914-1918,* Nisbet and Co., 1923

WARD, C.H.D. *The 56th Division (1st Territorial Division),* John Murray, 1921

INDEX

Other titles published by The History Press

Around Ruislip

MARIA NEWBERY, CAROLYN COTTEN, JULIA ANN PACKHAM & GWYN JONES

This glorious collection of archive photographs will delight visitors and residents alike. Bringing back fond memories for many, it is a rare chance to see the town as it once was, before the enormous changes of the twentieth century changed the face of the area, and of Britain, forever.

978 0 7524 0688 6

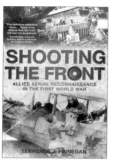

Shooting the Front

TERRENCE J FINNEGAN

Shooting the Front reviews the entire evolution of Allied aerial photography and photographic interpretation during the Great War, in a text packed with data and based upon meticulous research in archives worldwide. The photographs included are both informative and spectacular, charting perforce the early years of aviation itself.

978 0 7524 6052 9

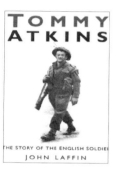

Tommy Atkins: The Story of the English Soldier

JOHN LAFFIN

Tommy Atkins is the English soldier who joking broke the cavalry of France at Minden, who singing marched with the Great Duke to the Danube, who grumbling shattered Napoleon's dreams at Waterloo, who sweating in his red coat tramped back and forth across Indis, who kept his six-rounds-to-the-minute at Mons, and who died in the mud at Passchendaele, the sands of the Western Desert, and the jungles of Burma. *Tommy Atkins* is his story - the story of this most versatile, most adaptable, most unmilitary soldier.

978 0 7524 6066 6

Mud, Blood and Bullets: Memoirs of a Machine Gunner on the Western Front

EDWARD ROWBOTHAM ED. JANET TUCKER

In 1915, Edward Rowbotham, a coal miner from the Midlands, volunteered for Kitchener's Army. Drafted into the newly-formed Machine Gun Corps, he was sent to fight in places whose names will forever be associated with mud and blood and sacrifice: Ypres, the Somme, and Passchendaele. He wrote these memoirs fifty years later, but found his memories of life in the trenches had not diminished at all. The sights and sounds of battle, the excitement, the terror, the extraordinary comradeship, are all vividly described.

978 0 7524 5620 1

Visit our website and discover thousands of other History Press books.

www.thehistorypress.co.uk